# Buying Business Services

Telephone: 020 7 487 7449
E-mail: library@regents.ac.uk

D1494300

# Buying Business Services

Björn Axelsson

&

Finn Wynstra

JOHN WILEY & SONS, LTD

*Other Wiley Editorial Offices*

John Wiley & Sons, Inc., 605 Third Avenue,
New York, NY 10158-0012, USA

WILEY-VCH GmbH, Pappelallee 3,
D-69469 Weinheim, Germany

John Wiley & Sons Australia, 33 Park Road, Milton,
Queensland 4064, Australia

John Wiley & Sons (Asia) Pte Ltd, 2 Clementi Loop #02-01,
Jin Xing Distripark, Singapore 129809

John Wiley & Sons (Canada) Ltd, 22 Worcester Road,
Rexdale, Ontario M9W 1L1, Canada

British Library Cataloguing in Publication Data

A catalogue record for this book is available from the British Library

ISBN 0-470-84302-0

Typeset by Mathematical Composition Setters Limited, Salisbury, Wiltshire.
Printed and bound in Great Britain by TJ International Ltd, Padstow, Cornwall.
This book is printed on acid-free paper responsibly manufactured from sustainable forestry,
in which at least two trees are planted for each one used for paper production.

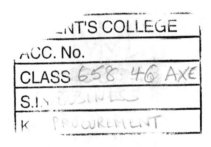

*Unfortunately, the tried and true rules for buying goods do not work when applied to the buying of professional services.*

(Wittreich, 1966)

# Brief Contents

# Contents

# Foreword

Over the past decades many Western countries have turned into real service economies. Most people in our modern economies now have their jobs in service companies, which over the years have grown significantly. One example is IBM, which currently reports that its income from services has surpassed the revenues related to sales of computers and hardware. The shift to a service economy has had a lasting impact on the structure of companies. More and more companies in their transition processes have been forced to focus on what they can do best. Non-core activities have been increasingly outsourced to specialist supplier firms. This is not only true for manufacturing companies, who have outsourced their component manufacturing; the trend can also be observed at large firms operating in the service sector. Facility and support activities such as catering, technical maintenance, security and even IT have in many cases been brought outside the company.

For this reason many companies have become more dependent on their suppliers for many activities. As a result, the strategic importance of purchasing and contracting has increased. Professional buying of products and services is a crucial factor in gaining a sustainable competitive position. Although this subject is covered by an increasing number of textbooks, the buying of services has until now received little scrutiny. This book tries to fill this gap and does so in an excellent way. Not only do the authors deal with the specific characteristics of different kinds of services, they also provide a new perspective on the role of purchasing in dealing with these. The authors contend that suppliers should be consistently challenged to support their customers' business strategies and that this is a crucial role for purchasing to play. Purchasing services, as they see it, is much more than negotiating and playing off suppliers against each other. Having gone through this book readers will be able to understand how they can make the most of supplier relationships in contracting for services, recognizing both internal service requirements and external supply market dynamics.

In writing this book both authors have drawn on their considerable academic knowledge as well as their practitioner networks. This makes the book a unique blend of pragmatic theory and structured application. The reader will benefit from the many case examples included in the text, which enable the book to generate a host of ideas on how to improve business and purchasing practices.

Prof. Dr Arjan van Weele
NEVI-Chair on Purchasing and Supply Management
Eindhoven University of Technology
Nyenrode University

# Acknowledgements

This book was mainly written in some short, intensive episodes at various places in Sweden and the Netherlands. Whenever possible, we combined it with some form of leisure, such as swimming near the island of Blidö, skiing in the mountains of Björnrike or dining in the old city of Dordrecht. We very much enjoyed writing this book, but in this way it even became fun.

It should be noted that the book might differ from most other textbooks, as it does not provide many checklists or dos and don'ts in relation to various phenomena. The book is largely written as a discussion with the reader; the attempt is to give direction and present a message, but without simplifying too much. To some readers it might appear as a blur, to others as offering some interesting insights. Needless to say, we hope to get the latter reaction. Partly this book builds on a previous Swedish version published by SNS. Comments by readers of that book have helped us in preparing this totally revised international version.

Many people have been extremely helpful in the process of writing this book. Several student research associates provided very useful help in the form of translations, case materials etc.: thank you Mikael Lövquist and Frédéric Claessen. Finally, we would like to thank the people at Wiley who prepared and delivered the book in the form as it is now.

Björn would also like to thank colleagues Håkan Håkansson, Jan Johanson at Uppsala University, Lars-Erik Gadde at Chalmers Technical Institute, Ivan Snehota, Stockholm School of Economics, Geoff Easton, Lancaster Business School and David Ford, School of Management, University of Bath, for having been such inspiring partners throughout the years. Much of the thinking presented in this book emanates from their original thinking.

In addition, Finn would like to thank Arjan van Weele, who provided a great deal of the inspiration and opportunities to do things like writing this book. He would also like to thank his other colleagues in Eindhoven for creating such a stimulating environment in which to work: Ferrie van Echtelt, Leo Haffmans and especially Frank Rozemeijer.

Many thanks also to our present colleagues at Jönköping International Business School, who have been able to refresh our thinking considerably.

Usually, this is also the moment to thank any wives or girlfriends. We doubt, however, that they will have the time to read this – they are too busy teaching schoolchildren or treating patients. They are the real service experts.

Björn Axelsson & Finn Wynstra
December 2001

# About the Authors

Björn Axelsson is professor in business administration, especially marketing, at Jönköping International Business School and Stockholm School of Economics, Sweden. He has for many years served at Uppsala University. His main research interests are in the area of business-to-business relations, both from the marketing and the purchasing and supply management side. He has published several books and scientific articles primarily in purchasing and marketing management, business networks and capability development of firms. For more than ten years he was managing the Uppsala Executive MBA Program, which, together with a long career in academia and frequent assignments in business firms, has positioned him as an academic with a close understanding of business practices. Björn Axelsson is strongly associated with the so-called IMP Group, a group of mainly European researchers who for more than 20 years have conducted studies of business-to-business relationships in network settings. He serves on the editorial board of the *European Journal of Purchasing and Supply Management* and has several other editorial and academic commitments.

Finn Wynstra is associate professor at the Department of Business Economics and Markets, School of Technology Management at Technische Universiteit Eindhoven, Netherlands and a research fellow at Jönköping International Business School, Sweden. His main research interests are in the area of supplier–manufacturer relations, innovation and industrial networks. He has been working with various European high-tech companies, mainly in the office equipment, medical equipment and mechanical engineering sectors, and has taught at universities in, among other countries, the US, the UK, Latvia and France. Finn Wynstra serves on the editorial board of the *European Journal of Purchasing and Supply Management*, the *Journal of Business-to-Business Marketing* and two Dutch practitioner journals. He is also a member of the Committee of the International Purchasing and Supply Education and Research Association (IPSERA), a global association of more than 300 academics and practitioners.

# Part I

## Introduction

# 1

# The Increased Importance of Buying Services

## The service society

Society goes through different phases of development. The industrial revolution transformed the agricultural society into an industrial society. This revolution involved the development of machines and equipment (steam engines, measuring equipment etc.) and subsequently led to an industrial organization of labour based on specialization and the use of production lines. Specialization, both within and between companies, started to increase. This internal specialization of labour tasks is sometimes called 'Taylorism' or 'Fordism', referring to some of its pioneers (De Geer, 1978; Piore and Sabel, 1984; Amin and Malmberg, 1995). Material welfare, infrastructure in terms of buildings and roads and other elements of social organization could be attained through this development, and a strong public sector was established.

Today, it is argued, we are on the verge of a new era. The industrial society has become a service society and is well on the way to becoming an information and knowledge society. We have experienced technological developments, which have enabled us, for example, to deal with large amounts of information. We are deeply interested in how knowledge can be derived from information, and we are trying to become better at exploiting and making money out of knowledge.

We can also observe that services are being produced and consumed more than ever before, partly as a consequence of the developments described above. This applies to most economic regions, although to some more than others. Services today are so obvious that we seldom think about them. Let us illustrate this with a short story: a tale about a day in the modern service society.

---

**Box 1.1   A day in the service society**

Today is an important day and you want to make sure you wake up on time. Therefore, you have arranged for a telephone wake-up call from your telecom operator. You get up, go to the door and pick up the newspaper from the mailbox. In the paper, you read that there has been an interesting development on Wall Street yesterday and that new developments were expected during the night at Tokyo's exchange. To see what has happened, you switch on the TV for teletext and the morning news.

After you finish your breakfast, well fed and well informed, you take the bus to work. The car is at the garage and you will need to pick it up later. When you get to the office, you read your e-mail, listen to the messages on your voicemail and start work. You are also informed that the computer network will be down for some hours later in the day. This is because the IT company that takes care of it has to do some urgent modifications to the network.

At 10 am, the organizational development consultant arrives. The two of you go to the cafeteria to start the discussion with a cup of coffee. Following that, there is a meeting where a project group goes through the company's new strategy, during which the consultant will present his analysis. The discussions continue during lunch, which is served in your company's own restaurant. The books you ordered as background information for the consultant's analysis arrive by courier. You make a note of the times of the flights later that week to Germany that the travel agency has booked for you. Then you make some important phone calls and write a memo on the company's strategy and the guidelines for the market research you are ordering from a telemarketing firm. In the afternoon, you eat an apple from the fruit bowl down the hallway. The fruit, flowers and plants in the office are taken care of by an external facilities management company.

You leave the office an hour early because your daughter has to go to the doctor and you have agreed to babysit your grandson. You take a taxi to the garage to collect your car and then drive to your daughter's house. On the way, you buy some sweets to please your grandson. You are going to be babysitting for the whole evening since your daughter's employer has invited her and her husband to the theatre. For dinner, you order pizza from a delivery service. When your grandson has gone to bed, you use your daughter's computer to do some electronic banking. You also download a movie you have wanted to see for a long time. Late in the evening, you drive home.

---

In terms of contents and activities, this is a normal day for many people in today's society – and that of the immediate future. The day is filled with the consumption (and production) of services. It is so natural that we normally do not think of the fact that we constantly consume services of different kinds. We do not ponder much over how these services are produced and by whom.

Neither do we give much attention to how they are bought. How were the services of the IT company procured? What about the travel company and the telemarketing company? Those of the management consultant? And how did the pizzeria acquire the resources to be able to deliver the pizza to your daughter's home?

Many of these services were bought by you personally, and many others you purchased – or came in touch with – in your role as an employee. Service companies can obviously address themselves to just one or both categories of customer. In this book, we will only deal with the services bought by companies or other (formal) organizations, and with how these organizations and their employees act in the procurement process.

## The service society: facts and figures

As an indication of the importance of the service sector, statistics indicate that nowadays between 60 and 75 per cent of the working population is active in the production of services. Table 1.1 provides more specific data on the growing importance of service production in a number of OECD countries. It is clear that in most developed economies, services account for around 65 per cent of civilian employment. At the same time, however, large differences exist, for example between the Netherlands (74.1 per cent) and Germany (60.2 per cent). Over the decade 1987–97, the share of service employment has increased around five percentage points for most countries, implying that service employment has risen about 10 per cent. Taking a look at the importance of services in relation to GDP (Table 1.2), a similar picture emerges.

Table 1.3 provides a more detailed overview of the various service sectors. Based on these figures, the fastest growing group is finance, insurance, real estate and business services. Community, social and personal services are also growing in many countries. In the retail and restaurant sectors, and in transportation and

**Table 1.1** Civil employment in services as a share of total civilian employment, for a selection of OECD countries, 1987 and 1997 (percentages)

| Country | 1987 | 1997 | Change |
| --- | --- | --- | --- |
| France | 62.2 | 69.9 | 7.7 |
| Germany[1] | 55.4 | 60.2 | 4.8 |
| Japan | 57.9 | 61.6 | 3.7 |
| Netherlands | 68.3 | 74.1 | 5.8 |
| Sweden | 66.3 | 71.3 | 5.0 |
| United Kingdom | 64.8 | 71.3 | 6.5 |
| United States | 69.9 | 73.4 | 3.5 |
| G7 | 63.9 | 68.2 | 4.3 |
| EU-15 | 59.0 | 65.2 | 6.2 |

[1] Former Federal Republic of Germany only.
*Based on*: OECD, 1999a.

**Table 1.2** The importance of the service sector: value added to GDP for a selection of OECD countries, 1987 and 1997 (percentages) [1]

| Country | 1987 | 1997 | Change |
|---|---|---|---|
| France | 66.9 | 71.5 | 4.6 |
| Germany | 64.0[a,b] | 69.9[a] | 5.9 |
| Japan | 56.8 | 60.2[c] | 3.4 |
| Netherlands | 67.8 | 69.8[d] | 2.0 |
| Sweden | 66.3 | 70.5[e] | 4.2 |
| United Kingdom | 66.1[f] | 70.8[d,f] | 4.7 |
| United States | 68.3[g,h] | 71.4[c,g,h] | 3.1 |

[1] Includes import duties and other adjustments and excludes imputed bank service charges.
[a] Publishing included.
[b] 1991
[c] 1996
[d] 1995
[e] 1994
[f] Includes repair services of consumer durables other than clothing.
[g] Sanitary and similar services excluded.
[h] Includes government enterprises.
*Based on*: OECD, 1999a.

communication, growth has not been that strong, and in some countries their share has actually decreased.

Another conclusion from Table 1.3 is that large differences exist regarding the importance of government as a service producer. In countries such as the UK, the US, Germany and the Netherlands government accounts for around 12 per cent of total service production, while in Sweden and France the corresponding percentages are around 17–20 per cent. Overall, however, government service production is decreasing, reflecting trends of privatization and outsourcing.

Figures such as these may differ depending on the kind of source, but the general trend is clear: the importance of the service sector is growing, to the extent that one can speak of the 'service economy'. A crucial comment, however, is that many of the services being produced are dependent on and closely related to production in the agricultural and industrial sectors. In this context, it could be argued that a considerable amount of current services production would not exist if those other activities had disappeared. On the other hand, services have become a significant driving factor in economic growth, to the extent that manufacturing can now be seen as flowing to those areas where the services infrastructure is well developed, rather than the other way round (OECD, 2000).

An important general phenomenon lying at the root of the growing importance of the service sector is firms' ongoing specialization, as reflected in the decrease in the amount of value that companies and organizations add internally. This leads to an ever-increasing amount of purchased goods, especially services.

Table 1.3 Contribution of services to GDP, by sector, for a selection of OECD countries, 1987 and 1997 (value added as percentage of GDP)

| Country | Wholesale & retail trade, restaurants and hotels I | | Transport storage and communication II | | Finance, insurance, real estate and business services III | | Community, social and personal services[1] IV | | Producers of government services V | |
|---|---|---|---|---|---|---|---|---|---|---|
| | 1987 | 1997 | 1987 | 1997 | 1987 | 1997 | 1987 | 1997 | 1987 | 1997 |
| France | 14.9 | 14.7 | 6.0 | 5.7 | 20.4 | 22.9 | 5.2[a] | 6.2[a] | 16.4[a] | 17.4[a] |
| Germany | — | — | 5.4[b] | 5.0 | 11.3[b,c] | 14.0[c] | — | — | 11.1[a,b] | 10.8 |
| Japan | 13.5[d] | 12.1[d,e] | 6.7 | 6.7[e] | 16.6[f] | 17.9[e,f] | 16.4[d] | 19.7[d,e,f] | 8.1 | 8.0[e] |
| Netherlands | 14.5 | 14.2[g] | 6.3 | 6.6[g] | 18.8 | 23.4[g] | 11.0 | 10.9[g] | 11.3 | 9.9[g] |
| Sweden | 10.9 | 9.9[h] | 5.6 | 5.9[h] | 17.4 | 21.4[h] | 4.4 | 5.3[h] | 20.2 | 19.7[h] |
| United Kingdom | 11.7[i] | 12.5[g,i] | 7.1 | 7.3[g] | 18.8 | 22.3[g] | 4.9[i] | 9.6[g,i] | 12.6 | 9.7[g] |
| United States | 16.9 | 16.8[e] | 6.3 | 5.9[e] | 25.5 | 28.6[e] | 9.8[j] | 11.5[e,j] | 11.8 | 11.4[j] |

— Not available
[1] Including other producers
[a] Other producers included in V.
[b] 1991.
[c] Business services and real estate except dwellings included in IV.
[d] Restaurants and hotels included in V.
[e] 1996.
[f] Business services included in IV.
[g] 1995.
[h] 1994.
[i] Repair services of consumer durables other than clothing included in I.
[j] Excludes sanitary and similar services.
Based on: OECD, 1999a.

## Increasing specialization

Large parts of what is now registered as service production have previously been produced without being accounted for as such. Security services, cleaning services and many others are examples of services that were previously produced internally, and registered as part of industrial firms' production costs. The service was produced but not registered separately as a service. In that sense, the economic shift towards services may be overstated – part of it simply represents a change in accounting (OECD, 2000). Let us briefly look at some examples of how specialization spawns the development of service companies.

---

**Box 1.2   Newly emerging structures in the IT sector**

While in the beginning there were several IT companies that were totally integrated, being responsible for both hardware and software (e.g. IBM), there has been a trend towards specialization, not only in terms of individual components for hardware (e.g. Intel) but also in terms of software (e.g. Microsoft).

In this way, previously integrated providers of IT products have cut the 'back end', but not only that: there have also been cuts in the 'front end'. During the 1980s, an IT service market emerged that pushed aside the original industry competitors. There are two important new market segments: facilities management and systems integration. Facilities management deals with the operation and maintenance of companies' (i.e. IT users') computer systems, in which the whole system is handed to an external company. Systems integration involves a company taking responsibility for the integrated implementation of a complete information system. These suppliers offer, among other services, analyses of the customer's need for information handling, an evaluation of available technologies and customization of products based on the customer's needs. This market has emerged partly due to the standardization of both hardware and software.

---

This illustration highlights the specialization that occurs between goods- and services-producing companies within the same industry. A second illustration comes from a firm that is active as a provider of marketing and advertisement campaigns.

---

**Box 1.3   The division of labour and specialization in the advertisement and media sector**

A promotional campaign can be set up in different ways. The company can turn to an advertisement agency that takes responsibility for the whole project. The company can also hire a number of firms, each with their own specialism. A traditional advertisement agency can contribute ideas and develop a newspaper advertisement or TV commercial. Then another company takes over, which specializes in selecting media and has knowledge of newspapers' circulation, type of reader etc. Some of these firms are mere 'brokering' companies, others give advice with a high knowledge content.

Given that companies in their marketing efforts are addressing increasingly small groups or niches, so-called micro-segments, knowledge about special media becomes very relevant. (This often involves 'multi-niching', i.e. targeting a large number of more strictly defined segments rather than a few large segments.) The more detailed knowledge, the better. This is why some advertisement agencies have reorganized themselves to establish new kinds of agencies with specific expertise in special media (e.g. so-called underground magazines), which address very specific audiences.

The above example illustrates how a division of labour develops between service companies in what can easily be perceived as one and the same business.

A common driving force of developments in these different examples is *specialization*. As markets are acquiring an increasingly wider geographical scope, opportunities are created for more specialized activities on the customer side. Companies are targeting ever smaller niches and searching for customers in global markets. On the supplier side, these specialization tendencies have forced companies to outsource activities that were previously performed internally. Firms are pressured to concentrate on core competencies, reduce costs and exploit external, specialized expertise more effectively. These changes are not only taking place in areas of new economic activity, but also within established, more mature sectors, thereby creating new conditions for purchasing and supply management.

## Services defined

Before we focus the discussion on purchasing and specifically the procurement of services, it is useful to look at some definitions of services. This section also looks at some of the (increasing) similarities between goods and services.

### Definitions of services

There have been various attempts at defining services. One popular definition is the following:

> A service is a process consisting of a series of more or less intangible *activities* that normally, but not necessarily always, take place in *interactions* between the customer and service employees and/or physical resources or goods and/or systems of the service provider, which are provided as *solutions* to customer *problems*.
>
> (Grönroos 2000, p. 46; emphasis added)

The following key words and their meaning should be specifically noted:

● There are activities involved.
● There is interaction, a meeting of some sort (physical or virtual, or machine to machine) between customer and supplier.

● There is a functional purpose, the service should (like goods) provide a solution to a problem or fulfil a need.

Most services fulfil all these criteria, but there are exceptions and borderline cases. There is a common alternative definition that also has some pedagogical merits: 'A service is something that can be bought and sold but that is not possible to lay your hands on' (Gummeson, 1987).

Grönroos (1979) emphasizes certain aspects of so-called business services (services delivered by companies and bought by other companies). He expresses this as follows:

> Business services are performed by qualified personnel, are often advisory and/or problem solving, and are also an *assignment* given to the seller by the buyer.

> (Grönroos, 1979; emphasis added)

We shall return to some of these specific elements of business services in Chapter 2, but here we want to emphasize the word 'assignment'. It has the important connotation that (at least part of) the content of the services is determined by the customer. Additionally, it involves a commitment – in future activities – to fulfil certain promises.

In defining services, the literature also tends to emphasize certain differences between services and goods. An overview is presented in Table 1.4.

There are examples of services that can be said to be exceptions to each and every one of these points, and therefore the list should not be seen as offering rock solid distinctions. On the other hand, these aspects give a broad overview of the most common differences between goods and services. There are, however, also significant similarities.

**Table 1.4**  Differences between goods and services

| Goods | Services |
| --- | --- |
| □ Tangible | □ Intangible |
| □ Can be demonstrated before the purchase | □ More difficult to demonstrate (not available) |
| □ Can be stored | □ Cannot be stored |
| □ Production occurs before consumption | □ Production and consumption simultaneously |
| □ Seller produces | □ Buyer/customer takes part in production |
| □ Production, sales, consumption on different locations | □ Production, consumption and (often) sales on the same location |
| □ Can be transported | □ Cannot be transported (but the producer and the customer can move) |

*Adapted from*: Normann, 1992, p. 31.

## Similarities between goods and services

The most important similarities between goods and services are:

- Both services and goods should fulfil a need, have a function for the customer.
- Both services and goods should be competitive, provide value to the customer, so that the customer may specifically choose this good/service from this specific supplier as compared with other functional solutions and other suppliers.

Additional similarities become evident when we look at both goods and services as products: 'anything that can be offered to a market to satisfy a want or need' (Kotler, 2000, p. 394).

In the context of this definition, a product is often defined as having different levels or layers (see Figure 1.1). The first level, or the nucleus, is the *core product* itself. This is what the customer primarily buys. It could be a drill with certain dimensions; it could also be a business trip. The core function in the first case is the possibility of drilling holes of a certain size in a particular material; in the latter case it is transport from A to B by a particular vehicle. It is therefore important to clarify what the main function of a good or service is. It should be

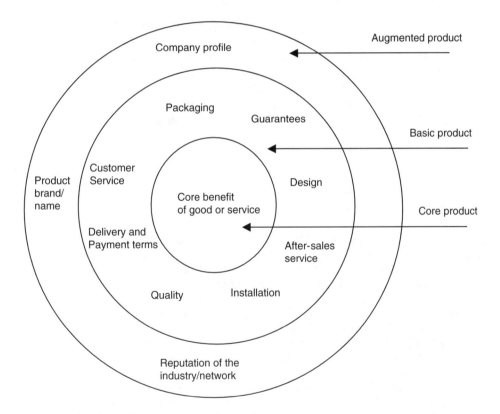

**Figure 1.1** The elements of an offering: core product, basic product, augmented product
*Adapted from*: Kotler, 2000, p. 394.

noted that one and the same product can have different main functions for different users and in different areas of application.

The attributes of the core product can be defined as the dimensions of the drill, its sharpness and durability or, in the case of the trip, duration, place of departure and arrival, departure time etc. The basic product also includes aspects such as packaging, technical information on the packaging, cleanliness of the drill, or (for the trip) being on schedule, a pleasant environment (clean train compartment, comfortable seat on the plane), kind treatment etc.

The middle ring in Figure 1.1 indicates under what conditions the product is transferred and made accessible to the customer. This can involve information before the purchase, method of delivery, warranties/guarantees and after-sales activities. These aspects are becoming increasingly important, according to several marketing experts. Some 20 years ago Theodore Levitt (1983) expressed this as follows:

> The new competition does not occur between what companies produce in their factories, but between what they add to these products in the form of packages, service, advertisements, financing, ways of delivery, stock policies and everything else that customers may value.

The outer ring in Figure 1.1 relates to the 'augmented product'. This consists of what we choose to refer to as 'meta-value', i.e. the values that go with a brand or company name without being specifically connected to a tangible function. The brand and the 'promise' it makes are also part of the product. This has to do with image and reliability. Think, for example, of the 'meta-value' of branding a line of clothing with 'Marlboro Country' or shoes with 'Caterpillar'. This kind of product value establishes the outer ring, the augmented product. This does not imply that this kind of value in general is more or less important than the other aspects; it can vary from product to product. Below are some examples of how service companies offer and use their meta-values.

---

**Box 1.4   McKinsey charges for its meta-value**

The world's leading management consultancy is undoubtedly McKinsey & Co. Its leadership can be illustrated in different ways, but the most salient aspect is that it charges higher fees than its competitors. A day of consultancy services from McKinsey often costs double the amount compared to other top management consultancies.

A professor from a high-ranking American business school argues: 'McKinsey and other consultancy firms recruit many of our graduate MBA students. The students that start working at McKinsey are in that context not specifically better than those that are recruited by McKinsey's competitors or other companies are. They are all top students, have had the same education and have done equally well. In short, they have the same qualities. In addition, they enter an organization that basically works like other good consultancy firms. Despite these similarities they manage to attract customers that often pay twice as much as the next most expensive alternative.' How is this possible?

To a large extent, the explanation lies in the company's legitimacy, its meta-value. The services discussed here are difficult to evaluate. In a truly uncertain situation, the customer can rely on 'this is what McKinsey has come up with', which is definitely a stronger argument (or signal) than 'this is what consultancy X has found'.

Meta-value can be important for other services as well, for example in the area of auditing. Whether annual reports have been audited by Pricewaterhouse-Coopers, Arthur Andersen or another well-known accountancy firm creates additional value compared to when the service is performed by a less well-known company or a company with a less impeccable reputation. This is true no matter if the work is carried out in exactly the same way and with the same recommendations and conclusions.

Besides illustrating that both services and goods have 'soft' and 'hard' parts, the discussion above also demonstrates that most product offerings contain elements of both services and goods. We can illustrate this with a continuum, putting 'pure goods' at the one end and 'pure services' at the other. In between, there is a large area that consists of products that are combinations of good and service (see Figure 1.2)

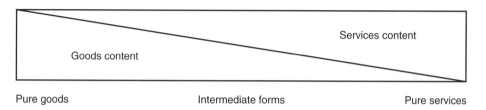

**Figure 1.2** Goods, services and intermediate forms

One example of services that are often part of a product offering is customer assistance. Common elements in such complementary services can be advice on how a product should be used, customizing the product to fit the customer's need, changing delivery times and including service offerings tied to the purchase, such as installation or maintenance. Sometimes the augmenting services can even be more important than the core product, as illustrated in the following example.

---

**Box 1.5   Plastic signs being bought as the result of the service content of a relationship**

Pricer, a company selling price signs for shop shelves, buys plastic tags or signs from a supplier. Through this relationship, however, it also gains access to a broad base of information and knowledge on its own customers, retailers all around the world. The supplier of the signs has a large market share and long experience. It knows the dimensions of the storage shelves, the layout of shops etc. for a large part of Pricer's current and potential customers. This is a very important service element. Perhaps this is what forms the core of the relationship, not the plastic signs themselves (see also Axelsson, 1996a).

No matter whether their content is dominated by goods or services, products should offer some value to their customers; this is the basic similarity between goods and services. A good is bought to fulfil a function, e.g. a spade is bought to function as a tool for digging ditches. A service is also bought because a customer expects to have a use for it. The spade can be replaced by buying a digging service, which is an activity delivered by a service provider. Clearly, different combinations of services and goods can (aim to) fulfil the same function. In that context, it is important to emphasize that the service content of a product can vary over time and in relation to different customers. Consider this illustration.

---

**Box 1.6  Stainless steel with high or low service content**

The product stainless steel has been moving along the continuum in Figure 1.3. When it was first introduced, it was a material that was difficult to handle. Among other things, knowledge of how to weld it was limited. In that situation, a great deal of assistance and customer training was necessary. When this knowledge became more widely spread, suppliers started to offer – to most customers – the product without this service; it was no longer requested.

---

Often suppliers and customers do not realize which services are in fact being exchanged, or they take them for granted. An increasing number of suppliers both of services and goods, however, have started 'pruning' their offerings, meaning that the core product is offered as a 'naked solution', to which customers can choose to add several 'options' (Anderson and Narus, 1995). This provides a starting point for targeting specific services that are part of the complete product offering to different customer groups.

This brings us to the concept of so-called service components. We define a service component as *a cluster of distinguishable activities within a total service package*.

This definition is in line with the concepts of 'bundling' and 'unbundling' that are used to illustrate how integrated a service is. Unbundling means that a service package is disintegrated; services are separated from each other. We choose to speak about service components that can be part of a standard offering or be 'unbundled', rather than speaking about 'naked solutions' and 'options' (see also Chapter 2).

As a final comment, technological advances seem to be narrowing the differences between services and goods. Information and communication technology enables people to enjoy a growing number of services in real or deferred time, without having to be physically present (OECD, 2000). Movies and other performances can be recorded, produced and distributed like manufactured products. Using the latest technology, even the consumption of TV broadcasts can be deferred to a later time that best fits the consumer. Similarly, some goods increasingly take on service characteristics, as in the case of dictionaries and encyclopedias that are made available through the Internet. We will look more specifically at the role of information and communication technology (ICT), especially electronic commerce, with regard to buying business services in Chapter 6.

## Development of the purchasing function

As an introduction to the specific topic of buying business services, this section takes a brief look at the changing significance and definitions of purchasing, and the difference between the purchasing function and purchasing department.

### Purchasing has become supply management

The development of the role of the purchasing function is sometimes described as a process from *buying*, via *procurement* to *supply management*. Purchasing as in 'buying' represents that specific purchasing activity dealing with buying things and making sure that a basic function is acquired for the lowest price. Purchasing as in 'procurement' deals with acquisition and a widened role, which implies (among other things) that logistical aspects are considered, and that not only price but also volume and time aspects are being taken into account. Purchasing as in 'supply management' increases the scope even more and includes the formation of supplier structures and the development of suppliers' and internal capabilities (resources, knowledge) in order to reduce costs and increase the creation of value in terms of product development and the like (Kraljic, 1983).

These developments have occurred in parallel with and partly as a consequence of the growing share of purchasing volumes compared to sales. Today, this so-called purchasing ratio lies more often above 50 per cent than below. Mechanical engineering had a share of approximately 50 per cent on average in the early 1990s. Other sectors have higher percentages, for example (petro)chemicals, food products, pulp and paper and construction lie around 70 per cent. The implication for many companies is that for each €100 of customer revenues, on average some €50–70 goes to paying for the efforts and resources of suppliers.

Many service companies also show high relative purchasing volumes. The purchasing ratio of trade companies is often around 80–90 per cent, which is not very surprising given the nature of this business. Trading is an important but, in terms of service *production*, very limited activity. Nevertheless, other types of service companies can also have high purchasing ratios.

It should be noted, however, that within one and the same industry large differences might exist. These differences reflect differing strategies with regard to specialization or vertical integration, but also differences in terms of the specific segments in which firms operate and differences in their specific value propositions. Table 1.5 presents an overview of the purchasing ratios of a number of Dutch companies, in eight different manufacturing and service sectors. For each sector, a company with a relatively high purchasing ratio and one with a relatively low purchasing ratio have been listed. The differences are substantial,

**Table 1.5** Purchasing ratios for a selection of Dutch companies (1997; external costs divided by sales)

| | | |
|---|---|---|
| **Construction** | | |
| IHC Calland | 76% | construction, off-shore |
| HBG | 69% | construction, dwellings and utilities |
| **Engineering/appliances** | | |
| Hunter Douglas | 80% | mechanical engineering |
| Océ | 48% | copiers and drawing room equipment |
| **Chemicals** | | |
| DSM | 75% | (petro-) chemicals |
| Akzo-Nobel | 53% | chemicals, pharmaceuticals |
| **Food** | | |
| CSM | 71% | food products, ingredients |
| Grolsch | 33% | beer brewery |
| **Retail** | | |
| Ahold | 80% | food retailer and wholesaler |
| KBB | 47% | department stores |
| **IT services** | | |
| Getronics | 61% | IT services |
| Cap Gemini | 10% | IT services |
| **Logistics services** | | |
| Pakhoed | 86% | storage and distribution |
| KLM | 30% | airline |
| **Media** | | |
| Endemol | 68% | TV entertainment |
| Elsevier | 42% | publishing |

*Source*: Van Weele and Van der Vossen, 1998.

but also explainable. For example, the difference between KLM Royal Dutch Airlines and Pakhoed can be explained by KLM's relative high internally added value in the form of wages for pilots and other personnel. Pakhoed's activities in the areas of (bulk) storage and distribution, of liquid bulk for example, require less (skilled) labour, and rely to a large extent on subprocesses that are subcontracted (transportation, cleaning etc.).

In general, however, there are strong indications that purchasing ratios may increase even further. One driving force is that many in-house service providers are more and more exposed to competition, compared to what external, more specialized providers can offer. In many organizations – manufacturing and service companies, public and private organizations – service activities previously performed internally have been outsourced to separate legal entities (see also discussion above). These units are created to take care of different support activities in a coordinated and professional fashion, for example in the areas of transport, printing/reproduction, library services, maintenance and catering services.

## Defining purchasing

Over the years various definitions of purchasing have been used. In the earlier literature, purchasing was often interpreted in a narrow and operational way. This led to a strong orientation on the position of the buyer and a narrow understanding of the organizational issues pertaining to the solution and organization of purchasing tasks. Heinritz *et al.* (1986, p. 9), for example, refer to purchasing as 'buying materials of the right quality, in the right quantity, at the right time, at the right price, from the right source'. However, following the trends of the last two decades the definition of purchasing has broadened considerably to a more strategic understanding of the underlying processes, leading to definitions such as 'managing the external resources of the firm' (Dobler and Burt, 1996; Van Weele, 2000). Gadde and Håkansson (1993, p. 13) describe purchasing even as broadly as 'a company's behaviour in relation to its suppliers'. We prefer to use the following definition:

> Managing the external resources of the firm, aimed at acquiring inputs at the most favourable conditions.
>
> (Wynstra, 1998)

This definition explicitly includes the possibility that inputs may be less tangible than goods or services (e.g. knowledge), and acknowledges that purchasing may involve activities that are only indirectly concerned with ('aimed at') obtaining inputs such as relationship building and supplier development programmes. The word 'acquiring' implies that the inputs may not only be bought, but could also be leased, rented, borrowed or traded (as in the case of counter trade). And 'favourable conditions' are key for all firms running a business in competition with others. Which conditions are important (price, delivery etc.) and what is the most favourable depends on the specific purchase and the specific customer firm.

Another very pragmatic but in most situations very suitable definition, which also fits very well with the scope of this book, is:

> Purchasing involves all activities that lead to an incoming invoice.

Many services are bought without much involvement from purchasing specialists, yet they still result in incoming invoices. This brings us to the distinction between the purchasing function (or process) and the purchasing department.

Note that, despite the discussions above, in this book we will use the words purchasing, procurement and buying interchangeably, purely for reasons of variety. Throughout the terms will mean the same thing: all (strategic, tactical and operational) activities aimed at acquiring (external) input resources.

## Purchasing function versus purchasing department

It is common to distinguish between the purchasing function and the purchasing department (cf. Axelsson and Laage-Hellman, 1991, p. 10) when discussing the internal actors. The purchasing department (if there is one) and its specialists may coordinate the basic processes of specifying, selecting, contracting, ordering, receiving and evaluating, but this does not necessarily imply that these activities should be carried out by this department. There are often groups of internal experts involved in different parts of the buying process covering various aspects. Therefore, 'the scope of the purchasing function is usually much broader than that of the purchasing department' (Van Weele, 1994, p. 10). For example, top management is usually involved in important make-or-buy decisions, and engineering probably has contacts with suppliers regarding the design of new products. These activities are also part of the purchasing function. In other words, purchasing processes cut across the entire organization.

Some purchasing activities may take place without any intervention by the purchasing department at all. In a US survey, researchers analysed the involvement of several internal units in the procurement of different products and services (Fearon and Bales, 1995). They found that, for the 158 public and private organizations they reviewed, on average purchasing departments accounted for some 41 per cent of total purchases and the other units for the remaining 59 per cent (see Table 1.6).

The figure of 41 per cent ascribed to the purchasing specialists would probably have been higher if a comparable study had been carried out more recently. There seems to be a general trend that purchasing specialists are increasingly putting their hands (and minds) on activities that are new to most (traditional) purchasing departments. These new activities often relate to the procurement of services, as we will discuss below. The growing involvement of purchasing specialists is closely related to the fact that they have increasingly become proactive and initiative taking, from having been more passive, 'order-receiving'

**Table 1.6**  Share in purchases by department

| Department | Share (in %) |
| --- | --- |
| Purchasing | 41 |
| Transportation | 9 |
| Finance | 9 |
| Administration | 6 |
| Personnel | 6 |
| Service | 3 |
| Production | 3 |
| Marketing & Sales | 3 |
| Other | 20 |

*Source*: Fearon and Bales, 1995.

**Table 1.7** The passive and the active purchasing organization

| The passive purchasing organization | The active purchasing organization |
| --- | --- |
| ● Waits to be visited by suppliers and to be informed of possible solutions | ● Searches and visits supplier actively to find the best resources. |
| ● Alternatives are presented and evaluated by the purchasing organization. Problem solutions are developed only by the supplier. Purchasing chooses from the 'market menu'. | ● Informs about its own needs and desires and 'creates' problem solutions together with suppliers. |
| ● Spends money. A dominating drive to save on expenditures. Low costs for the purchasing organization and lowest possible expenditure are striven for. | ● Creates value for the benefit of the company. Cost efficiency is important, but also 'business development'. |
| ● Needs to be convinced by supplier that the solution offered is best. Passive reactions in the form of a 'yes' or 'no' to proposals. | ● Convinces suppliers that the company is an interesting partner with interesting needs. A relationship can be stimulating, rewarding and a learning experience. |

administrators. This can be illustrated with the general distinctions presented in Table 1.7.

Purchasing can thus be seen as a buying function in which purchasing specialists and/or other functional specialists, often in some form of collaboration, work for the company's resource procurement. Resources of many different kinds can be bought without any collaboration from purchasing specialists. The basic driver is that the company needs resources in the form of personnel, production equipment, raw materials, components and services of different kinds in order to be able to develop, produce and deliver value to its customers. These resources are developed partly internally, but are also to a large extent procured from external sources, and purchasing specialists can have a more or less important role in that process.

## Buying business services

> Unfortunately, the tried and true rules for buying goods do not work when applied to the buying of professional services.
>
> (Wittreich, 1966)

This book is about buying *business services*: services delivered by firms or other organizations and bought by other firms or organizations. The *suppliers* are either public or private service providers; the *customers* can either be different types of manufacturers, or private or public service providers. In other words, we focus on services being sold, bought and exchanged in business-to-business and government-to-business (and business-to-government) markets.

We make a deliberate choice not to speak about *professional services*, as these usually have the connotation of involving a high knowledge content, provided by skilled professionals (consultants etc.). These are just one category of business service, as discussed in Chapter 2.

This introductory section on buying business services takes a first look at the underlying reasons for buying services, the different types of service bought by different types of customer, and the different people and departments involved in buying business services.

## Reasons for buying business services

Earlier we discussed how on-going specialization implies that each firm creates less added value internally. At the same time, this leads to a richer environment to buy from as more goods and services are produced by specialized firms, thereby contributing to an ever more sophisticated supply market. Specialization and outsourcing thereby become a self-reinforcing phenomenon. But why bother to outsource, subcontract or buy services at all? Partly the answer to this question has already been given: to acquire resources to which the company otherwise has no access. But this answer is not complete. The company could perhaps internally produce the services it is buying, but it cannot do so in a competitive way. Or the people responsible do not want to spend energy and resources on producing certain services, and therefore they choose to buy these from an external supplier.

It is possible to list a host of reasons why any firm buys services, but they all come down to three reasons. The buying firm does not have sufficient:

● capabilities to perform the service effectively with the right quality; or
● scale or ability to perform the service cost efficiently; or
● capacity to perform the service (completely or at all).

Box 1.7 presents a specific example of a buying firm that lacks specific capabilities and that is looking for these capabilities in an external service supplier.

---

**Box 1.7   Buying services, buying capabilities**

In a study of three international market establishment efforts by the Swedish telecom operator Telia, there appeared to be a common pattern (Malmgren and Olausson, 1997). In all three cases a consortium was established and in the consortium there was a coordinator (not Telia) that kept the network of participants together. A characteristic of this coordinator was that it did not have operator experience, and hence lacked credibility.

Subsequent analysis resulted in the interpretation that one reason for Telia's being invited to collaborate in the different consortia was that the company was a recognized and well-known operator in those countries. There are specific reasons for this. During many years, units within Telia have given training to the public authorities in these countries on how to run and control telecommunications operations. In addition, it was also one of the first European state-owned operators to be privatized and consequently it has extensive experience in deregulation and competition.

The decisive reason for the consortium and especially the coordinating actor 'buying' Telia's collaboration, according to the analysis, was not only that they required the operator's experience and competence, which they could have obtained from other actors as well, but that they wanted Telia's *legitimacy*.

Obviously, in the long run, a firm could decide to build the required capability, ability or capacity, but it may decide not to do so because it feels that performing the service does not fit within its strategy. This fit is often related to what the firm perceives as the most effective and efficient use of its (scarce) resources. Chapter 4 discusses the various issues around outsourcing – and insourcing – in more detail.

## The importance of buying business services

Overall there has been strong growth in business services. Table 1.3 already demonstrated that finance, insurance, real estate and business services account for a growing share of total service production. There are several reasons for this growth, akin to the driving forces for the general growth in service production:

● Specialization and increased division of labour.
● Outsourcing by established firms of many of their former activities. In a national survey on purchasing practices in Sweden, around 35 per cent of the 261 respondents indicated that they had been outsourcing at least part of their ICT and facility services in the period 1995–98 (Brandes *et al.*, 1999, p. 15). Also, nearly 25 per cent of the respondents had been outsourcing design and engineering services, while more than 15 per cent had been outsourcing logistical services.
● The need for greater flexibility within firms.
● The rise of the knowledge-based economy, with its reliance on expertise and specialised service inputs.
● The growth of smaller production units and firms that use external services to supplement their internal resources.

Focusing on so-called strategic business services (this excludes most cleaning and catering, as well as transportation and distribution services), total turnover in these services is estimated to have exceeded €1 trillion for the 19 OECD countries in 1995. At the current average growth rate of 10 per cent, this turnover may well have been around €1.5 trillion in 2000. Total employment in these service sectors was around 10 million in 1995, more than twice the employment in the entire OECD motor vehicle industry, which is one of the largest manufacturing sectors (OECD, 2000; OECD, 1999b).

This leads to the question of how important business service purchases are in relation to goods purchases. A US study involving 116 organizations (59 manufacturing companies, 23 service companies and 34 public authorities) found that on average, services account for more half of total purchasing spend. However, this share is substantially higher for companies involved in service sectors than for manufacturing companies, as is shown in Table 1.8.

The obvious conclusion from these figures is that in quantitative terms, the procurement of business services has become a substantial element in firms' total acquisition of external resources. However, it is important to emphasize that 'the impact of the services themselves on the success of the organisation's operation is far greater than the impact of the dollars spent' (Dobler and Burt, 1996). This is also true for some goods purchases such as capital investments in new equipment, which enable the production of a new range of final products, but holds more widely for business services. For example, a market research service may cost €10 000, but could ultimately result in €1 million in extra sales.

Chapter 2 and especially Chapter 6 deal with the impact that different business services may have on the buying firm's operations. We will propose a classification of business services purchases that takes this differing impact into account.

## People involved in buying business services

At many companies, non-purchasing specialists still mainly handle services, for example from marketing (marketing and advertisement services), finance (financial and auditing services), production (technical maintenance) or top management (consultancy). Table 1.6 already pointed to the relatively large amount of purchases carried out in general, for example, by transportation and finance departments; many of their purchases will involve services.

As these purchases are done without the involvement of purchasing specialists, they are probably handled less professionally from a commercial point of view. Given that the volumes involved are high and the management of the purchasing aspects is likely to be imperfect, there is reason to assume that purchasers could

**Table 1.8** Relative importance of purchases of goods and services in different sectors (in percentages)

|  | Type of purchases | |
| --- | --- | --- |
| Sectors | Goods | Services |
| Manufacturing companies | 61 | 39 |
| Service companies | 19 | 81 |
| Government authorities | 38 | 62 |
| *Weighted average* | *46* | *54* |

*Source*: Fearon and Bales, 1995.

contribute useful knowledge and skills, and that they will become increasingly involved even in these purchases.

There are some indications that purchasing specialists are increasingly active in buying business services of different kinds. This is also due to the fact that in many firms, purchasing specialists are increasingly focusing on so-called non-product-related (NPR) purchases. Not all but many business services such as facility, marketing and business organization services are usually treated as NPR purchases.

One example comes from the so-called OCOO project at Philips Electronics. This project, initiated in the mid-1990s, focused on saving on the 'other costs of organization', i.e. NPR purchases. At Philips these purchases involve a relatively large share of services, such as temporary labour, lease cars and consultancy.

---

### Box 1.8 The OCOO project at Philips Electronics

In the mid-1990s, Philips spent some €7 billion per year on 'other costs of organization', approximately €4 million every working hour and an equivalent of more than 20 per cent of total sales. The initial savings target was some €600 million – 12.5 per cent of current expenditure – based on internal and external benchmarks. Supported by a letter from then CEO Cor Boonstra, dedicated resources and specialist support, a programme was developed covering more than 45 spend categories, at 400–500 Philips sites and over 14 countries and all product divisions. The various categories included a large number of services:

- Accommodation/facilities – cleaning, security, utilities/energy, building maintenance.
- Personnel – temporary labour, travel, catering, training and courses, leased cars.
- Marketing and sales – media services, printing.
- Distribution – transportation, transport insurance, warehousing.
- Automation and communication – IT services, telecommunication services.
- Professional services – consulting, insurance, legal, financial services.
- Production/development – maintenance, inspection.

The most important strategies for achieving the potential savings in these various spend categories were standardization, supplier rationalization and cross-national supplier agreements.

During this process, various difficult issues needed to be tackled:

- NPR and especially services are often far less definable than direct purchases.
- Performance measurement needs to be more sophisticated than for most direct, bill of materials purchases (mainly goods).
- Some business units were reluctant to give up their independence, especially for those categories that were seen as critical to key business decisions (e.g. consultancy).

In 2000–2001, Philips turned the initial project organization into a permanent organization, the so-called NPR Global Service Unit, stressing the continued importance of NPR buying.

*Source*: various Philips documents.

## Specific issues in buying business services

On page 10 we gave an overview of the most common differences between goods and services. It is clear that these differences imply that in relation to services and service companies, a number of specific issues have to be taken into account. These include the ways in which services are or can be purchased. Issues that become more important, more difficult or at least different in the case of purchasing (and marketing) services include the following:

- *Identifying the content of the service.* One problem here is that the service does not yet exist when the customer buys it. Unlike a good, it cannot be looked at or played around with. Customers may therefore have problems in defining and evaluating *a priori* the contents of (alternative) service offerings. In addition, purchasing a service is very dependent on which category of service is chosen, whereas buying a good usually involves choosing from a limited number of alternatives within a well-defined category. For the supplier, identifying the most suitable service content often requires a fundamental understanding of the business processes, especially for the more 'strategic' or 'professional' business services (Wittreich, 1966).
- *Capacity and demand management.* Services can normally not be made to stock. For the buying company, it becomes important to evaluate and assure that there is enough capacity when it is needed, especially for those services that are particularly sensitive to this problem, such as call centres. It is essential for the supplier to match its own needs with the customer's ability to adapt concerning the (time of) delivery of the services. It is not uncommon for the customer to be able to influence the moment it needs the supplier's services by rescheduling some internal routines. In those cases, even the costs of the supplier's production – and thereby the price of the service – can be affected positively.
- *Quality definition and assurance.* The production of services consists of recurrent activities, often in close interaction between the customer and the supplier. Failed production can often not be put aside, but will lead to a bad service delivery to the customer or a bad purchase process from the customer's perspective. For the buying company, this implies that the evaluation of this aspect of the supplier's efforts right from the beginning becomes very important. However, it is also important to see how much and what kind of efforts the customer should invest itself, so that the interaction or collaboration with the supplier becomes as fruitful as possible. Think, for example, of a management consultancy service. In order to prevent a bad service, a customer may put a heavy emphasis on selecting a particular consultancy firm, but it may also choose to invest a great deal of time in meeting with the consultants during the project, in order to assure the quality of the service. With respect to the perceptions of quality, it is also crucial to *mutually adjust expectations.* For the supplier, 'right' means a compromise between a high level in order to create interest in the client for the service and a low level in order to prevent future disappointment. For the customer,

'right' means clarifying certain demands and coordinating expectations in a dialogue with the supplier.

- *Recovery.* It is also important to clarify what is to be done when, despite all efforts, the initial service delivery is not satisfactory. The supplier's willingness and ability to recover, to repair things when a defect arises and – obviously – to prevent this from happening the next time (i.e. the ability to learn from its mistakes) are crucial in this respect.
- *Pricing issues* are different compared to purchasing and marketing goods. It can be more difficult to see the connection between the price and the value of a service.
- *Personnel.* In many service providers, the majority – often up to 80 per cent – of total personnel has direct customer contact. One striking example is a university, where virtually everybody is on the organization's interface with customers, be they students, clients of research projects, clients for executive training etc. Since the quality of a service is strongly affected by the quality of the interaction between supplier personnel and customer personnel, this implies that front-line personnel from both sides are greater in number and that the quality of their meetings is becoming more important. For a buying company, this means, among other things, that in evaluating one or several suppliers, it should put relatively more weight on the competencies of the supplier's employees.
- *Physical environment.* Service production, to a large extent, takes place in interaction between suppliers and customers. This means that these processes become important and also that the physical environment in which they take place is quite relevant. Bitner (1992) has coined the concept 'servicescape' to capture this environment. The servicescape, be it a place where two or more parties meet face to face or a virtual meeting place (Web interfaces), is also important in business services.

One additional specific problem in buying services is highlighted in the following illustration from a purchasing manager of a large company.

---

**Box 1.9   Has the service arrived yet?**

The purchasing manager argues that services, less tangible as they are, create problems in internal coordination within the company. For incoming goods, there are well-developed routines for quality inspection. The good that arrives at the buying company is registered as 'received'. In this way, the company knows that when the invoice arrives, it is paying for something that has actually been delivered. With services, it is different. 'They arrive at different locations in our organization and the routines for administering them are not as well developed. When we receive an invoice, it is often difficult to know whether what we are paying for has really been delivered – and in the amount as specified in the invoice. This may sound very amateurish, but it is a real problem for services.'

There are many new payment procedures that do not use incoming goods registration, such as pay-on-production (paying your component supplier when the final product with that component leaves your factory or is sold to the consumer). However, these may be much more difficult to implement for services, partly because many services do not become part of a company's final product. Also, such procedures would not solve other coordination problems such as quality control. In Chapter 9, payment issues are discussed in more detail.

These are just a few of the aspects that in one dimension or the other can be expected to be different in exchange processes dominated by services, as compared to those dominated by goods. All these issues create specific conditions for and have an effect on the buying company's way of working. How should it handle these issues in its purchasing strategy and behaviour? These and related topics are discussed in the remainder of this book.

## Summary and book overview

In this first chapter, we have given a brief overview of the growing importance of services in today's society and economy, followed by a discussion of the differences and similarities between services and goods. One important conclusion has been that at the general level of the economy, manufacturing and service sectors become increasingly interrelated, to the extent that their differences become blurred. This also applies to individual product offerings, which more and more are combinations of both product and service components.

Against this background, it is not surprising that the purchasing of services is a growing business. The growth is, first, a matter of a growing share of purchases relative to the company's total sales. Secondly, it is qualitative growth, in the sense that purchasing issues and purchasing experts are more and more involved in a growing part of the firm's overall purchasing activities. This includes especially the purchasing of services, which were usually dealt with previously without the involvement of purchasing specialists. This development should also be seen in the light of the growing interest and importance of the purchasing function. Nevertheless, while it is easy to identify a growing and more strategic role for purchasing in general, it is often argued that developments are not going fast enough and are not taking place everywhere.

This book consists of 12 chapters, divided into four main parts: Part I, Introduction; Part II, Analysis: Business Services as Functions and Activities; Part III, Application: The Process of Buying Business Services; and Part IV, Reflection (see Figure 1.3). Part I provides an introduction to the – very heterogeneous – phenomenon of business services. Part II analyses business services in terms of the functions they serve and the activities they require, and then uses that perspective in discussing issues such as outsourcing/insourcing and producing and delivering business services. In fact, Part II sets out the specific perspective that *we* have when studying and analysing business services. Based on this analysis, Part III deals with specific steps in the process of buying business

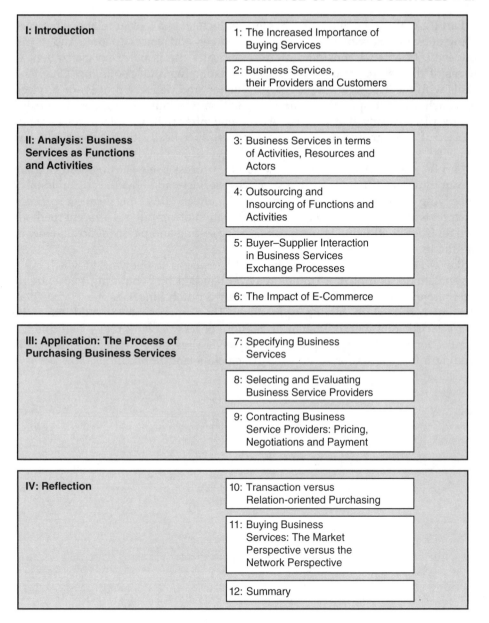

**Figure 1.3** Overview of the book

services: specifying, selecting and contracting (Van Weele, 1994). Part IV provides a last reflection on the previous discussions.

Part I, Introduction, sets the scene. After the current introductory Chapter 1, Chapter 2 deals in more detail with the nature of business services and their providers.

Part II, Analysis, begins with Chapter 3, which takes a look at relations between companies in terms of the activities, resources and actors (people and firms) involved. Chapter 4 considers more specifically the issue of specialization, in terms of the key (decision) processes of outsourcing and insourcing. Chapter 5 deals with the actual development, production and delivery process of services, in which we put special emphasis on the role of buyer–supplier interaction taking place during that process. At the end of Part II, Chapter 6 looks at the impact of e-commerce on business services, specifically their production and delivery.

Part III, Application, focuses on the service process itself, starting with Chapter 7 examining the different ways of specifying services and how the critical issue of specifying and managing service quality affects this specification process. Chapter 8 deals with the selection and evaluation of suppliers. Different methods and tools for contracting issues, such as price setting and payment arrangements, are the topic of Chapter 9.

Part IV, Reflection, starts with Chapter 10, focusing on the ways in which inter-organizational (supplier) relations may be handled by comparing two extreme alternatives: transactional and relation-oriented purchasing. Chapter 11 considers the outer context of buying operations. This outer context could have the characteristic of a market system or be more or less network-like – and this has implications for the buying process. Chapter 12 presents a summary of the book, leading into a discussion of its main conclusions and implications.

# 2

# Business Services, their Providers and Customers

In the previous chapter, the growing significance of purchasing business services was discussed in the light of the increasing overall importance of services in today's economy. We defined business services and discussed the reasons for and specific issues related to purchasing business services. This chapter examines the various types of business services and business service providers. It also takes a brief look at the differences between the various customers or clients buying these services. Finally, we analyse the different forms that business services may take in terms of the characteristics of the activities taking place in the relationship between the provider and the client of the service.

## Types of business services

In Chapter 1 we emphasized that purchasing, ultimately, is a matter of acquiring resources for the company's operations. The suppliers in these resource markets supply buying companies with goods and services that they do not own themselves, do not control and do not create. Obviously, it may be necessary to acquire different types of services (and goods) for different businesses. What is being bought depends primarily on what the business needs, and this differs strongly between different types of firms and organizations.

The wide variation in service needs also implies that the associations, the mental images that different people have of 'business services' or 'purchasing business services', will vary. We believe that most people have a very biased perception of the types of business services that are being bought. Let us review three examples of typical reactions from people with experience in industry.

---

**Box 2.1: Stereotypes of business service purchasing**

**Stereotype 1: Business service purchasing is about buying travel, cleaning and going to restaurants**
'Yes, we buy lots of services. Cleaning, travel, transportation and lots of other stuff. Altogether, it may be a lot but it is still not worth investing substantial resources in. Services are services, and services are not very complicated or advanced.'

**Stereotype 2: Business service purchasing is about outsourcing IT**
'What is really exciting is the outsourcing of IT services. The question is whether this is a fashion trend that will level off, or a lasting phenomenon. An important issue is for which companies it is feasible to maintain an internal IT unit. Myself, I believe that the line lies at roughly 100 people; companies with an IT unit smaller than that should not have that in-house. They should buy those services from external suppliers that are more capable of following the (technological) developments.'

**Stereotype 3: Business service purchasing is about buying consultancy services**
'You don't have a clue how many strange and expensive service purchases I have seen during my time on management teams or boards of directors. It seems like there is an incomprehensible magic around certain consultants. Company management is prepared to pay whatever the price, despite the fact that consultants often come up with things you already know. It is much like the old saying: "The task of the consultant is to find out what company management thinks, tell this to them, and then send a large invoice because they actually explained to the management what their position is." That is what I see as buying services.'

---

Because, in contrast to these quotations, there is such diversity in the category of 'services', we need to develop a more structured overview of the different types of services. One such an overview would be the following (OECD, 2000; OECD, 1999b):

● *Facility services*: cleaning, catering, security, real estate maintenance.
● *Financial services*: banking, finance, salary administration, insurance.
● *Information and communication technology services*: hardware implementation, customization and maintenance, telecommunication services, software development and implementation.
● *Business organization services*: management consultancy, environmental consultancy, risk management, public relations, accounting and auditing, legal services.

- *Research and development and technical services*: technical maintenance, repairs and assistance, development, engineering.
- *Transportation and distribution services*: warehousing, value-added logistics, transport.
- *Human resource development services*: training, recruitment.
- *Marketing services*: sales, reselling, advertisements, agents, franchising etc.

This is by no means the only possible classification of business services. As discussed in the following section, services are also often classified in terms of their provider. Later in this chapter we propose yet other classifications – or rather, characterizations – of services that are based on their internal characteristics.

It is also clear that certain packages of services may be hard to classify in just one category. Think for example of the design and maintenance of a website oriented towards customers: is that an ICT service or a marketing service? Similarly, consultancy services and the subsequent implementation of an enterprise resource planning (ERP) system usually consist of both business organization and ICT services. The integration of these types of services is also reflected in the trend for management consultancies to integrate with ICT providers, such as in the case of the Cap Gemini/Ernst & Young merger. This leads us to consider the different types of service providers.

## Types of business service providers

Nearly all companies sell services. Even those that would be undoubtedly classified as goods-producing companies sell products that have some element of service in them. General Electric and IBM, for example, generate more than half of their revenues through services, while they are usually perceived as goods manufacturers (OECD, 2000). In this section, however, we will focus on companies that are generally perceived as predominantly service providers.

Service production is done by all sorts of companies. Transportation companies, advertisement and media agencies, insurance providers, banks, attorneys; they are just a few examples. All these companies show both similarities and differences. In some aspects the similarities dominate; in other aspects the differences are more obvious. The great variation implies that it is difficult to find clear and useful groupings of service companies. Useful would mean that there are similarities *within* a group (homogeneity) while there are significant differences *between* groups (heterogeneity). One popular and useful classification distinguishes *routine service* providers from *professional service* (or knowledge) providers. Normann and Ramirez (1994) use the terminology 'relieving' and 'enabling' services for more or less the same distinction.

## Routine service providers

The traditional service provider is characterized by the ability to solve relatively simple problems for its customers, i.e. each separate transaction is rather simple.

The creative moments in the direct contacts with the customer are short even though they could be frequent. Usually, the service involves a great number of similar transactions with many customers and requires the involvement of only a few people in each transaction. That each transaction or contract is simple does not mean, however, that it is an easy task to get such a company working well. In order to succeed, the company normally has well-developed systems for handling personnel, information and other support functions. Production is usually highly standardized and the services are often bought and delivered as a 'task' to perform a certain function during a particular period of time. Some examples of services of this kind are:

- Cleaning.
- Travel.
- Security.
- Mail.
- Transportation.
- Administration.
- (Basic) banking services and insurance.

In many cases, the buying firm knows its needs and what kind of service production it takes to fulfil those needs. Furthermore, it may have sufficient knowledge to carry out the service but, for various reasons, prefers to buy it. It relieves itself of these efforts.

## Professional service providers

A professional service provider – or knowledge provider – is characterized by an ability to solve complex problems. Each separate transaction, or contract, is substantial and involves considerable creative moments in the direct contacts with the supplier. Often several people from both parties are involved in the problem-solving process (see Riesling and Sveiby, 1986). The assignment is normally on the basis of a specific project. Companies that can serve as an example are an engineering firm, an architect, a university or a consultancy firm. These companies have, compared to service companies, a non-standardized production process. Competencies and the abilities to solve problems reside largely in specific individuals, the 'professional' – the engineer, architect, the consultant – rather than in the organization itself (see also Wittreich, 1966). Despite the strong dependence on individuals, the so-called structural capital, i.e. the organization and its capabilities and resources, is not without importance even for this type of company. The administrative routines, the network of customers and other actors, systems, working procedures, the image of the organization, management's ability to lead and develop the company are all important ingredients.

Examples of knowledge companies and the type of services that are often seen as being knowledge and problem solving include:

- Temporary labour agencies with a focus on specific competencies.

- Lawyers.
- Advertising services.
- Technical consultancy (engineering).
- Architects.
- Media companies that provide creative services ('content providers').
- Management consultancies.
- Recruitment (headhunters).
- Special banking services such as special financing.
- Special stock trading and placement services.
- Special insurance services such as professional insurance.

Many of these services are difficult to grasp and frequently the customers have only vaguely defined needs. The solutions are developed in a process where the supplier and customer interact and step by step come to understand the real need and forge appropriate solutions. These services often enable the customer, in its turn, to deliver better value to its own customers.

It is important to note that many services and service providers do not meet all these criteria. In other words, there are neatly fitting, clear examples, but also many hybrids and borderline cases that are more difficult to categorize according to this distinction. Some service providers can, for example, operate like a routine service provider in some areas and like a professional service provider in others. Firms can also act as both at the same time in different markets. Additionally, even routine service providers solve problems that can be quite complex. The difference, however, is that these solutions, after they have been well defined, lead to long phases of more routine behaviour. The knowledge provider, as defined above, is more continuously oriented to creative problem solutions.

Hence a strict classification based on these two categories can be misleading or wrong in some cases, but what is important is to illustrate the broad differences and the underlying criteria.

## Types of business service customers

In Chapter 1 we defined business services as services provided by firms or other, formal organizations to other firms or organizations. In other words, business service customers can be either manufacturing or service companies, government authorities or organizations such as associations, foundations etc. In this book we will primarily focus on firms as customers, be it in a manufacturing setting or a service setting.

As briefly indicated already in Chapter 1, the relative importance of the different business service categories may differ across sectors, industries and individual companies. To give some illustrations of service procurement at different companies, consider the following four examples.

### Box 2.2: Service procurement in different industries

**Service procurement in a manufacturing company**
Some years ago, an IBM printer factory was buying the following services: surveillance/security, catering services, travel, facility management, telecommunication services, property management, translation, programming and advertising. Internal suppliers delivered transport, warehousing and administration services.

**Service procurement in a service company**
The insurance company Skandia, in a study several years ago, showed a comparable picture of purchased services. Especially important were IT services of different kinds: software, software development, computer maintenance, network support etc. Other essential items were advertising, security, training and property rental services.

**Service procurement in local government organizations**
The work of local governments consists largely of the production of services. This can involve road and building maintenance, healthcare, public transportation and schooling. In Sweden, some 50 per cent of the total purchasing volume by local government consists of service procurement, such as construction work, maintenance, transport, garbage collection, social care and consultancy (Bryntse, 2000).

**Service procurement in a knowledge-oriented company**
Ericsson Infocom Consultants, which is now differently organized within the Ericsson group, used to have a purchasing-to-sales ratio of about 50 per cent (Axelsson, 1996b). The core of the company's activities is development and engineering work, leading to the development of new services in telecommunication. Considering that it is not a normal manufacturing company that buys raw materials and components for processing, this high ratio may be surprising. However, a business like this needs to buy information technology, training, travel etc. The most important category, though, is the various types of consultants. The company was contracting external resources to a high degree, in order to have sufficient manpower to carry out its assignments.

The US study referred to earlier categorizes services into eight groups: advertising, construction and engineering, consultancy, healthcare, insurance, legal services, travel and facility services (Fearon and Bales, 1995). Table 2.1 shows the relative quantitative importance of those eight categories, for respectively manufacturing companies, service companies and public authorities. Overall, facility services, insurance and marketing/PR services are the top three services in terms of volume, but large differences exist. Transportation, for example, ranks number 2 for manufacturing companies, but only number 8 overall.

These figures should be interpreted with considerable care, however. First of all, there may be differences between similar sectors and organizations across different countries. Some figures in Table 2.1 may reflect typical US characteristics, such as the high rank of insurance, which should be seen in the light of that country's more legalistic, claims-oriented economy.

**Table 2.1** Most important service spend categories for various sectors

| Rank | Manufacturing companies | Service companies | Public authorities | Weighted average |
|------|------|------|------|------|
| 1 | Marketing/PR | Insurance | Insurance | *Facility services* |
| 2 | Transportation | Facility services | Banking | *Insurances* |
| 3 | Banking | Air travel | Construction services | *Marketing/PR* |
| 4 | Facility services | Healthcare | Personal insurances | *Healthcare* |
| 5 | Construction services | Consultancy | Cleaning | *Travel* |
| 6 | Healthcare | Hotels | Facility services | *Construction services* |
| 7 | Advertising | Copying | Garbage collection | *Consultancy* |
| 8 | Personnel | Telecommunication | Consultancy | *Transportation* |
| 9 | Cleaning | Banking | Architect services | *Banking* |
| 10 | Consultancy | Car rental | Auditing services | *Copying* |

*Source*: Fearon and Bales, 1995.

Furthermore, there are probably strong differences between individual companies in each of these types of sector. Each company or organization is unique and develops its own business idea with accompanying resource needs.

The main point, however, is to give an idea of the different types of business services being bought and which types of services are generally important.

## Different forms of business services

Services can be categorized in many different ways, as will have become clear by now. To conclude this chapter, we want to illustrate some ways of characterizing services based on their internal characteristics (rather than those of the provider). Again, the idea is that the services *within* a group should be very similar and that there should be significant differences *between* groups. Such differences are also important starting points for the buying company's behaviour.

We briefly discuss the following characterizations, partly based on existing classifications, partly on our own insights:

- Long-term versus short-term business services.
- Standardized versus non-standardized business services.
- Simple versus complex business services.
- Creative versus non-creative services.
- Fluctuating versus non-fluctuating business services.
- Business services targeted at individuals versus business services targeted at organizations.

In our view, the long-term/short-term classification is the most generally applicable and can be used in combination with any of the others.

## Long-term versus short-term business services

Long-term services are often services based on a contract. They are usually paid on the basis of annual agreements with a fixed price, within certain performance limits.

---

**Box 2.3: Examples of long-term services**

**Security and reception services**
Securitas sells surveillance and security, but has expanded its activities to the more general area of access control. A common alternative is that the customer has its own employees who work together with Securitas people in a security guard centre.

**Bank services**
Some banking services, such as the administration of wages for the company's employees, are based on annual contracts. The bank and the company agree on how the administration should be handled and what the conditions, such as the interest rates, should be.

**Park maintenance and garbage collection**
A supplier of park maintenance in a city can also be managed through a contract. The city representatives and the supplier agree on what is to be done, e.g. the frequency of cutting the grass in the summer, pruning of trees in the autumn or spring etc. Another example from the public sector may be the contract for garbage collection over a number of years. Local government and the contractor agree on the terms and the operating methods, such as collection frequencies, which will apply during the contract period.

---

There are also examples in this group of services that are characterized by a combination of an annual contract and a premium based on how often and how intensively the service is being used.

---

**Box 2.4: Examples of long-term service contracts with possible fluctuations**

**ICT service agreements**
ICT service agreements can be designed in many different ways, not least depending on the buying company's need for those different services. Is the need continuous and small or big? Is there a need for emergency services when a failure arises or is the time aspect not that critical? Is there some internal competence to take care of small failures?

---

Based on these considerations, the requirements and conditions for a service agreement are formulated, which are then set out in a contract for one or several years. The contract may stipulate the demands of the supplier regarding how the customer should collaborate, e.g. by giving the supplier access to its facilities during the night, in order for the agreement to work. The contract may also specify a basic level of service, which may be expanded for an additional fee.

**Car rental agreements**
Companies often sign long-term contracts with preferred agencies for rental cars. These usually include the basic conditions for the service: quality and type of cars, pick-up and drop-off places, design of the invoices, rebates etc.

**Telecommunication services**
Telecommunication services are often contracted on an annual or even longer basis. The agreement may include the system's availability, the traffic volumes that will be run on it and the conditions for rebates. Additional conditions can concern the number of extensions, possibilities for increasing or reducing the number of extensions, and the cost and availability of other communications such as Internet access and e-mail facilities.

**Psychiatric services**
Local government often contracts the services of private providers of psychiatric care. In the contract, there can be conditions concerning the number of different types of patients that can be treated, the kind of treatments to be given and the cost of treatments.

It will be clear that different types of long-term service deliveries occur in different situations.

Another common category of services includes short-term, project-like assignments. However, even those may take place within the context of a long-term contract or relation.

**Box 2.5: Courier services**

One example of a service that is often ordered, supplied and invoiced for each separate occasion, like a single transaction, is a courier service. A normal process would be that the person desiring the service contacts the supplier – a bike courier, a car courier etc. The supplier is informed about the pick-up and drop-off addresses, size of the package, required pick-up and drop-off times and other (special) information. The supplier quotes the price and the job is done, the service performed and the invoice drawn up and sent to the customer.

There are obviously variations to this 'one-off' version, especially for regular or large customers. There may be regular deliveries, for which the invoices, for example, are consolidated monthly, and there may be some special price negotiations when the courier knows that several packages have to be delivered to the same area and so on.

This service differs from those mentioned in the previous two boxes mainly by the fact that it is limited in time. However, we want to emphasize here that some of these services have *effects* over a long period, as demonstrated by the following illustrations.

---

**Box 2.6: Short-term services with long-term effects**

**Financial advice**
One service that is produced and delivered within a short period, but that can have effects over a very long period, is financial advice. This can include recommendations to secure a loan at a certain interest rate for a longer time, or making certain guarantees in the case of a takeover or stock issue. These services can have both positive and negative consequences over a long period.

**Recruitment**
Recruiting a manager or a certain type of specialist is another example of a service that is bought and performed over a limited period of time, but that has often effects during a longer period. The person recruited may stay for a relatively long time (compared to that taken for the actual recruitment) and may affect the company's activities to a high degree, for better or for worse.

---

## Standardized versus non-standardized business services

Another common categorization is between standardized and non-standardized services. Both can include long-term and short-term services. Two examples of services that are often highly standardized are school transport and cleaning.

---

**Box 2.7: Standardized services**

**School transport**
In many countries, local governments often negotiate school transport, which frequently occurs on the basis of an annual contract. In the contract, the transportation company agrees to supply buses (or vans/cars) travelling according to certain routes and timetables. The supply is required on each school day during the year.

**Cleaning**
Cleaning services that are negotiated by companies and other organizations are also often very standardized. Surfaces, precision and frequency are all parameters that are defined for the actual performance of the cleaning service.

---

A closely related distinction that can be made is between services that have substantial creative elements and those that are mainly identical from one occasion to the other. Some examples follow.

> ### Box 2.8: Financial advice and marketing campaigns – examples of creative, non-standardized services
>
> Financial advice can be very creative. The possibilities for a supplier to offer a financially interesting service that is also well adapted to the customer's financial situation can play an important role and require a great deal of creativity.
>
> A specific example was the proposal by financial advisers to split the Swedish pharmaceutical company Astra (now Astra-Zeneca) into a division for the successful medicine Losec and a division for all other activities. The idea behind this was that Losec should be able to stand on its own feet. Calculations of the results of this split for the shareholders were very positive and were thought to increase the value of their shareholdings considerably. This advice involved a substantial amount of creative thinking.
>
> To design a marketing campaign is something that is often perceived as obviously being creative. The aim is to get a message across that reaches the right target audiences and is noted among all other campaigns, is perceived in the way it was meant to be, and achieves the right effects in terms of interest, attitude changes, purchases etc.

The following example demonstrates that creative (non-standardized) services (and obviously also non-creative, standardized services) may involve either long-term or short-term services.

> ### Box 2.9: Development services such as engineering
>
> An advertising campaign can continue for a relatively long time as a project. Other creative services with a long-term nature are services in the context of major development projects, such the design of a new type of fighter or passenger plane. Other creative design and development services, such as the design of a new label or package for a fruit juice, may have a considerably shorter time span.

A special variant of non-standardized services is that offered in 'modules', see Chapter 3.

## Simple versus complex business services

Another distinction that is sometimes made is between simple and complex services. Even these can be a subgroup of long-term and short-term services; both of these can consist of simple and complex services. Furthermore, simple is not the same as standardized and complex is not the same as non-standardized. Consider the following example.

> **Box 2.10: Cleaning services – sometimes complex standardized services**
>
> Many cleaning services are such that they do not require any substantial professional training, but some can be very advanced. There are environments, such as laboratories and different types of production facilities, in which the demands regarding the amount of dust particles etc. are extremely stringent. In such an environment, cleaning can be a very complex and advanced service.

Even within these categories of complex and simple services, we can obviously find a broad range of different services.

## Fluctuating versus non-fluctuating business services

Many services are characterized by demand that fluctuates over time. For some these fluctuations are regular: weekly, monthly, seasonally or annually (think of outside painting, lawnmower repair and tourist information centres). For others the fluctuations are irregular. For a third group there are no fluctuations at all. Even this dimension can be seen as a subcategory of long-term and short-term services.

> **Box 2.11: Conference centres, tax forms and annual reports**
>
> Conference centres often wrestle with the problem that their capacity is underused during long periods, especially weekends, holidays and so on.
> Auditing services follow a natural annual cycle and high demand coincides with the tax authorities' demands that companies should present their income statements and other accounts. Similarly, companies that assist firms (and individuals) with filling in their tax forms experience regular cycles in demand.

## Business services targeted at individuals versus business services targeted at organizations

This criterion – whether the service is primarily oriented at the individual employee or the organization as a whole – again can be seen as a subcategory of those defined previously. Some illustrations follow.

> **Box 2.12: Business services targeted at individuals**
>
> **Medical services**
> Often companies negotiate medical services for their employees. This can involve, for example, pre-contracted physiotherapeutic treatments at special rates or annual health

checks for all employees. The agreement specifies what is to be checked and what treatments may follow from the checks. There may also be agreements that provide priority specialist treatment (such as surgery) for key personnel and so on.

**Domestic services**
More and more companies offer domestic (housekeeping) services to their employees. This is a secondary benefit that relieves employees of some of their domestic chores and, in that way, helps them meet their professional obligations and gain more valuable spare time. The Scandinavian insurance company Trygg-Hansa offers this service to employees with small children. The service is contracted by the employer and is a employee benefit just like a leased car, and is therefore subject to taxation.

These services are directed at and consumed by individuals in the company. Other services are targeted at the organization as such, or parts thereof.

**Box 2.13: Services for organizations**

**Auditing services**
Annual reports and accounts need to be audited and verified by registered accountants. These services follow guidelines on what is to be controlled and under which conditions the auditors can approve the accounts. These services can be complemented by others, such as advice and recommendations on the improvement of certain administrative routines. These services are often negotiated for a specific period, say a number of days and hours that the auditing company should be or actually has been investing in the assignment.

**Advertising services**
Advertising services are often negotiated within the framework of an ongoing collaboration. The advertising agency has the customer as an account. Campaigns are discussed, planned and executed based on a dialogue between the agency and the customer.

That certain services are aimed at individuals in the company – as employees or private individuals – and others at the company as a whole can be a very important distinction. It may, among other things, affect the way payments are made, for example an agreement for a specific period, based on actual consumption or a combination of these.

Through the different classifications we have presented, we have emphasized one of our earlier statements: services are a very differentiated and varied group of products, with different characteristics. As a consequence, they are often hard to define. Nevertheless, the characterizations listed here can be of assistance in a practical purchasing situation, in helping to describe and analyse the actual service according to the distinctions made above. Following that, one needs to evaluate the most important aspects to consider given the type of service in focus, in addition to the general characteristics of business services as discussed in Chapter 1.

## Conclusions

This chapter has tried to identify the differences between various business services, their providers and their clients. The main conclusion is that business services are not homogeneous, and an important aim of the chapter has been to illuminate the wide spectrum of business services. First, we discussed this spectrum in terms of the type of service offered: facility services, financial services, information and communication technology services, business organization services, research and development and technical services, transportation and distribution services, human resource development services, and marketing services. Then we discussed the services spectrum in terms of routine based vs knowledge based.

Finally, we described the spectrum in terms of the internal characteristics of business services. These internal characteristics include one main dimension – time – and a number of subdimensions. For example, both long-term and short-term business services may also be described in terms of simple vs complex, and many other subdimensions.

Thus we have drawn a multidimensional picture of services that also tries to address the common conception that people have of the services that companies buy: that they either involve mundane things like cleaning, or IT services or management consultancy. The reality is much more complex than that.

The reason for discussing the different types and forms of business in such detail is obviously that for the buying company it can be important to realize which type of service and service provider one is dealing with. In Part III, we discuss some guidelines for how purchasing behaviour and purchasing strategy may be adapted to the specific type of service being bought. First, Part II considers how to analyse business services.

# Part II

## Analysis: Business Services as Functions and Activities

# 3

# Business Services in Terms of Activities, Resources and Actors

In Chapter 2, services were defined and illustrated in a number of different ways. Services are essentially made out of one or a number of activities, or one or a number of chains of activities. Earlier, we also discussed service components in terms of bundles of activities. The point is that no matter the size of the assignment or what it involves, *activities* must always be carried out, *actors* must be mobilized for the assignment and they must have access to relevant *resources*. In this first chapter of Part II, Analysis, this terminology will be introduced as an analytical tool for various parts of the discussions in the following chapters.

## Services described as activities and functions

One way of describing what services and the production of services consist of is illustrated by the following example.

> **Box 3.1   Jensen safari**
>
> Some years ago, the Executive MBA program at Uppsala University (Sweden) purchased a packaged service for a seminar for 35 delegates in South Africa. This was

a 'service production', which involved a large number of chains of activities, many actors and, overall, a considerable number of different kinds of resources and competencies. A description of how the complete service production emerged and how it was carried out provides a good starting point for discussing service production in terms of *activities*.

### Actors and general activities

The work was initiated when the MBA course management group, in collaboration with the course participants, discussed the preferable direction of the study trip, its scope, contents, location etc. Thereafter, the question was which *actors/suppliers* could help in carrying this out. Wits Business School in Johannesburg and the Swedish Export Council in the same city were two very competent partners in finding individuals and companies to provide the desired profile for the content of the seminar. Travel agent Nyman & Schulz's unit for conference travel had carried out a number of similar arrangements, with good references. Hence they were hired to take care of all transport, logistics and social (tourist) activities.

Uppsala University thus established contacts with each of these three actors. Subsequently, a connection between the Swedish Trade Council and Wits Business School was established as well. The trip had two main destinations, Johannesburg and Cape Town, with a full programme of activities.

This may seem easy enough and principally only a question of buying three major service productions: one travel and tourism production and two business (professional) content productions. However, it was not that simple.

### Service content (general activity structure)

Let us consider two of the service productions in more detail:

- The travel service turned out to involve travelling by plane from Stockholm to Johannesburg, plane from Johannesburg to the Kruger Park, car transport to the lodge in Ulusaba, a safari event, similar return transport by car and plane to Johannesburg, bus from the airport to the hotel in the city, and in addition hotel reservations and bus transport to and from Wits Business School (in Johannesburg) as well as some other visits, including an excursion and an educational visit to an operating goldmine. Subsequently, a flight to Cape Town was needed, a bus from the plane to the wine district with transportation between boarding houses and hotels (the group was spread out over different accommodation) and so on. Other excursions involved the Cape of Good Hope and Cape Town's Waterfront district. The trip was completed by bus transfer to the airport for the flight back via London to Sweden. Obviously, all this travelling involved a number of actors and activities.
- The production of the professional content was done (apart from the university's role as the actor placing orders) by two important actors: representatives from the Swedish Trade Council and Wits Business School. The MBA group spent three days following a course at the school. Through a project manager, the school's president arranged the first day, containing lectures from the school's most prominent professors. The Trade Council was responsible for the other two days. The first involved a number of representatives of Swedish companies who talked about their own and their companies' experiences in doing business in South Africa. An additional event was a party at the Johannesburg Country Club with the Swiss/Swedish multinational ABB as host. The third day was spent with South

> African companies and important South African institutions. Finally, the Trade Council arranged the visit to the goldmine. The production of these professional services also added a number of actors.

This description still gives the impression of relatively few problems, even though by now the complexity has increased. The allocation of work and responsibility between the actors is still clear, as are their different functions. But when we take an even closer look it becomes clear that there were important delineation and execution problems to be solved in the production of the complete service package. Let us illustrate this by describing one of the more problematic service components.

---

**Box 3.2  The booking problem – a service component**

An important issue in the relationship between the people responsible for the MBA programme at Uppsala University, the course participants from around 20 companies and the travel agency was who was in fact responsible for reserving the tickets. From experience, the university people knew that in these kinds of groups there will be a number of individual wishes: to combine the trip with another trip, for example to arrive directly from the US, to be able to leave a day earlier or later, to be able to postpone the decision to participate, to be able to change one's mind since there are matters beyond one's control that may need to be taken care of and so on. Who should handle these changes to plans?

One possibility is that the people responsible for education should collect all the changes and keep track of them so that they can inform the travel agency when necessary. The other alternative is that all course participants have direct contact with the travel agency so that all changes can be handled directly between them. There is also an economic aspect to this: who is financially responsible for possible deviations and what is the cost?

In this case, the responsibility was given to the travel agency. The course participants were obliged to handle their own contacts in connection to their trip directly with the travel agency. The MBA course management in turn was informed by the travel agency about the course participants' choices of routes and times of arrival etc. This can be seen as an additional component of the agency's service production.

---

This description illustrates how the procurement of a service can include the purchase of a large number of activities, to be carried out at different times and in different situations. Those who carry out the activities can be referred to as actors who are expected to have abilities in the form of knowledge, time, supporting staff and other important resources to carry out the activities. These activities require that the actors (the executors) have access to different resources (premises, transportation, personnel and knowledge). When the activities are carried out, certain resources are consumed, such as individuals' time in the preparation and realization of the activities, and the utilization of vehicles for transport. Other resources are not consumed but are still important prerequisites for carrying out the services. The consumption of resources can be – and often is – attributed with a certain monetary value. Yet other resources are *created* in the execution of the activities. This may entail increased knowledge among the actors involved of how to carry out these kinds of arrangements. A service production can thus be described in terms of *activities, actors* and *resources*.

This description is based on the so-called network or A-R-A model, developed by a group of researchers in the area of industrial (business-to-business) marketing and purchasing (Håkansson, 1982; Håkansson and Johanson, 1992; Håkansson and Snehota, 1995). In this model or approach, the three concepts of activities, actors and resources are used as key elements. We return to this model in more detail later.

The line of reasoning in the A-R-A model is also closely related to mainstream research on services. There are well-established models on how to determine the nature of a certain service through mapping the activities involved in its creation. One of the best-known is the 'blueprinting method' (Shostack, 1992). This method involves the activities constituting a certain service being mapped in detail. The activities constitute the *design* of the particular service.

This view can be related to Grönroos's terminology (2000, p. 166), in which a distinction is drawn between:

- *Core service(s)* – the basic function that the service is to achieve (the trip, the course programme).
- *Supporting service(s)* – different additional functions that add value (help with check-in at airports and hotels etc.).
- *Facilitating service(s)* – important prerequisites to make it possible to produce and deliver the service (design of premises, access to mobile phones to enable fast communication etc.).

Core and supporting services can be related to our discussion on activities, while facilitating services have more to do with the discussion on resources. Later in this book we describe the process of buying services as an interplay (exchange process) over time between customer and supplier (Chapters 4–6) and as a decision process, the actual buying (Chapters 7–9). In the negotiations and agreements regarding service purchases, both the actual service as well as the interplay between customer and supplier may need to be clarified. Here, we give a complementary perspective in which the production of services is described in terms of activities, actors and resources. At the end of Chapter 1 we discussed some of the special characteristics of (buying) business services. In the following sections we return to that discussion.

## The A-R-A model

The A-R-A model is often described as in Figure 3.1. It was developed as a tool for describing and analysing business activities in industrial systems. The idea is that there are different actors in the industrial system who have control over

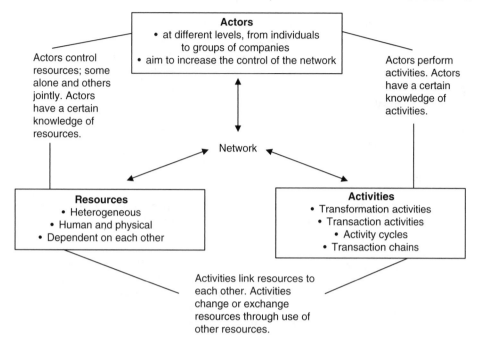

**Figure 3.1** The Activities-Resources-Actors model
*Source*: Håkansson, 1987, p. 17.

resources and who carry out different activities. When they perform their activities, e.g. production/manufacturing activities or transaction/exchange activities, their own resources or those of others are used.

The general starting point for descriptions according to this model is the pattern of activities and the way the activities are linked or connected to each other. Subsequently, one examines what resources are used in or tied to these activities when they are being performed, and which of these resources are most critical. In addition, an analysis is made of which actors control these (more or less critical) resources. Finally, it is important to examine how the actors involved are connected through different kinds of *bonds*: social, technical, legal, economic etc.

A service can consist of anything from a single activity to a number of connected activity chains, a series of more or less extensive activities that are tightly related to each other. In any case, activities involve something more structured than just single events; they form the substance, the essence of the service.

Service activities are usually *preceded* by a sequence of actions. Returning to our example of the study tour, the description is focused on the actual service activities taking place and the functions or purpose that they fulfil. But in the preparation, many actions and initiatives had to be taken to realize these activities. One type of action, for example, was the negotiations between the various actors.

Services are produced – and activities performed – by different kinds of actors. An actor can be anything from a single individual to a big company or even a major corporation. This depends on the system of activities being studied and the chosen level of detail. When actors perform activities, they use different kinds of services. A simple example can illustrate how activities, actors and resources are related to each other.

---

**Box 3.3   Distribution of flyers**

A football team accepted the task of distributing flyers for a pizzeria. The pizzeria planned its operations for the production of pizzas based on its experience of how great a demand the distribution of 2500 flyers would create. If the football team only managed to distribute half the flyers, the agreement was that the pizzeria would only pay for half of the service.

This was a highly risky undertaking. The entire effort could have become a severe loss, since the pizzeria had planned its resources in order to meet a high demand, specifically in terms of personnel to bake and distribute the pizzas. An activity that partly 'disappeared' (the distribution of half the flyers) would therefore generate consequences for both resources as well as actors – and these could be quite serious. The resources mobilized cost almost as much whether they are used (for baking pizzas etc.) or not.

---

The A-R-A model is useful for describing and analysing economic activities within and between organizations. Actors perform activities for which resources are used, and there are often strong requirements for synchronizing the activities and resources between two or more actors. In the following section, we discuss the different activities and actor structures that are created in the production of different services. In later chapters, we will return to the model in more depth.

## Allocation of activities between actors

We stated earlier that services are often formulated as an assignment, which the supplier accepts to perform alone or together with the customer and/or other actors. The activity systems in which these accepted assignments result can differ depending on what functions are requested, which actors are responsible for which activity/activities and so on. Below, we review some important aspects and illustrations of how activities can be organized and how roles and responsibilities can differ between different actors. The purpose is to demonstrate the possible variety of activity patterns and divisions of labour underlying the production and consumption of business services (of which a wide variety exist, as discussed in Chapter 2).

### Vertical allocation of activities

An allocation of activities that is mainly based on the assumption that the tasks of actors are allocated *along* the value chain, in terms of a short or long distance

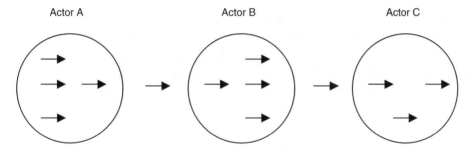

**Figure 3.2**   Vertical allocation of activities

away from final consumption by the consumer, can be called a *vertically dominated* division of labor. Often terms such as *upstream* or *downstream* are used to indicate different positions on this value chain. Upstream means that the specific operation or activity is close to the extraction of raw materials, while downstream means that it is close to the end user. Figure 3.2 illustrates this kind of allocation of activities.

This means that the responsibility for the activities performed is regulated between the customer and the supplier in a traditional sense. The supplier is at a greater distance from the consumer and at an earlier stage of the value chain. The customer handles activities that are based on tasks performed by the supplier at an earlier stage. It is, however, also common for one and the same actor to be active in two stages. For example, actor A has responsibility for the entire service package and starts with performing certain activities, but then actor B performs part of the package. As soon as their activities have been completed, A regains the initiative and performs some remaining activities.

These kinds of division of labor can be distinguished in a variety of situations. There may be a division of labor within a continuous relationship, in recurrent activity cycles or within a temporary project. Examples of these situations will be given below.

*Continuous activity chains (long-term assignments)*

---

**Box 3.4   Permanent vertical allocation of activities**

Amersham Pharmacia Biotech works together with the global delivery service company DHL in the area of logistical services. When any of Pharmacia Biotech's sales offices in Europe places an order with the production unit in Uppsala (Sweden), a consignment note is automatically transmitted to DHL and the goods are delivered within 24 hours, often even faster. A parcel collected in Stockholm by 19.00 can be delivered in New York by 10.30 the next day.

This is a continuous process. DHL has an activity system that works as a basic infrastructure. The activities of Pharmacia are then linked to this, according to a specific pattern. There is a specified 'closing time' in the evening by which the orders must be placed to reach the addressee the next day. If the company keeps its structure of activities within these boundaries, it will harmonize with the activities of the supplier.

With the help of this arrangement, Pharmacia has been able to cut both its distribution costs and its costs for expensive fresh goods, which before then did not reach the customer in time. Previously Pharmacia had 14 warehouses around Europe. Chemical samples and substances have a short life cycle and many of these used to exceed their use-by date before they were sold.

These continuous operations, implying that identical activities are continuously repeated, can in certain cases be described as circles of activities instead of as a straight line. In that case they could be illustrated as in Figure 3.3, which provides a picture of ongoing activity loops that are different from the activity lines in the previous illustration.

*Recurrent activity chains (short assignments frequently repeated within a permanent relationship)*
Consider the following example.

---

**Box 3.5   Hiring super-pilots for critical manoeuvres**

Gulf Agency Company (GAC), which works all over the world but has its headquarters in Stockholm, offers a number of services for customers in the field of shipping. Through its concept GAC Cargo Systems, it offers a complete logistics package, which includes transport, logistics and distribution services.

An especially interesting service is 'ship-to-ship transfer', where GAC offers 'coaches', e.g. when a large oil freighter, which cannot port, needs to deliver oil to a smaller freighter out at sea. The task of the coach is to give directions to the boats so that they can dock and begin transferring the oil. This is a difficult operation. The boats must be very close to each other at a certain angle, in order not to bounce off each other or collide. The insurance companies involved demand that this operation be led by a coach certified by them. Such coaches are supplied by GAC. In practical terms, this may mean that a coach travels from Sweden, is put aboard an oil freighter in Kuwait, leads the operation, returns to the mainland and travels back to Sweden. Thereafter, the normal captain can regain command of the freighter.

Another specific service is that GAC personnel also work as 'load masters', with responsibility for measuring how many tonnes of oil have been transferred from one ship to another, the measurement then being approved by both parties involved. If the seller thinks that 100 000 tonnes have been transferred and the buyer argues that it is only 99 000 tonnes, for example, this may seem a marginal difference but it represents a very large sum of money.

*Source*: Interview with Ulf Eriksson, UE Engineering, 1997, and information from GAC's home page.

---

These two services are, when described in terms of activities, of the type 'actor A leaves over to actor B who in turn leaves back to actor A', i.e. actor A uses help from actor B for a certain part of its activity chain.

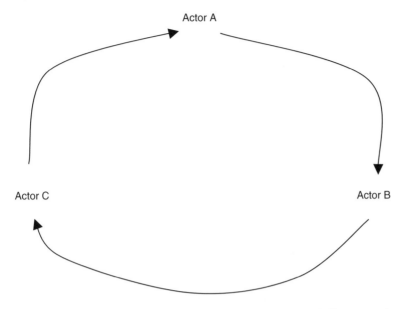

**Figure 3.3**  Continuous activity chain between three actors, vertical allocation of activities

*Temporary activity chains (a substantial task, limited in time and possibly not repeated)*

---

**Box 3.6  Temporary allocation of development and production activities**

Ohmae (1995, quoted in Van Weele and Rozemeijer, 1996) presents a good example of a global division of labour. Certain Japanese companies develop new products (in terms of design etc.) in a research network involving American and Asian researchers. The sketches are then developed in detail by engineers/programmers in Bangalore or Bombay in India (lower salaries). The details are sent electronically to Singapore; the components for production are constructed in Taiwan and then shipped to Tianjin (China) for assembly and inspection; and finally the products are sold in Europe and the US.

---

It is evident that the network model works quite well as a tool to describe these different activity chains or patterns.

## Horizontal allocation of activities

A different pattern is created in situations where the activities are placed in parallel, i.e. performed at the same time and by actors working at the same level upstream or downstream, at the same distance from the final consumer. These kinds of division of labour can be illustrated as in Figure 3.4.

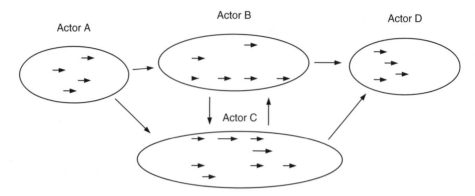

**Figure 3.4**  Horizontal allocation of activities

Also in this case it is important to recognize the differences between more or less continuous deliveries and activities, and project-based, shorter business transactions. The sequence 'actor C who leaves over to actor B who in his turn leaves the ongoing assignment back to actor C' is common in these kinds of structures.

*Continous activity chains (long-term assignments)*
Consider again two illustrations.

---

**Box 3.7  Resource pooling for combined leverage**

A good illustration of a horizontal division of labour is resource pooling by distributors in order to gain a powerful joint system, as in the case of American distributor of industrial equipment Grainger Integrated Supply Operations (GISO), reported by Narus and Anderson (1996).

Since the mid-1990s, the company has been striving to offer its customers deliveries of a wider range of articles, repairs etc. than had earlier been the case. The company realizes this by, among other things, cooperating with three groups of suppliers:

● The traditional distribution channels.
● Other independent, prominent distributors.
● An internal purchasing group (within the Grainger group) with many contacts and the ability to obtain unusual products.

Products that are made available from these sources can either be delivered directly to GISO customers or be consolidated into a package. When GISO receives an order, the purchaser involved directly accesses the computer system and checks if the articles are available at the company's traditional distributors (group A). Parts that these distributors cannot deliver are ordered from group B, the independent distributors who have a complementary range of products and parallel activity structures to GISO. Group B suppliers are paid by GISO for their products. To be included in the GISO system, they pay an annual fee, delivery costs and a small transaction fee in relation to the particular transaction. If the suppliers in group B cannot deliver, GISO's own unit starts searching for the unusual products (group C suppliers). For the purchasing unit, computerized searching and a broad range of contacts form the foundation for success.

This is an illustration of how a specialized distribution company organizes activity structures to create a capability, an organized system of resources and knowledge, to be able to handle logistical problems effectively.

---

**Box 3.8  A global helpdesk**

For companies with globally dispersed production facilities, the ability to provide service is important. In many cases service functions locally, i.e. one or a number of service units, take care of problems that appear in that city, country or continent.

Thanks to technological developments, these functions have changed in many organizations as well. A centrally placed helpdesk function can now handle all the problems that arise within a large geographic area. For some companies, like Ericsson, it may be important to follow the developments in connected networks over the whole world, 24 hours a day. For such companies, it is rational to organize helpdesk functions as a sort of 'relay race' where the unit, which operatively is manning the function, varies between different time zones. Two or more service organizations can also divide the assignments between them, depending on the type of service (specialization). In this way, the work rotates around the globe and one unit relieves the other as time passes.

---

In continuous, horizontally aligned activity chains, the activities are repetitive and there is a well-organized activity structure according to which responsibilities and authorities have been divided between actors. The actors involved have thus developed a common structure of activities, which are repeated according to a specific pattern. The operations are continuous and the actors know at what point their own responsibility is passed on to the next party.

As in the case of continuous activity chains with vertical allocation of activities, horizontally aligned continuous activity chains are probably more clearly described in terms of *circles* of activities, as in Figure 3.3.

*Recurrent activity chains (short assignments within a permanent relationship)*

---

**Box 3.9  A bank's purchase and development of study material**

A European bank wanted to develop flexible study material based on specific cases or situations for the personnel in the local branches to work with, e.g. in connection with their weekly internal meetings. This service was purchased in the following way.

The bank first approached some possible consultants to develop the content of the idea and to see if there was a coherent and reasonable basic philosophy. A consultancy firms was selected and the work was done interactively with an internal work group. The work resulted in a document called 'Our Business Culture'. This was presented to the bank's board of directors and was, after certain editing, subsequently approved.

In phase two, material consisting of interesting and informative situations was to be created. This phase was seen as a routine job by the bank and thus it was assigned to its normal consultants who were often hired for this kind of assignment. The bank had a blanket contract with these consultants, meaning that they were less expensive than the consultants hired in phase one. Together with these consultants, film actors and so on, a package was completed that described some 20 situations. The material was stored on CD-ROM discs. At the branch offices, employees choose a suitable moment to practise one or several of these situations. They will then consider different courses of action and discuss the implications of the bank's business culture for the situation described.

*Temporary activity chains (a substantial task, limited in time)*
A final type of horizontal allocation of activities involves more temporary activity chains.

---

**Box 3.10   Purchasing resources and activities for a development project**

In certain situations, development services are purchased according to a special technique, where the services are broken up at the right point and divided between many actors. One reason is to gain time. For development projects this may mean that the creative thinkers work as long as they are needed, then they assign an army of less-qualified 'programmers' for the routine work.

At the start the scope of a development project is often unknown, and it is thus hard to define and price its contents exactly. A possible activity structure is first to hire a consultant paid on an ongoing, hourly basis. When the consultant has worked about 20 per cent of the estimated total time, they should be able to divide the project into a number of smaller work packages. These are transformed into fixed assignments (lump-sum contracts) and can, in certain cases, also be performed together with consultancy firms that were not involved from the beginning.

Each of the different work packages, A, B and C, is then allocated a fixed price. Different work packages get different prices depending on scope and difficulty. In this way the company can go from variable to fixed prices and consequently avoid buying idle hours. Equally, the buying company wins time since the projects can be finished at an earlier stage, because they can be divided into well-defined packages that can be carried out in parallel. In practice, the division takes place gradually as the project develops. As the work package is defined as a subproject, payments can also be connected to particular events/performance.

---

## Allocation of activities: horizontally and vertically at the same time

An activity system can be organized according to different principles. Four main variants are as follows:

● One actor takes overall responsibility for holding the network together. This is exemplified by contractors in the building industry, systems integration companies in the IT industry and other project coordinators of this kind.

- A number of actors join and decide actively together how they want to organize operations.
- An organized structure emerges organically; no single actor or group of actors controls everything, but it still works in an organized manner.
- 'Laissez faire': the market decides and no active coordination takes place.

Hence there are clearly allocations of activities that are both vertical as well as horizontal, and the classifications in the previous two sections are only simplifications. The image of a value chain along which a product is successively refined before getting to consumers is very simplistic. An alternative metaphor sees the company as an arena where activities flow together from several directions. At the intersection of these activities, the company shapes its contribution to value creation. This can be illustrated as in Figure 3.5. The metaphor of the company as a value constallation (Normann and Ramirez, 1994) or the industrial business system as a network can be seen as more relevant the more downstream one gets. There is, in different contexts, an assumption that both complexity and the amount of knowledge and resources (and thereby actors) an actor needs increase the further away one comes from the raw material stage.

This illustration presents the company as an actor in a relatively complex network of activity structures and actor groupings. If we then also recognize that it takes resources (internal or those of others) for the actors to perform the activities, it means that the structures also consist of different kinds of resources and resource constellations.

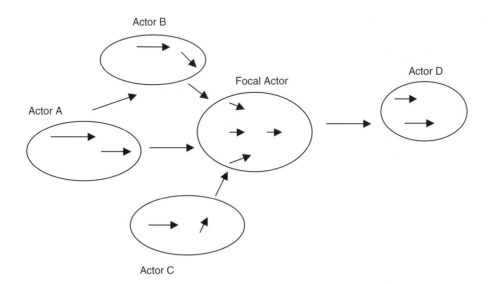

**Figure 3.5** The company as a point of contact where activities are joined from several directions

## Conditions for allocation of activities: production technology

Different production technologies create different conditions for the division of labour. It is easier to separate some activities from each other than others. One way to discuss this structurally is by using Thompson's (1967) classification of production technologies. Thompson distinguishes *serially connected technologies*, *mutual technologies* and *intermediary technologies*.

Serially connected technologies are characterized by one of the activities having to be carried out before the next can be performed. Consequently, there is a sequential dependence between them. Mutual technologies are characterized by activities being carried out simultaneously and interactively. This means that it is hard to tell them apart – if one activity ceases to progress the other activities also stop. Intermediary technologies are different from the other two in that there is no clear connection between subsequent activities.

The specific technology involved consequently influences the possibilities for the division of labour between the actors. The easiest way of separating the activities is in the case of intermediary technologies, then serially connected technologies; the hardest to separate are activities involving mutual technologies.

With these implications, this classification has been used to discuss the possibilities of transferring operations from one place to another, for example decentralizing certain activities (Axelsson and Berger, 1989). Certain dependencies between activities can in some cases be handled or coordinated from a long distance; in other cases they must be executed in close proximity. However, it should be pointed out that in many situations, information and communication technology (ICT) has changed the conditions for the division and (geographic) distribution of work, not least for information-related activities. ICT has thereby influenced what activities and for which technologies activities can be separated. Hence, the technologies now differ in the *degrees* of freedom when it comes to organizing activities. In Chapter 6, we will take a closer look at the impact of one application of ICT – e-commerce – and its impact on the allocation, production and buying of business services.

The issue of production technologies has also been recognized in research about possibilities and limitations to use outsourcing, i.e. to contract out to an external supplier activities that have earlier been carried out internally. The *boundaries* between different activities have in these situations been presented as substantial hindrances and/or enablers (Blomgren, 1997).

The issue is also relevant for suppliers that, in a more efficient and customer-oriented manner, want to supply their customers with packages of service offerings. They want to be able to offer their customers 'naked solutions with options'. For this to work, it is necessary for activities to be able to be grouped and controlled. This is easier if the supplier learns how to work 'modularly': when a customer wants a certain package of supplementary services it should be easy to execute these additional services. They are produced as a 'module of activities' (Anderson and Narus, 1995). Production technology influences the conditions for carrying out these strategies. If a particular module is created through a mutual technology, the supplier cannot handle the execution alone.

The customer must be involved and activated and in that way, the process (execution) can become more complex and difficult to organize.

## Analysing and changing activity structures

Activity structures as we have described them can evidently be hard to change, depending among others on the production technology. This does not preclude, however, it being an important aspect of all services that activity structures may – and sometimes should – be changed. The changes can be induced by new conditions in the form of new technology, changed market structures or changed customer demands. Therefore, for internal and external actors involved in certain activity structures, there are always more or less evident and important reasons to reconsider the functionality of the current activity system. A tool for this kind of analysis can be the following checklists (Axelsson, 1996a; adapted from Gadde and Håkansson, 1993, 2001).

## Activity analysis

The goal of an analysis as discussed here would be to identify the business service process that should be changed or redeveloped by mapping and analysing the activities of which the process consists. Relevant questions would be:

- What does a complete chain of activities look like, from the first step of the process to the last?
- Can a certain activity be eliminated or moved to another position in the chain or to another actor?
- Can coordination between the activities be improved?
- How can a single activity be adapted to the others?
- Can a certain chain of activities be exchanged for another?

A company that poses these questions and extracts information to assess and answer them will have a basic foundation in the form of a general picture of the current business service process. For the analysis to be really useful, it is imperative that the mapping is done thoroughly.

After this process mapping, one can start to think about possible redesigns. As a mnemonic, one can think of the word *CARRIER*, which stands for a series of seven questions:

- C = Change – Can certain activities be changed?
- A = Align – Can certain activities be aligned better?
- R = Rearrange – Can the activity sequence be altered?
- R = Reduce – Which activities can be shortened or reduced in frequency?
- I = Integrate – Can certain activities be combined or even integrated?
- E = Eliminate – Which activities can be left out?

- R = Reapply – Are there are activities that could be redirected for other purposes?

These CARRIER questions can create a good starting point for capturing new ideas.

## Resource analysis

The goal of the subsequent resource analysis would be to map and analyse the use of resources in the business service processes being studied. Relevant questions include:

- What are the total costs of the resources (including knowledge) required to carry out the (service) process?
- Which are the most critical resources for the process? What makes it possible to achieve the basic function of the process?
- Which of these critical resources does the company need to control itself, and which ones can be acquired externally?
- What resources would an alternative (design of the) process require?

The activity and the resource analysis may be complemented by an actor analysis.

## Actor analysis

Relevant questions to map the actors involved are as follows:

- What actors are involved in the process and what activities are they carrying out?
- What actors control the critical resources for the current process and for the possible alternatives? In what way do they control them?
- What relations does the company have to these actors? What forms of cooperation are possible in order to get access to these resources (or to get *better* access, e.g. to become more prioritized by a partner)?
- Can the current partners be influenced to change in a direction that makes it possible for us to access a wider resource base?

By carrying out such a relatively simple activity, resource and actor analysis, a general picture can be created of the relevant (business service) process and its activity chains, which forms the reference point for future improvements.

## Buying business services as resourcing

Irrespective of whether the business service/assignment consists of a temporary project or a continuous task, from the buyer's point of view it requires that actors be involved. These actors must have the necessary means to carry out the required activities in the desired, competent manner. When the customer starts to engage actors for the assignment, this creates a foundation for linking activities and connecting resources. The company is involved in what can be seen as a more or less continuous 'resourcing process'.

In this book, the word *resourcing* is given two complementary meanings:

- The company attracts surrounding actors' resources and interests in order to *get access to resources* as needed. It may be with the aim of building resource structures for the current needs, or for all larger and smaller future needs for business services. This is, for example, done through building relations with those suppliers that have control over important resources and are willing to make these available for the customer. Resourcing by the buying company consists of relating to such actors.
- The company, on its own or in (interactive) collaboration with its suppliers, *develops resources*. In relation to various assignments, more or less far-stretching improvements take place continuously together with the suppliers. Resources are being developed. The buying company can, to a varying extent and with differing ability, be focused on using these kinds of possibilities. The purchasing company's resourcing process consists of being part of and driving this kind of resource development.

With regard to resourcing as a process of getting access to resources (meaning A), the company may apply a certain division between current, routine assignments and occasional assignments. To be able to handle this kind of mixture of needs and assignments, there is a requirement to try to create a structure of suppliers that the company can mobilize when necessary. Consider these two illustrations.

---

### Box 3.11   Mobilizing supplier networks

**A basic structure in the form of a supplier list**
A manufacturing company has the policy of working with fewer suppliers; the target is three per buying area (product range). The company has also grouped its suppliers according to quality levels: A, B and C. In time, it wants to be able to exclusively use group A suppliers and it tries to influence the suppliers in groups B and C to improve so that they can qualify as a group A supplier. The reason for this is that the company wants a supplier network that has strong resources, and it also wants to be an important customer for its suppliers and consequently have a better chance of having its voice heard and its specific needs met. This is a basic structure, which the company wants to achieve and mobilize in order to handle its own challenging assignments, both today and in the future.

**A basic structure in the form of an address book**
Within many businesses, the supplier network consists of a looser structure of actors that may need to be mobilized every now and then. Training companies arranging courses have, for example, a need for address books, which hold names, addresses and certain notes about the characteristics of 'resource individuals' (speakers, chairpersons etc.). This can involve knowing ten individuals who can give a lecture about relations with the media, ten who can lead exercises in presentation techniques, ten who know a lot about doing business in Japan etc. From time to time, the training company will need to mobilize a number of actors among these, who can assist in performing a service production.

Resourcing as in *developing* resources (meaning B) implies that the company more or less actively tries to take advantage of the opportunities to develop resources that exist in the interplay with other actors. A common experience from business-to-business markets is that a new product, a new supplier, or a changed routine does not work as it should. An important issue is how the companies involved will handle such situations. It usually is a question that what seemed wrong from the beginning turns out to be the right thing. The reason for this is that problem solutions are *formed* as work progresses and as parties invest more energy and resources in order to create functional problem solutions.

This is an important point to note and it is connected to the fact that transactions between companies are often multidimensional. It is not only a question of buying or selling a product but of having well-functioning cooperation. This has a certain resemblance to a marriage or friendship: the parties discover what they are good at and what they can achieve together as the process progresses. To be aware of this and have the ability to leverage opportunities and improvement potential can be an important part of the company's resourcing process.

Firms are to a great extent a platform for combining resources, both internal and external. Through combination, something new is created at the same time as knowledge and resources develop. This aspect of business is probably underestimated, not only with regard to service companies but also in the case of manufacturing companies (Snehota, 1992).

## Activities, resources, actors and the concept of supply chain management

An increasingly popular management theme that is very interesting from a purchasing perspective is supply chain management (SCM). The basic argument in this concept is that companies, either on the initiative of a dominating actor or in a collaboration of (more or less) equals, try to coordinate activities across several links in the market system. Flows of activities are not only to be organized within but also between companies. This can involve simple coordination, implying that the customer's customer simultaneously informs its supplier and the supplier's suppliers regarding its prognoses of future purchase requirements, or more advanced integration. Regarding this more advanced type of integration, consider the example of Hewlett-Packard.

---

**Box 3.12  Hewlett-Packard – an example of supply chain management**

In cases where it is important for the customer to have immediate access to the desired products, service in terms of the availability of products is very important. The dilemma for the supplier is to handle this without having large stocks of finished products and products in different stages of manufacturing across the supply chain. Some factors in this case complicated the issue, since we are dealing with: a) many products in different variants, b) a lack of standardization of components, c) high demands on service, d) short product life cycles and e) low profit margins.

ECR (efficient customer response) – which could be seen as a specific form of supply chain management – is a philosophy and method that should assist in coordinating activities across the whole system, from consumer to raw material supplier. An important element in this thinking is that sales data are distributed across everyone involved, as soon as possible. When a product leaves the store, the supplier of raw material hears about it immediately. This requires different solutions in different environments and many actors may need to adapt their behaviour.

Against this background, Hewlett-Packard (HP) has worked very hard to get all the functional units and activities that are involved in this whole chain to work together in a harmonious way. Some important elements in this collaboration have been:

- Reorganize the distribution itself into central and local warehouses and the division between them.
- Standardize and design the components in different end products in such a way that a component can be used in different products and/or is easily adapted for a specific area (plug-and-play products).
- Change the point in the supply chain where the products are customized and 'locked-in' for specific customers ('postponement'). Previously, HP used to produce customized products for different segments on the basis of forecasts. Nowadays, its production is identical for a much larger part of the chain. Segment-based adaptations are made later, which reduces the risks of forecasts and maintains the company's ability flexibly to adapt its product at a later stage of value creation.
- Direct information from the store (point of sale) is going further up the chain so that the whole chain can adapt to the most precise and early information.

*Source*: Lee and Billington, 1995.

---

Clear effects of this change have emerged. Some aspects have been easy to measure quantitatively (such as stock reductions of different kinds), others are more qualitative. The important point to note here is that efforts like these include several internal and external units, and that there is a great deal of coordination taking place across a whole supply chain. An important aspect is that notable *bull-whip* effects have been reduced. Bull-whip effects arise as imbalances that are created by actors at different steps in the chain forming their own expectations (forecasts) based on their own, limited information (Forrester, 1961). These effects can be quite substantial, and can be reduced by spreading information from the final customer level immediately throughout the chain.

The phenomenon of supply chain management has been the subject of many attempts at definition (see e.g. Chopra and Meindl, 2001; Lee and Billington, 1995; Schary and Skjött-Larsen, 1995; Christopher, 1992). Our own synthesis and reinterpretation of some of the popular definitions is the following:

Supply chain management is a matter of coordinating activities and resources within a network of actors and resources (equipment, transportation vehicles, knowledge etc.). The chain can include all activities from the mining of raw materials to a product at the level of the final consumer, but should at least comprise activities that tie together the business of three actors.

The whole idea of supply chain management assumes that each activity (and actor or company) is a link in a chain, that certain activities have preceded and others will follow the specific activity that is in focus. A classic way to illustrate this idea is the expression 'from wheat to bread': the perspective that stretches from the growing of wheat and other grains via various steps until it reaches the consumer's loaf of bread. Philips Electronics used to have the expression 'from sand to customer' (*van zand tot klant* in Dutch), illustrating the 'path' of a light-bulb (the glass of which is made of silica, i.e. sand).

What is interesting is that the logic of ECR (see Box 3.12) starts with the bread and goes back to the wheat. Hence supply chain management is now increasingly termed 'demand chain management'. In such a system there are various dominating sections along which value is added to the product by various actors and at various levels of the product's creation.

In describing these kinds of systems, the reference point (besides agriculture and logging) is often the production of cars, electronics and steel. Service companies and the services that are part of the overall value chain in these cases are noted as contributing several support services, such as transport, accounting, facilities management, insurance, financial services etc. (Axelsson, 1996a). However, there are supply chains of services in their own right. An example of one such chain provides a very different illustration of the principle 'from bread to wheat'.

---

**Box 3.13  Service providers as a supply chain in the production and distribution of films**

A system with a slightly different emphasis is, for example, the media sector. The activity chains we engage in when we watch a movie on television, in the cinema or on a rented or bought video are quite large. Before the movie has reached that far, a large number of service companies has carried out a variety of important activities and functions.

In the stage immediately before consumption (the actual watching), there are buyers of certain rights. This can be a TV channel or another media company that buys broadcasting rights, cinemas buying the rights to show the movie, distributors that buy the right to put the movie out on video, and perhaps even other companies that want to distribute the movie through new media such as the Internet or video-on-demand.

In the preceding stage, a distributor segment sees to it that the movie comes out, that it is seen and that it gets money on the different end markets. Before that, the movie has to be produced. Various people play a role in production: the script writer, the director, camera operators, actors, stunt performers, special effects people, costume designers, location scouts and different kinds of investors. The value chain often starts with an idea in the work of a writer. The writer has produced a book that for some actor in the whole system becomes the starting point for the idea for a movie. Before the book is produced, a similar value chain has performed the whole process from an idea for a book to the finished product (Silander, 1997).

This describes a complex network of actors whose activities and resources complement each other. Together they form chains of suppliers that, in this case, apply to the majority of service-providing companies.

We will not go into supply chain phenomena much more deeply, but it is important to note that a supply chain perspective does not cover everything. Some observations:

- An individual company can be part of different chains that can involve other actors than those participating in the particular chain that is in focus (see Figure 3.6). This, in its turn, can create prioritization and loyalty problems: which chain(s) should the individual actor prioritize when its resources are not sufficient or when what is desirable from one chain's perspective is less desirable from that of the others?
- This can also imply that several chains have different points of optimization. The organization of activities that is optimal when the chain includes the stages from raw material to the component placed in the end product may become suboptimal. If the chain is stretched to include the recycling of the component, or other aspects such as the use and handling of transportation packaging, then this may very well be the case. What is optimal depends on where the chain's beginning and end are located.
- One and the same chain can also be perceived differently, depending on who is doing the observation. This is obvious, considering the two previous points. The actor who finds himself at the beginning of a chain probably sees the whole chain in a different way to the one who is at the end. Actors in such network-like systems are therefore likely to have different 'network horizons' (Anderson *et al.*, 1994).

An additional, very important aspect is that at different stages of the chain, various encounters of different actors' products occur and concurrent interactions take place. An individual firm usually is a meeting point of many different value chains. Suppliers of different kinds 'meet' and are brought together in the individual company's business, and that is why an alternative image, the metaphor of value constellations (Normann and Ramirez, 1994), is in many contexts a better (if not more complex) representation of reality than that of supply or demand chains. We return to this point in our reflections on markets as systems of mutually dependent actors (i.e. firms and other organizations) or, in

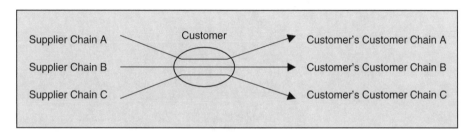

**Figure 3.6**   A firm may be part of various value chains

other words, as networks (Chapter 11). It is, however, interesting to note here that the concept of supply chain management deals in fact with the organization of activities that occur between (and within) different actors in an industrial system, and that it is basically a matter of process orientation that does not stop at firm boundaries. This implies that a supply chain integrates and ties together the more or less complex interfaces of actors.

## Conclusions

Services can be described as activities and service producers as actors. Actors cooperate in different ways in order to create functions (services) in different areas of the economic system. The distribution of activities can vary according to a number of basic patterns.

The allocation and pattern of activities are dependent on the actors' needs, desires and capabilities, but also on the technological relations of dependence. Some activities are easy to separate whereas others can be substantially more difficult to separate.

To be able to perform the different activities it is necessary that the actors have the adequate resources at their disposal. Resourcing, to fill an activity structure with resources, means that the actors involved have to ensure that they have the necessary resources at their disposal. This not only applies to continuous and recurrent activity chains, but also to temporary activity chains, for example in the form of a large project.

# 4

# Outsourcing and Insourcing of Functions and Activities

An important consideration is the balance between internal production and purchasing from external suppliers. This balance has often been the subject of debate or even conflict between purchasing and production managers. Purchasing managers have questioned existing internal manufacturing and, instead, argued for using external suppliers, for example because of potential cost savings. Manufacturing managers, in turn, have disagreed and have sometimes also posited that some of the functions (products, services, activities) that are currently being purchased should be produced internally, for example because of delivery or quality problems. In principle, this discussion is about the division of labour between companies. In that respect it is related to the discussion in the previous chapter, with the difference that 'make-or-buy' decisions are often seen as more significant and having longer-lasting implications.

For a number of years the make-or-buy issue has been framed as one of outsourcing vs insourcing. It has often been put in a strategic/organizational context. Outsourcing is a processual concept, which implies making a change. Here we define it as:

> The decision and subsequent transfer process by which activities that constitute a function, and that earlier have been carried out within the company, are instead purchased from an external supplier.

'Activities' is a broad concept that includes everything from producing a component or producing a service such as quality control to the creation of an invoice. The phrase 'that constitute a function' means that it often is a question of a number of activities, but also that it is not only a question of exactly the same activities being transferred from one actor to another; it can also mean (and usually does) that the activities are partly changed.

In the following section, we present a number of examples of companies and the various outsourcing and insourcing measures that they have taken. A discussion follows of some of the main underlying factors explaining why firms tend to outsource or not.

## Some illustrations of outsourcing and arguments for and against

Outsourcing has become something of a trend. Companies seem to be contracting out complete functions (integrated outsourcing) and/or parts of functions (split, partial outsourcing) to a greater extent and more rapidly than before. Some of the reasons for this supposed development are:

- Faster technological development, which implies that the company must focus on what it is good at and purchase everything else. If not, the company risks falling behind in technical development.
- More complex products that are based on several technologies, e.g. biotechnology, electronics, computer science, mechanics etc. It is becoming much too resource demanding to maintain and develop all knowledge by oneself within all these knowledge/resource areas.
- Less continuous, 'jerky', customer-derived demand, which increases the need for flexibility. The company needs to be able to handle ups and downs in a flexible way.
- More substantial global competition on the world market, which among other things means that it can be hard to keep a reasonable level of profitability when continuously facing different kinds of crises. By using external resources the company does not need to commit itself as much as it would need to do otherwise.
- Newly specialized and flexible companies are developing in the market, which can effectively handle the functions that the company wishes to contract out to external suppliers. This has successively created an infrastructure that makes it possible to purchase many more services than previously.

An important distinction with regard to outsourcing is presented by Van Weele (2000, pp. 54–5) when he divides the concept of outsourcing ('contracting out') into two different types:

- Turnkey (integral).
- Partial (split).

The former case applies when the company contracts out an entire function to an external supplier, while the latter means that only a part of an integrated function is outsourced and the coordination of the function is still operated by the purchasing company.

Examples of turnkey outsourcing could be a so-called 'build-operate-transfer' (BOT) contract, where a supplier delivers a fully tested and operational building or plant to the customer (see Box 4.1), or a completely outsourced catering function. Examples of partial outsourcing include distribution logistics, where an external forwarder provides the trucks and drivers but the customer still does the planning or billing, and factoring processes, where the customer sends its clients the first invoice but an external factoring firm sends the second reminder and collects outstanding debts. Let us consider some examples in more detail.

---

### Box 4.1  Turnkey outsourcing

**An IT supplier instead of an internal IT department**

It is a very common theme for both large and small companies to let specialized IT companies take responsibility for the analysis of what functions the customer needs, how these can be done and by what technology they should be supported (so-called systems integration). It is also common for IT companies to be responsible for running operations for all those systems. The supplier takes over and develops the functions, but it also takes over a large part of the current personnel and equipment. The supplier changes, develops and handles the functions in question according to the contract.

**Skanska as prison warden: the British government outsources the treatment of prisoners**

In Bridgend (UK), Swedish construction company Skanska has been building one of the world's most modern prison facilities. Skanska not only received the commission to construct the building, but will also run the facility as a prison for 25 years. This is an example of an operation within the company's BOT process.

The prison is part of the British government's private finance initiative (PFI), where the government contracts with private companies not only to build but also to run facilities once they are built. As purchaser, the customer develops elaborate specifications for how the building should look and how the operations should be run. The supplier must have the capability to perform all parts of the contract. In this case Skanska will cooperate with different partners with which it has different forms of relationships, including jointly owned companies. An especially important partner is security company Securicor, which will be responsible for the actual handling of the prisoners. The commitment means that the British government pays a fee per prisoner; 'as if it were a better hotel', says Skanska manager Gunnar Samuelsson.

*Source: Dagens industri, 24 June 1997.*

---

These two examples illustrate the outsourcing of relatively complete (integrated) functions. The following case illuminates the factors characterizing split or partial outsourcing.

---

**Box 4.2   Partial outsourcing**

**The service component 'changed bookings' in earlier illustration**
An example of an outsourced function has already been illustrated in the example of the booking problem (Box 3.2), where the customer contracted out the problem of changed bookings to the travel agency, after having handled this function internally for earlier purchases of this kind.

---

All of these examples have concerned outsourcing, i.e. the concept of companies contracting out activities and functions to external actors. To underline the fact that the process also can go in the opposite direction, i.e. that activities and functions can be insourced, consider the following.

---

**Box 4.3   Insourcing**

**The internal banks of major corporations**
For a number of years many major corporations have successively built their own internal banks. An example of this is ABB Financial Services, which conducts many of the services that were earlier purchased from external banks. This has led to a new division of labour where the customers themselves have started to take care of and develop the services. This is an obvious example of insourcing.

**Pharmacia & Upjohn's education of clinical test managers**
Clinical test managers are project leaders for testing new medical substances. This demands extensive scientific competence, good knowledge of mathematics etc., social competence and a kind of marketing competence. For a long time clinical test managers have been a scarce resource. Within pharmaceutical company Pharmacia & Upjohn they were seen as a bottleneck.
   Pharmacia & Upjohn's solution to the problem was to arrange courses itself for future clinical test managers. In this way, the company not only created more tailored training, but also managed to avoid *ad hoc* behaviour for solving the problem. Currently the initiative operates in the form of an education programme for a number of managers each year.

---

What, then, are the pros and cons of outsourcing? To give a brief hint we provide the overview in Table 4.1, which can be seen as a relatively typical picture (Van Weele, 2000).

In this chapter we explore these advantages and disadvantages in terms of three aspects of outsourcing decision processes. The first element that influences how important the various (dis)advantages are for a specific company is the company's core competence. This involves what we call *strategic* aspects. Other important aspects to consider before and during an outsourcing process are what we have chosen to call *performance* and *organizational* aspects. By performance aspects we refer to whether a supplier is (over time) likely to be better than an

**Table 4.1** Advantages and disadvantages of outsourcing

| Advantages | Disadvantages |
| --- | --- |
| ● Investments can be focused on the core operations | ● Increased dependence on suppliers |
| ● Optimal usage of knowledge, equipment and experience of third party | ● Continuous follow-ups of the costs related to the supplier and the handling of the supplier relationship is often necessary |
| ● Increased flexibility; fluctuations in the workload can more easily be absorbed | ● Risks of communications and organizational problems during the transfer of activities to a third party |
| ● Outsourcing leads to easier and more obvious primary processes in the organization | ● Risk of leakage of confidential information |
| ● Input through an independent party's point of view which lessens the risks of introvert short-sightedness in the organization | ● Risk of social and legal problems |
| ● Diversion of risks | |

*Source*: Van Weele, 2000, p. 89.

internal unit and whether the customer can access the external resource in an efficient and effective manner. By organizational aspects we refer to the internal, structural (im)possibilities of outsourcing. In the following three sections, each of these aspects is explored further.

## Strategic aspects

In order to create a sustainable competitive advantage, firms forge strategies, deliberately or emergently. An increasingly central element in this forging process is the definition and development of core competencies. But what is a firm's core competence? How can it be identified and how can it be exploited in the best way? What does the possible connection between out/insourcing and core competence look like? Hedberg *et al.* (1994, p. 109) provide an expressive illustration of the connections between core competence and outsourcing and insourcing. The authors note:

As the old gardener trims his fruit trees, picks out branches and sprouts, grafts, and makes them grow, in the same way competent business management uses insight in the company's core competence to support growth, dominance and perfection.

The hard part in a real company is to know which branches to cut and which should be taken special care of. It is in these situations that it can be especially valuable to have identified the core competencies of the company.

## Definitions of core competence

Discussions about core competencies or core capabilities are often based on Prahalad and Hamel (1990), who emphasize the competence that is unique, distinct to the specific company. Another interesting definition has been presented by Long and Vickers-Koch (1992, p. 13). We have slightly modified their definition (with the text in brackets), but it remains in line with their overall argument:

> Core capabilities are the most critical and most distinctive resources a company controls and which are the hardest for others to copy when they are (in a number of processes) connected to the relevant strategic goals which the company pursues.

There are some aspects in this definition that need to be emphasized. The first is that it is a question of the *critical* and/or the most *distinctive* resources. In some definitions of core competence, only the resources that are *distinctive* are emphasized, which is often a very limited set of the total resource base. In other definitions, *all* the resources that are important for the company's functions (the company's main processes) are emphasized, which normally gives a wider base of core competencies. In the definition given here, these two factors are combined.

It is also interesting to note that core competencies are part of a system, i.e. they are combined with other resources and abilities, and that this combination must work properly in order to create efficient processes. This means that the question of outsourcing should not only be viewed mechanically. We would like to emphasize that our conception of this 'system' is not merely technological but also social. This means among other things that social 'ties' can be important 'boundaries' between activities and processes in an organization. The boundary is not just of a technical nature, which may be one way of interpreting the definition. The wider conception of the systems and its boundaries increases the complexity of the core competence issue.

Furthermore, the definition puts some emphasis on *direction*, i.e. that the company is going somewhere. It strives to fulfil different goals. Knowing what the core competence consists of facilitates the allocation of the company's limited resources, including human energy, to the most important activities. The company can concentrate on the activities and resources that can create 'unique value'. The basic idea is that this will secure competitive advantage in the long run. The company should also identify those activities that can keep core competencies vital and developing. It should, according to most views, concentrate on what it does best and contract out those activities that others do better (Quinn and Hilmer, 1994).

## Core and peripheral competencies in the company

An interesting model, which also considers the system character of resources, knowledge and competencies, has been suggested by Long and Vickers-Koch (1992, pp. 13–14) and is illustrated in Figure 4.1.

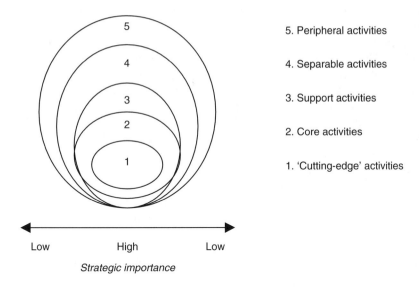

Figure 4.1 Different activities in the dimension peripheral–core
*Source*: Long & Vickers-Koch, 1992, pp. 13–14.

The authors emphasize that it is always a combination of knowledge/resources and processes that creates the abilities of the company and they try to separate these by using a scale from core to peripheral:

1. *Cutting-edge activities/functions* are those that determine the competitiveness of the organization from a long-term perspective. These are capabilities that must be developed today and that are a source of tomorrow's core competence. The competence must also continuously be prioritized and developed.
2. *Core activities* create the foundation for the organization (main processes) and its possible competitive advantages. It is consequently around this competence and these activities (functions) that the company forms the rest of its operations.
3. *Support activities* are those activities that are directly connected to the core competence (core activities, core functions). The support activities must be a part of the organization as a support in order for the core competencies to function properly.
4. *Separable activities* are those activities that are part of the main processes, e.g. as a component, but they are easily separable and do not relate as an active part to the core competence.
5. *Peripheral activities* consist of those activities that do not concern the current main processes. For a manufacturing company, for example, the activity 'to supply a cafeteria function' can be very peripheral in relation to its main process. On the other hand, such an activity can be central in a museum or shopping mall.

This kind of classification of activities/functions, competencies/abilities and underlying resources/knowledge can give the company a more detailed classification to determine what activities are important and what are less important. This can in turn give guidance on questions about outsourcing and insourcing. It is often argued that the activities that are closest to the centre (core) should be carried out and controlled internally, while the activities on the periphery can be more suitably contracted to an external partner.

To use a scheme like this in practice is probably not as easy as it might seem. Many judgements are difficult to make, the boundaries can be very fluent and the overall situation is much more complicated. Nevertheless, as a starting point for systematic discussions it can be fruitful.

A next step in this kind of analysis can be to try to distinguish the resources/knowledge that make it possible for the company to perform the activities that are of special value (the core functions).

## What kind of resources and capabilities create core competence?

Based on the previous discussion, two central questions for those operating in companies or organizations are:

- What are the specific skills, knowledge, abilities and processes we use to meet the needs of our customers and other stakeholders to create competitive advantage?
- How can we use these abilities as a base for building future competitive advantage?

However, before these questions can be answered, we need to know what the relevant resources, knowledge and abilities are. Let us begin with the firm's capability. Organizational capability should, just like the concept of core competence, be seen as task oriented:

> An organization is competent if it has the 'right' capability to perform a certain (or several) task(s).

The task does not need to be decided and limited to anything that *de facto* is performed today, it can rather be expressed as 'to develop an operation that will solve certain problems'. The organization that can manage this under reasonable conditions is competent for the task. Often the abilities of the company must be viewed in relation to those of other companies. The competencies of a company can in certain cases decrease even though, for example, productivity increases. If the competitive advantage of competitors increases at a faster rate it can lead, in comparison, to a deterioration in the company's capabilities.

Resources and knowledge together should create the company's capabilities in a context that is strongly influenced by competitors, customers and social systems and so on.

The relationship between resources, knowledge and activities can be illustrated as in Figure 4.2. Resources and knowledge give the company its organizational competence. This competence is used for tasks, implying that activities and processes are performed and functions carried out.

Against this background, some important questions are:

- What is seen as resources, what kind of resources are there and which are relevant, for what and for whom?
- What is knowledge, what different kinds of knowledge are there and which are relevant, for what and for whom?
- What are the connections between the following concepts: resources and knowledge, knowledge and resources, resources and capability, knowledge and capability, capability and activities/assignments?
- What are the activities and functions for which the company needs to have sufficient capabilities?

In Chapter 8, when we discuss supplier evaluation, we will return to these topics in more detail. We will continue here with a discussion of some of the features of corporate capability.

## The system character of organizational competence

We have thoroughly defended the view of the company as an organized system of different kinds of resources, including knowledge. It consists, among other things, of technical and human resources; it constitutes a technical and social system. A system is an entity, connected in a specific way. A company that tries to use Long and Vickers-Koch's model (1992) according to the earlier argument,

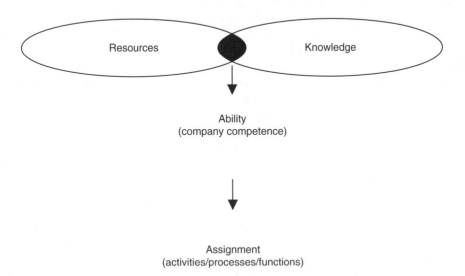

Ability
(company competence)

Assignment
(activities/processes/functions)

**Figure 4.2** The connection between knowledge, resources, capability (company competence) and assignments (processes)

and tries to go in the direction of a 'right' degree of separation, has several delicate matters to consider:

- Knowledge is often composed of a number of related core areas: biotechnology, electronics, molecular science etc. How can one be separated from the other? It is often the combination that makes knowledge valuable and useful.
- Resources and knowledge that can be divided in terms of technical resources into peripheral, support and core (or another categorization) may not go hand in hand with the social systems. Those who adopt an anthropological perspective on companies emphasize the social interplay. A company does not have a culture, it *is* a culture according to some researchers.
- Inertia to change. What is relatively easy to contract out to an independent supplier today can be hard to incorporate in the future, if it turns out to be desirable. What is hard to contract out today can be easy to incorporate again in the future. How do we consider such aspects?

It is obvious that there are no simple answers to these questions. Nevertheless it is, especially in relation to the discussion earlier in this chapter, important to review these questions critically. Outsourcing or insourcing is not only a question of a simple calculation with one-dimensional pluses and minuses.

## Core competence varies between companies and over time

Core competence is partly a matter of the basic functions that are needed to carry out an assignment and partly a matter of emphasizing the activities/functions that differentiate a firm against its competitors. Therefore it is obvious that core competence varies between different companies and contexts. It is also crucial once more to emphasize the systemic nature of the company's abilities. It is, in other words, usually a combination of resources and knowledge that creates the whole system. Consequently, it is always difficult to differentiate between single resources and knowledge and group them into important and not important.

Here we want to stress in particular that the resources and knowledge that give a firm a differentiating competence at a certain point in time do not have to have the same effect at a different stage of the company's and the market's evolution.

Time is always an important factor. What was a core competence a couple of years ago may no longer be a core competence today. What is central today does not need to be central tomorrow. What is peripheral today can be central tomorrow. What was central yesterday and is peripheral today can be central again tomorrow, and so on. How do we judge and weigh up such aspects? These points may seem trivial, but it is worth pointing out and underlining them. It often comes as a shock to a company when it is realized that what was the company's unique competence yesterday is obsolete or common knowledge today. What used to be a unique resource becomes a standard resource or one without significance. This has been experienced in many situations, as the following example demonstrates.

---

**Box 4.4    The limited life span of core competencies**

Consultants who want to offer their clients leading-edge knowledge must continually develop themselves. For many this is a demanding process, which is made more difficult if the consultant is not working in a stimulating and developing environment. It is also more difficult if the business is going 'too' well. Then there is a risk that development is forgotten and that it, in time, will lead to the customer seeing the consultant as only contributing old ideas.

---

These mechanisms also work in the opposite direction, in that what used to be a less valuable resource or knowledge base is becoming important today. This is illustrated by the following interesting example.

---

**Box 4.5    Design is making a comeback as a core competence for train manufacturing**

According to traditional methods, train manufacturers purchase their requirements for the design of trains from designers on the market. This was also the case for Adtranz. In the early 1990s, however, design was increasingly becoming seen as an important resource. The train manufacturers started to work in closer alliance with the designers and to view them as their own, permanent subcontractors. To be able to handle these subcontractors more professionally the company built what it called 'architect knowledge', so that it would have better control over the specifications given to the external design companies.

One step towards even greater involvement was taken when the company found out that it had bought a great deal of designer time, which had become expensive. By coincidence, the company had come into contact with a trained designer who worked very well. When it also sometimes proved hard to find the right competence at short notice, e.g. when making offers to final customers, it seemed logical to insource parts of this function. A company policy has now been established that the target for design work should be to use 50 per cent internal resources and 50 per cent external resources.

The reason for insourcing is that the company increases its ability to handle and integrate designs into the final product. It is a competence in itself to be able to construct designs so that the final product reflects the thoughts and ideas that were at the basis of the design. Through doing this part of the work in-house, the company increases its ability to have a good relationship with the designers, who are then also more dedicated to their work. That half of the design work is still purchased externally has the advantage of external designers also being involved in other situations, as they have different customers and thus have a better feel for what current and future trends will be. However, it is pointed out that design is still not seen as a core competence by the train manufacturers, even though the trend sees its importance increasing.

*Source*: Fasth *et al.*, 1997.

---

In the above example, the company has incorporated the resource 'design capabilities' in a very conscious way. This also becomes apparent as the company has substantial resources to both work with design itself as well as purchase external design services in a professional way.

This is not a unique example; other businesses show similar developments. It is sometimes said that the core competencies for a car manufacturer today are design, marketing and distribution rather than engineering and production. Even within the truck manufacturing industry, similar evaluations are being made (Box 4.6).

---

**Box 4.6 Scania's insourcing of the market channel**

During recent years, marketing managers at truck producer Scania have experienced customers starting to put higher demands on the company as well as its importers, retailers and workshops. The demands concern higher efficiency, availability, service and that the supplier (Scania) has a deeper insight into the business environment and the core operations of the customer. Customers have also become more international and are often running their operations over large geographic areas. At the same time there is a trend towards higher concentration in the haulage business. The development of customer offerings has entailed trucks becoming more of a standard product, at the same time as additions in the form of complementary products and services have become more important.

This means that a deep knowledge of the customers' situation appears as a more and more important competence. In turn, this means that Scania's distribution strategy is changing. It will become more common for the company itself to own the retailers. Within a couple of years, Scania expects to own directly half of all its retailers and importers, substantially more than before. Direct contact with the market is seen as a better way to access the core competence of customer knowledge and to develop and exploit it.

*Source*: Adermalm *et al.*, 1998.

---

## Performance aspects

In the context of performance aspects related to outsourcing/insourcing decisions, there are two key questions:

- Are there any *capable suppliers available* for the desired function? What are their capabilities and what is their interest (willingness) to work with the issues on which we are focusing? This is a rather basic aspect, which sometimes disappears to the background in discussions about core vs non-core.
- Do we and/or will we have enough internal *competence to purchase* the function professionally? (Or is that kind of competence available to be purchased on the market as well?)

Needless to say, a decision to outsource should benefit from a previous understanding of what alternatives are available. Likewise, it would benefit from an analysis of the kinds of skills needed to be a competent buyer of the services in question. The issue of having the competence to purchase has in several studies proved to be a very important factor that needs to be taken into account.

The term 'performance' refers to the short-term and long-term costs for different actors to perform the activities in question. Such a judgement should be based on an evaluation of different categories of costs, but also values. One category should be the different costs for the potential supplier of producing the service, compared to internal production. This category of costs can be explored using traditional micro-economic theory. A second important category would be transaction costs, using theories on transaction cost economics (e.g. Williamson, 1985). This is based on contract theory and institutional economics and focuses on the different contracting costs of different governance structures, such as internal production and external supplies.

A third category is formed by what we call 'transaction values'. These are central in interaction and network theory (Chapters 3, 5, 10 and 11), which builds on theories from the field of business administration, with special emphasis on how companies interact with each other. This adds other aspects than merely costs, such as the effects of a change from own manufacture to external purchasing on a company's network position.

The different theoretical perspectives mentioned here are sometimes seen as conflicting, sometimes as complementary; we will treat them as the latter and discuss each of the three categories of costs and values below.

## Production and factor costs

Production and factor cost theory is always an important starting point for understanding the division of labour between actors in the economic system. The fundamental question is based on the thought that the unit that has the best possibility of performing certain work should do it. Through a combination of factors, which have been acquired from a number of resource markets at certain costs, production is made possible. The conditions that exist (prices are, for example, a result of supply and demand) are important prerequisites for both the factor markets (resource markets) as well as the sales markets. The company's own ability to combine resources and to use possible economies of scale also plays an important part. In this way, the optimal division of labour can logically be derived using cost theory.

Three important notions within this theory are:

- The division of labour becomes optimal if the market's supply and demand match and the supply ends at the point where the marginal costs and marginal revenues meet (marginal cost is the cost of producing one additional unit; marginal revenue is the revenue given by one additional unit sold).
- Economies of scale and scope exist thanks to specialization of different kinds, which influences who is and will be the best source in each field of activity.

- Industry structures arise as a result of the basic conditions of the business environment, which influence the behaviour of organizations and eventually the efficiency of the entire economic system.

Of the three issues we will deal in more detail with the second.

*Economies of scale*

There are many possible resources and knowledge (competencies) from which a competitive advantage can be created. It can be about having access to and exploitating the possibilities of:

- *Size*. The company with a large capacity in the form of premises, personnel etc. has the possibility of allocating the costs of this to several units, which will lower the unit cost.
- *Technology*. A company with the possibility of accessing new technology providing better performance can utilize this and offer performance that is cheaper than that of competitors and/or of higher quality than the customer's own production.
- *Product development*. A company can be more skilful than others conducting product development. The factors facilitating this can be that the company has more highly skilled personnel or a better methodology, but also that it has better technical equipment.
- *Brands* are another possible and important competitive advantage to exploit. An established brand simplifies communication and enables higher or alternatively better targeted sales.
- *Distribution channels*. Access to an existing or possible distribution channel to which others do not have access, possibly because they have too small an operation to afford it, is also a possible and exploitable resource in many situations.

There are apparently many possible factors that singly or in combination can result in economies of scale and thus influence the division of labour in the production system. In Box 4.7, we present one example of a situation where a lack of economies of scale leads to an outsourcing decision.

---

**Box 4.7   Scania outsources IT because it lacks a critical mass of knowledge**

Some years ago Scania and WM-data agreed a long-term cooperation concerning Scania's IT function. WM-data entered as a 50 per cent owner in Scania Data AB.

The starting point was when some of Scania's senior managers felt that Scania Data was not functioning properly. One of the reasons was that the unit, which consisted of 200 individuals, was too small to be able to keep up with the fast pace of technical development in this area. It also showed that the company had difficulties in recruiting new competent personnel and that the unit was not big enough to create the necessary dynamics in the form of interesting career paths, including developing work rotation. Furthermore, staff turnover was high (10 per cent), which was becoming costly.

The outsourcing process was carried out in two steps. First the current organization was developed. Thereafter a production and development company was created, which in dialogue with the internal line functions developed specifications for internal requirements, which were later used in the ordering process. Only after that was the joint company created.

At that stage Scania had a strong competence in ordering, which was subsequently judged to be very valuable. The alternative would have been for the company, which was to take over the function immediately, also to be responsible for making an inventory of current needs etc. In this case, the purchaser of the outsourced services turned out to be stronger in the dialogue with the supplier.

*Source*: Adermalm *et al.*, 1998.

*Economies of scope*

The difference between economies of scale and economies of scope is that in the latter it is not scale in itself but the possibility of combining different operations and different assignments that lays the foundation for the company's competitive advantages. In other words, there can be said to be a difference between which operations are connected by a particular company. Depending on how it combines its operations it can possibly gain advantages. An example is provided in Box 4.8.

## Box 4.8 Economies of scope – outsourcing of meter maintenance

At every property, both private and commercial, there are meters for electricity, water, gas etc. Every meter is considered as a delivery point and utility companies serving large cities may have between several hundred thousand and a few million such delivery points. Utility firms have traditionally had a special department for the installation and maintenance of meters; it is rather important that the meters are continually in a good condition. Over specific periods, meters will be put through a revision programme and be repaired or replaced. Several of these utility companies have started to reconsider their routines and found them to be very inefficient. After many unfruitful attempts to improve the situation, some companies have decided to outsource the whole process.

As an example, Stockholm Energy has outsourced a large part of such operations to Backlund, a small electrical installation firm with some 80 employees, and has achieved considerable cost reduction and productivity improvement. One of the main explanations is that Backlund has gained some flexibility from Stockholm Energy to perform the maintenance activities at times that fit best with Backlund's other workloads, leading to a more even capacity utilization. In other situations, utility companies have outsourced these type of activities to companies that combine the maintenance of electricity, gas and water installations, which often leads to economies of scope in client administration, house calls etc.

*Source*: Helmer, 1995.

All of the above means that the company's organizational ability does not only relate to production costs and economies of scale, but also to its scope, i.e. what customer and supplier operations the company links together. Panzar and Willig (1981, p. 286) describe economies of scope as 'cost savings that arise when it is less costly to combine two lines of production in a company than producing each separately'.

The efficiency of the company depends on how well it succeeds in exploiting its resources and knowledge, including different contact networks, and the trust from other actors built up over time. As an aside, we have frequently noticed that economies of scope seem to be an important explanation of structural changes among service firms, be it expansion in general, insourcing or internationalization (Erramili, 1989). There are frequent cases when certain resources could be exploited in different businesses (different scopes). This could be to exploit the customer base for more than one business (e.g. auditing plus advising) or any specific knowledge or other resource.

## Costs of contracts and transactions

An important complement that can sometimes be seen as an alternative to structure and factor cost theory is transaction cost theory. The general assumption of this theory is that transactions (exchanges) between actors are based on some kind of contract and that the establishment and control of contracts entail costs. The transactions themselves carry costs. The basic theoretical work of two authors is often mentioned as the core of transaction cost theory: Coase (1937) and Williamson (1975 and 1985).

The question from which Coase started was: 'Why do companies exist?' His answer was, greatly simplified, that it would be too expensive always to apply market mechanisms, for example for companies to auction their needs for personnel every day. It was substantially more efficient to close long-term contracts and integrate them (and other functions and resources) within the company. Against this background there are reasons to see the functions (activities) that companies choose to handle internally by themselves as the result of 'market failures'.

Williamson and many other researchers developed these thoughts when they were trying to understand the factors that have the highest influence on the choice of a certain market solution or 'hierarchy solution'. In connection with in/outsourcing, the question becomes why the company chooses to abandon a hierarchy solution in favour of a market solution and vice versa. Williamson points out some especially important factors:

● The level of transaction-specific investments, i.e. to what extent the supplier and/or the customer has invested in production equipment and other resources, including knowledge, which are only useable (have any value) in a specific customer–supplier relation. The greater these investments are, the greater is the driving force towards vertical integration (i.e. hierarchy and insourcing).

- *Frequency of transactions.* The more often the partners perform different kinds of exchange processes, the higher is the drive towards vertical integration.
- *Level of insecurity.* The more insecure the purchasing situation, the higher the contract and other transaction costs become, which is more in favour of vertical integration.

Here is an example of what transaction costs can consist of in practice and how they arise.

---

**Box 4.9   Transaction costs**

A manufacturing company made an analysis of its needs for IT services. It found out that one alternative to its extensive internal IT unit would be to purchase these services from one or several external suppliers. The calculation was used as a base when the company decided to outsource its IT unit consisting of 100 individuals. The company kept three individuals who would act as purchasers/orderers from the IT company.

After about a year it was evident that these three individuals would not be able to handle their tasks. Their resources were not sufficient either in time or in competence to be able to perform professional purchasing activities. To create a stronger unit, which also would be a more attractive and developing workplace, the manufacturer strengthened its purchasing function. After about a year the unit consisted of 20 employees who in essence purchase IT services from the 100 individuals who left the company a couple of years before.

---

In this case each unit's production costs, i.e. all the costs that the service production generates, only constitute a part of the total costs. Other costs are the costs of doing the purchase, staying updated on the market and seeing to it that the supplier is fulfilling its obligations, including that it is developing in the desired way, are all to be seen as transaction costs.

In the case illustrated above, the customer was probably able to foresee the main transaction costs from the beginning. But it is not impossible that subsequently these (transaction) costs will prove to be substantially higher than expected.

## Transaction values

Transaction cost economics mainly looks at transactions between two organizations. Business relationships between companies, the so-called dyad, the interplay between two parties – customer and supplier – and what influences this kind of interplay have been extensively studied. But, as discussed in Chapter 3, there has also been a great deal of research regarding the interplay between several actors in industrial systems, according to the so-called A-R-A or network model. Some general issues for researchers adopting this model have been the following:

- The environment of the company is not an anonymous mass of companies, rather it consists of other mostly identified, well-known companies.

- Companies do not change partners in the way presumed in the traditional market model; instead to a large extent they work within the framework of relatively stable relationships over time.
- Actors, companies and/or individuals are heterogeneous, which means that the choice of partner matters.

Based on the A-R-A or network model, we can discern two main types of transaction values (or, more correctly, the conditions under which they arise):

- Transaction values created by *market heterogeneity*. Heterogeneity means that the suppliers are different and that this is relevant. It can be seen as a possible positive effect of market transactions. Through the existence of a dynamic market, which makes it possible to change suppliers, the company has the possibility of purchasing renewal through variation. This can be especially obvious in cases where there is openness from the purchasing company towards the new supplier's ideas, at the same time as the supplier gladly shares its knowledge. This openness enables renewal. This is a form of innovation resulting from who is cooperating with whom.
- Transaction values created in interplay as so-called *team effects* (Håkansson and Snehota, 1995, p. 37), which emphasizes interaction as a possibility for developing these values. This can be seen as especially important when purchasing services created in interactive processes, for example education: everything that has substantial moments of creation and thus depends strongly on which actors (individuals, business units, companies) interact. The basic idea is that through interaction and learning to know each other the partners will gain deeper knowledge about each other and each other's abilities. Over time this leads to substantial team effects (Nonaka and Konno, 1998). Technical development has often been shown to be the effect of such cooperation. An important prerequisite for development and thus high transaction values through interaction is that the relationship is kept creative and vital over time and is not left to stagnate.

These two types of transaction value are complementary to the two types of cost influencing the division of labour in a business system (production and transaction costs).

## Organizational aspects

We have already noted (in Chapter 3) that it might be difficult to separate certain activities from one another because they are strongly interrelated. There are several theories dealing with other relevant organizational aspects that could be related to outsourcing and insourcing as a problem area. These include the following:

- Interorganizational theory, i.e. theories of interplay between companies, which partly overlaps but also complements aspects of interaction and network theory. In addition, those parts of decision theory that have been directed towards reverse inertia (degree of reversibility or irreversibility) and such are dealt with. Interorganizational collaboration patterns can also foster or hinder outsourcing processes.

● Production and organization theory, with special emphasis on how activities are organized and what the connections between activities look like. This can also be seen as a clarification of important aspects of interaction and network theory. Dubois (1998) describes an activity-based system for analysing what activities should be carried out inside and outside the company. On the basis of Richardson (1972), she uses two concepts that are important in this context: complementing and similar activities. Complementing activities are defined as activities that 'represent different phases in a production process, which in one way or the other, need to be coordinated'. This means that there exists a sequential dependency between complementing activities. 'Similar' activities are those that 'need the same capabilities to be carried out'. This means that a specific resource is used to perform more than one activity. Complementing activities can also be similar, which means that two sequentially dependent activities demand the same type of resources or capabilities. Consequently, performing activity and resource analyses (see Chapter 3) is one way of identifying these complementing and similar activities and identifying possible combinations – and separations – of activities. Another important aspect, which can be judged based on these kinds of analyses, is how easy or how difficult it is to change partners (suppliers) seen from the different ways in which activity chains can be linked and resources connected.

● Organization and decision theory, with special attention to understanding influence and change, i.e. what actors have the ability to influence and change the organization and how this influences the internal interplay between actors' assessments of insourcing and outsourcing. Internal collaboration and conflict patterns can also facilitate or hinder outsourcing processes.

There are obviously a great number of possible organizational aspects that might have an impact on the issue of activity distribution between actors in a business system. Adding these aspects to the previously discussed strategic and performance aspects, we can easily see that a great deal of complexity is involved in such decisions. To illustrate this, consider the following example.

---

**Box 4.10  Contamination risk**

A technology-intensive firm in the biotechnology sector had identified certain knowledge areas within ICT as a core competence. In the initial situation, this competence was bought from external suppliers at a very high price. An analysis indicated that this involved a core competence that should be available internally. It also turned out that such a field of expertise could continue to grow (qualitatively) within the firm, and that it would be economically advantageous to have an internal group of ICT specialists in this area.

Despite all these observations, the firm explicitly decided not to insource this particular function. As the responsible manager explained: 'To be able to recruit these resources, which are in high demand, we should pay rather high wages. It would have been cheaper than the fees we currently pay to ICT consultants, but the problem arises in the following stages. If we pay these people a high wage, it will successively 'contaminate' our other employees. In a short while, we will have to pay, overall, a considerable amount of money for this solution.'

## Deliberate versus emergent outsourcing

The literature on outsourcing and insourcing is to a large extent decision oriented. It focuses on a rational calculation of the pluses and minuses. This may not always result in successful outcomes. One essential requirement is that the delivery process – and the interorganizational processes in general – function well. Outsourcing/insourcing is not just a matter of taking a decision of one kind or the other. Let us discuss this aspect in more detail.

Earlier we discussed illustrations from Adtranz and Scania (Boxes 4.5 and 4.6) to describe various aspects of outsourcing. For Adtranz an analysis was done of six outsourcing and insourcing decisions. In this case, Fasth *et al.* (1997) systematically describe:

- The interpretations and evaluations that were made before the respective outsourcing or insourcing decision and how these opinions had been reached. What were the driving forces behind the change? How the outsourcing decision worked out, for better or for worse.
- What the results had been so far. Had new arrangements been made, or had new changes been carried out? Or had things even reverted to the old situation?
- How could the experiences in the different cases be explained by economic factors (economies of scale, economies of scope, transaction costs) or other factors?

The authors conclude that in all six cases, production costs and the access to or lack of competent personnel were the main factors in the outsourcing or insourcing decision. Outsourcing processes were initiated by a perceived lack of internal capabilities to perform a function as well as external actors were expected to. The authors also conclude that out/insourcing decisions, in the instances studied, did not occur against the background of a predetermined strategic plan, but rather that they emerged through a sequence of events.

In one such case, a person with a certain specialist competence was hired so that the firm could act more like a competent buyer. Right after that, a thorough cost analysis was done (for different reasons), which demonstrated to senior management how expensive it was to buy this function (component). The decision to insource parts of this function was facilitated by the fact that there happened to be a suitable person available internally. This illustration – and the other five cases – demonstrate that *events*, rather than strategic decisions, cause a *gradual* change in a firm's purchasing behaviour.

Fasth *et al.* (1997) relate their observations to Mintzberg's (1992) argument that strategies are not often planned and then remain like that, but that rather they *emerge* and are subsequently modified. Mintzberg refers to the handicraft of a ceramic artist, whose vases and bowls 'grow' on the turntable.

Fasth *et al.* also point out that the traditional literature usually assumes that there is a number of potential suppliers interested in taking over different sorts of functions. In many cases, however, this is not true. Let us turn, again, to the Adtranz case.

---

**Box 4.11   Adtranz's experiences with supplier markets**

Adtranz can only offer relatively small volumes to its suppliers. In some cases, there are very few or no suppliers at all for the products that Adtranz needs: the products are not available on the market. In one of these cases, Adtranz first had to develop the supplier in order to be able, in a later stage, to place an order with it. In another case, a supplier first had to invest considerable resources in its development activities to be able to perform the desired (production) function. In both cases it puts strong demands on the knowledge transfer capabilities of the supplier, but it also requires that the supplier has the courage and can be motivated to take the necessary measures. In a third case, a supplier offered to take over certain functions, but the offer it made was not attractive to Adtranz. Fasth *et al.* (1997) concluded that 'the high price level is a signal that the supplier is not interested in producing such an odd product'.

---

In a situation where a firm has several suppliers to choose from for a specific product, it is possible to use the existing literature (i.e. theory on economic factors) to decide on outsourcing/insourcing decisions. If that is not the case, a more thorough analysis should be carried out. Especially in those cases, a firm should consider the following aspects:

- *Geographic location*: proximity facilitates, for example, social and technical exchange.
- *Time*: in many cases, the time needed for establishing an effective supplier relationship is underestimated.
- *Boundaries*: a simple and clear boundary between different activities is a prerequisite for outsourcing to be successful.
- *Expert knowledge*: to be able to handle and 'control' a supplier, it is often important that a firm possesses so-called architectural knowledge.
- *Employee participation*: if the people who are to carry out an outsourcing or insourcing process are not motivated, it does not matter how well management has analysed the situation.
- *Speed of change*: large changes may be difficult to carry out in a short period.

Fasth *et al.* (1997) finally argue that there is no simple recipe for outsourcing or insourcing that makes companies successful every time. They point out that in some of the cases they studied, things went wrong even though the decision and the implementation process were handled very professionally, including all the calculations. In one case suppliers had retreated due to personal issues, and in another changing ownership structures led to major problems. There are always a number of factors that are impossible for a firm to foresee and that can come to affect the course of events (Fasth *et al.*, 1997, p. 76).

This discussion may seem to result in a very irrational picture of business practice, but it is much more realistic and appropriate than many of the more simplistic decision- and calculation-oriented evaluations discussed in other contexts. As Blomgren (1997) also demonstrates, it is often a matter of 'what was right, became wrong' and 'what was seen as wrong, can become right'!

## Summary checklist

Much of the previous discussion of the different aspects to consider in relation to outsourcing and insourcing can be summarized in the overview or checklist in Table 4.2. The theories and concepts considered earlier give some support and guidelines for the evaluations of each aspect.

For each aspect, evaluations need also to be done for the three different time perspectives. After formulating these evaluations, the different market, economic, organizational and other aspects need to be weighed up.

As we argued in the previous section, outsourcing/insourcing decisions usually emerge through a process, during which, at various times, a checklist like this may be used. In the study on Scania referred to earlier (Adermalm *et al.*, 1998), the authors used the checklist from Table 4.2 and found that it was useful in mapping and analysing any given situation that may occur during (emerging) outsourcing/insourcing decision processes.

**Table 4.2**  Overview of considerations in outsourcing/insourcing decisions

| Aspects | Short-term effects | Medium-term effects | Long-term effects |
| --- | --- | --- | --- |
| **Strategic aspects** | | | |
| 1. Evaluations of core business and core competencies, related to competitve position | | | |
|   – Core competencies | | | |
|   – Underlying resources and capabilities | | | |
| **Performance aspects** | | | |
| 2. Supplier availability | | | |
|   – Supplier market structure | | | |
|   – Supplier capabilities | | | |
|   – Supplier improvement potential | | | |
|   – Strategic fit | | | |
|   – Conditions for collaboration | | | |
| 3. Internal sourcing capability | | | |

**Table 4.2**  *Continued.*

| Aspects | Short-term effects | Medium-term effects | Long-term effects |
|---|---|---|---|
| 4. Production costs | | | |
| – Factor costs | | | |
| – Economies of scale | | | |
| – Economies of scope | | | |
| – Specialization advantages | | | |
| 5. Transaction costs | | | |
| – Transaction frequency | | | |
| – Uncertainty | | | |
| – Transaction-specific investments | | | |
| 6. Transaction values | | | |
| – Activity structures | | | |
| – Resource structures | | | |
| – Potential resource development, incl. 'team effects' | | | |
| – Actor structures, incl. dependencies, potential relations | | | |
| – Ties: social, legal, economic, technical etc. | | | |

**Organizational aspects**
7. Control
   - Power/dependency
   - Flexibility/lock-in
   - Inertia/reversibility/irreversibility
8. Production/technical and organizational connections
   - Clear/ambiguous boundaries
   - Type of production technology
   - Organizational logic
   - Internal collaboration, inter-functional boundaries
   - Alternative use of resources
9. Influence
   - Hierarchy
   - Initiative
   - Relative power

**Other aspects**
10. Non-economic factors
    - Social policy
    - Environmental policy
    - Aesthetics

**Overall evaluation**

## Conclusions

Viewed from the perspective of a single company, the question of outsourcing or insourcing of activities, which in the end is a question of division of labour in a business system, is often presented as an assessment of whether the function in question is a core competence in the organization or not. The clear-cut recommendation says that what does not constitute a core competence can be outsourced and what does constitute a core competence should be performed and maintained internally.

In this chapter we have shown that the reasons to outsource or not are much more complex and comprise a vast range of aspects. We have concluded that it is often hard to determine what is core or not core since the company is an organized technical *and* social system. The question of outsourcing and insourcing could also emphasize strictly production-economic and/or organizational issues. The chosen perspective and emphasis are likely to have consequences for what is suitable (and possible) to do in terms of outsourcing and insourcing.

# 5

# Buyer–Supplier Interaction in Business Services Exchange Processes

We have previously discussed services as activities and assignments. Different patterns of activities arise when various services are produced. We have also pointed to the corresponding requirements for resources to produce the desired services (activities, functions). The previous chapter involved actors, in terms of who should do what, which was discussed as a matter of outsourcing and insourcing.

This chapter deals, in general terms, with buying behaviour and, in more detail, some of the factors that affect (condition) this behaviour. More precisely, we look at the interplay between seller and buyer and the need for contacts between actors from the two organizations to handle the interaction. In this respect, we rely on two main sources: the customer relationship management literature (Grönroos, 2000; Gummeson, 1999; Reichheld, 1996; and others) and the approach represented by the IMP Group, a major group of researchers who have developed their thinking based on industrial marketing and purchasing (Ford, 1997; Ford et al., 1998; Håkansson, 1982; and others).

At the end of the chapter we also take a look at some other factors than merely the kinds of services – such as power – that can have an impact on buying behaviour and the interplay between the parties involved.

## Exchange processes between buyer and seller

One description of buying behaviour characterizes this behaviour in terms of three important elements:

- Which alternatives are being considered?
- Which type and amount of resources are being deployed, e.g. which type of competencies (managers, specialists) are being involved and how many?
- Which issues dominate in the dialogue with the supplier (and internally within the buying group or decision-making unit)?

This categorization can be carried out for both the long and the short run, which results in a matrix as in Table 5.1. Naturally, there should be a link between the content aspects of buying behaviour in a certain transaction and the purchasing strategy, i.e. purchasing behaviour in the long run. Essential elements in long-run behaviour are the position taken regarding the number of parallel suppliers that should be aimed for, the relation to these (i.e. competition or collaboration oriented, see Chapter 10), the necessary qualifications of the people dealing with the suppliers etc.

The type and amount of resources involved and the dominating issues are all aspects of what we call the 'exchange process' between buyer and seller.

The exchange processes and how they are handled obviously vary, depending on what is being exchanged and what one wants to obtain from the transaction or the relationship.

However, purchasing behaviour is not only a matter of handling individual purchasing processes (transactions). It is also a matter of continuously dealing with supplier relationships. As we have argued, some services are contracted at a certain point in time, but then require a continuous interaction over time to manage the *interactions* between the parties involved (Chapter 2). To give a more concrete illustration of this point, which in our opinion is a critical one, we give two illustrations of communication and contact patterns in business relationships involving services.

**Table 5.1** A matrix for describing a firm's purchasing behaviour

|  | Short-term, the single transaction | Long-term, purchasing strategy |
| --- | --- | --- |
| Number of alternatives under consideration |  |  |
| Representatives involved; type and quantity (number and time) |  |  |
| Important issues in the dialogue with the supplier |  |  |

## Box 5.1   Communication and contact patterns

**The manufacturing customer and the insurance supplier**
A manufacturing company discusses its relationship with a major insurance company as follows: 'They have a customer account team. This team includes everyone from their company that has contacts with us. This involves experts on different types of insurance: personal insurance, fire and other property insurance, product liability insurance etc. Similarly, we have a team to deal with the supplier in a coordinated fashion. Depending on the specialism needed and the responsibilities of various people, the communication patterns will vary. Our human resource department has the most important contacts with their specialist on personal insurance, including the insurance on our key personnel. Our production people have contacts with their fire insurance specialists etc. The contacts vary in intensity, partly according to an annual cycle of planned visits and other meetings, partly depending on important events such as damage and accidents or new investments that may change the situation.'

**The manufacturing customer and the advertising agency**
The relationship between a manufacturing company and an advertising agency is described as follows: 'From our side, it is primarily the marketing and sales managers that select an agency and divide our budget among alternative suppliers and campaigns. They have contacts with the customer account managers from the advertising agency and – especially within the different projects – with the important creative people of the agency. During the execution of the project, other people from our side will actively participate. The frequency of the contacts varies, but we have at least one meeting annually in which we present the main elements for our joint projects for the coming year. We "book time" with each other on an overall level. What happens in addition to that are mainly the contacts occurring during specific campaigns.'

These examples illustrate the different contact patterns that can occur in business relationships as a consequence of the characteristics of the service and other basic conditions (the nature of the business, the formal organization etc.), both at the buying and the selling company. In this chapter we will investigate these issues in more detail.

The characteristics of the products or services that are being exchanged create different problems and opportunities. Purchasing and selling a standard and simple component, or a simple service, puts no or few requirements on the technical competencies of those arranging the transaction, while such competencies are obviously important when the exchange involves a complicated piece of equipment. When the product is simple, it is most often the purchasers (or the internal users) and the salespeople from the supplier who take part in the interaction, while in the case of more complicated products and advanced services (such as engineering services, management consulting etc.) collaboration from other employees on both sides is required. It is even not uncommon in many transactions, as indicated in Chapter 1, for purchasing specialists not to be involved at all. In Chapter 7, where at various points we will look at purchasing as a rational decision process, different contact patterns between customer and supplier for the 'daily routine' are discussed, to signify that the decision process and the execution of the assignment are two important aspects of the purchasing job.

Characteristics of the product thus have an effect on the interaction and information exchange pattern. When the product or problem solution is complex, intensive and broad communication is often necessary. This usually implies the following:

- More questions are being discussed.
- More employees from both sides are being involved.
- The duration of communication becomes longer.

Fundamentally, interaction should be functional. The reason for interaction between people from the buyer and seller is that there is a need to make certain competencies available in order to handle problems of various kinds.

If that is true, it should to some extent be possible to predict which interfaces between two firms are likely to emerge in order to fulfil the functions requested. If we apply this reasoning and first of all look at the buying party, the customer and the competence that this actor is likely to bring into the relationship, the frame of reference in Figure 5.1 (cf. Fisher, 1976; see also Van Weele, 2000) should be relevant.

Two important dimensions are the technological importance of the business service in question and its financial importance. By 'technological' we mean not just biotechnology, mechanical engineering and the like, but also other issues related to the technology of a business in a broader sense. It could be about understanding children's play habits and the pedagogical aspects of that, something that could be a vital technology in a childcare business (Fisher, 1976, calls it 'product complexity'). The buyer or buying team that is to supply such an

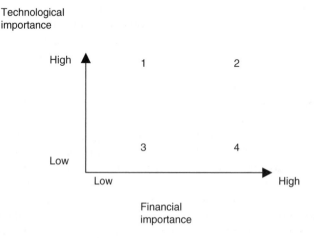

**Figure 5.1** Two basic dimensions of competence involved in specific buying processes
*Adapted from*: Fisher, 1976.

operation with for example toys needs to understand this technology. The technological importance, or more precisely the importance of defining and understanding the technological dimensions of the purchase, could be high or low related to the specific purchase situation. The other dimension is the financial importance, e.g. in terms of order volume and/or required investments, which also could be high or low.

In this frame of reference it would be natural if a situation of low–low (quadrant 3) were dominated by the purchasing specialists and the interaction with the supplier primarily focused around the buyer of those products. If we have a situation of high technological and low financial importance, we would most likely find dominance by the technology specialists. A situation of high–high (quadrant 2) is likely to be very much characterized by teamwork, with a multitude of specialists involved. Finally, quadrant 4 would imply dominance by financial experts and people in top management. Switching to the supplier side, we could apply the corresponding arguments. In for example a low–low situation the interacting people from the supplier would be a salesperson and so on.

Following this basic argument, we could argue that clear regularities exist in interaction patterns. Business relationships are, in our view, not just a matter of 'relationships' and 'interaction': they are a matter of *what kind of* relationships and *what patterns of* interaction and – for the practitioner – how to *understand and handle* them.

Before we focus on the effects of service complexity and service application on the interaction pattern and exchange process between buyer and supplier, we briefly take a look at buyer–supplier interaction processes in general, and some ways of describing them.

## Describing and understanding business interactions

Relationship marketing – and we could easily apply this to relationship purchasing – is based on 'a distinct view of the relationship between a firm and a customer. It is not a number of tools that can be included in a marketing mix toolbox' (Grönroos, 2000, p. 39). It is, rather, a perspective on how value is created in interaction. Gummeson (1999) argues that relationship marketing (and thereby relationship purchasing) is marketing based on relationships, networks and interactions.

In business-to-business contexts these interactions are often enduring and long term. Interaction processes are functional: they exist and involve people to create and deliver problem solutions. They are conditioned by a number of influencing variables. A broad picture of the factors that affect the content and extent of interaction processes has been formulated in the so-called interaction model (Håkansson, 1982). The aim of that model is to describe and analyse in a systematic way the interaction processes and relations between firms. The model consists of four main groups of variables: the interaction process (both in the short and long term), the characteristics of the parties involved, the atmosphere in the relationship and in the individual transactions, and environmental factors. The model is represented in Figure 5.2.

We will discuss each of the four groups of variables in turn.

## Interaction processes and relationships in the short and long run

Regarding the interplay between buyers and sellers, a distinction is made between the individual transaction ('episode') and the more or less long-term relationship within which the business is taking place. According to previous discussions, transactions can be described as a series of exchange processes. The relationship can be described in terms of the adaptations that the parties have made in relation to each other, and the institutionalization and expectations that have been created. In a systematic analysis, different patterns, for example regarding the form of interaction, can be investigated and understood: which type of information is being exchanged, which type of employees are involved, how many and with which qualifications.

As indicated earlier, exchange and adaptation processes can be seen as an effect of the relationship: parties having experience with each other and thereby being able to collaborate more easily. This also works the other way round: relationships develop based on individual transactions. One example may illustrate this notion.

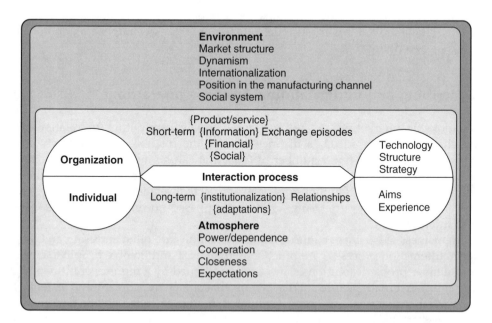

**Figure 5.2**  The interaction model: a tool for systematically analysing business transactions and relations

*Source*: Håkansson, 1982, p. 24.

---

**Box 5.2   A failed assignment as the start of a successful relationship**

A major service provider used a law firm that was new to the company, but had especially good references within the area of antitrust laws. The law firm perceived the odds of a positive result of a lawsuit in which the service provider was involved as very high. The law firm and the company representative prepared their case well and worked out a well-defined line of defence. Then the lawsuit took place.

Despite the successful collaboration and the sound line of defence, the client lost the case. The customer had to pay the legal expenses both for itself and for its counterpart, and also had to pay financial compensation to the counterpart for losses incurred. The customer was not satisfied with the result, nor with the evaluation that the law firm (the supplier) made at the beginning. Despite all this, it became the start of a long-term collaboration. The customer thought that the supplier was very professional and that the collaboration had worked well. The customer argued that the things both parties had learned about each other during this process would be of value in any future business. The result of this episode was therefore negative in the short run, but very positive in the long term.

---

## The customer's purchasing strategy, production technology and purchasing organization

Purchasing strategy can affect purchasing behaviour and, in doing so, the long-term development of the supplier relationship (in terms of institutionalization, adaptation and investment). If the strategy implies that the buying firm actively wants to exploit competition and wants to avoid committing itself to a specific counterpart, this will obviously have a corresponding effect on the relationship. However, it also will affect the way the individual transaction is handled: what is being discussed, which communication patterns will arise etc. This will be discussed in detail in Chapter 10, and therefore at this point we will only state that there is such a connection.

We also know that the production technology of the buying firm, whether it is large series or unit production for example, as well as its organization have an influence both on the need for purchased items as well as the collaboration with the supplier. This would, for example, be reflected in the type of contacts between the customer and the supplier that are especially important to the customer, the dialogues that need to be pursued and the conditions for the desired functionalities to be realized. Here is an illustration of the role of organizational aspects.

---

**Box 5.3   Procurement of training for management development**

In company A there is a coordinated human resource management department, with broad responsibilities. When the company is contracting management development in the form of training and education, this department forms a strong central actor. Communication is facilitated. The supplier knows 'who decides' and can adjust its behaviour accordingly.

---

In company B there is no such department. The procurement of management development training is spread across all business areas and is carried out locally. This implies that the contacts between the supplier and the customer have to be adjusted to this situation. The contacts become larger in number and more difficult to coordinate. Patterns in the behaviour of both sides and the pattern of the mutual contacts are in this way affected by the customer's organization.

It is obvious that the internal organization of the companies involved actively affects the collaboration between them. Conditions like these can either facilitate or hinder, and sometimes even prohibit, the business relationships between customer and supplier. Conversely, a change in the content of a relationship (e.g. the purchasing or marketing tasks) often requires adaptations in the organizations of both parties.

To summarize, the customer's purchasing strategy, its production technology and the organization have an important impact on how the interaction between buyer and seller takes place.

## The influence of atmosphere

In a similar way, it can be argued that the atmosphere and the broader context (environment) of the relationship help us to understand and/or to predict how the collaboration between customer and supplier will or can take shape.

### Box 5.4  Delivery impossible

Over the past five years, publisher XYZ has concentrated its purchases of typesetting and printing services. Currently it has only two suppliers in this area. In return, the publisher has achieved better prices (through volume discounts) and a more stable production flow. At one of the suppliers, printing company A, the publisher accounts now for 40 per cent of the total production.

An important activity for publisher XYZ is the publication of education material. During August in a recent year, something happened that is not uncommon. An overambitious author and an overloaded editor at the publisher went past their deadline for a new course book. Camera-ready originals were not available during the first week of August, as previously agreed. The third week of August seemed more realistic, but in the meantime the publisher had made a strong promise to educators that the book would be ready for the new school year, starting in September. When the publisher informed the printing company that the situation was problematic, but that it assumed the printing company would do its best to arrange that the book could be printed within two to four days, the immediate reaction was very negative. The production manager of the printing company argued that two to four days was impossible and declared: 'I refuse to do it!' What now?

Within the publishing company, internal discussions took place that (among others) included the managing director. Educators and the author were informed and received a comforting message despite the dramatic situation: 'We will fix it.' New contacts were made with the printing company, this time at a higher level than previously. Within a couple of hours after the second contact, news comes from the printing company: 'We will do it, we will help you this time – but please do not put us in a similar situation next time!'

An obvious question regarding this example concerns which of the variables from the interaction model discussed so far has the greatest explanatory value for those who want to understand this behaviour. Probably the power balance has an important influence and that (im)balance has been created by, among other things, the buyer's change in purchasing strategy.

## Environment

The environment of a business relationship is usually described by factors such as the characteristics of the market system in terms of market structure and the number of available alternatives (the structure of the supplier market), but also by the nature of the social system in which the business takes place. The latter aspect affects conditions such as business culture, norms etc., and as such, indirectly, the purchasing behaviour of the firm.

The first group of aspects directly affects the conditions for purchasing activities. When the environment of a specific supplier relationship acts like a competitive market, this has a positive impact on the possibilities a customer has to exploit the competition between suppliers ('play the market'). When there is only one alternative supplier, the ways of working have to be adjusted to that. The conditions for performing purchasing activities within different market structures will be discussed in more detail in Chapter 11.

## Individuals

The interaction model even considers the characteristics of the individuals concerned. Personnel from a buying company who participate in a particular business relationship can – often strongly – affect both the exchange processes and the long-term relationship. Therefore, in order to understand and exploit the opportunities that exist in a specific exchange process or business relationship, it is important to know what experiences these individuals have had with transactions of a certain type and/or with specific suppliers. It is also important to know their individual goals, which may be derived from how they are rewarded for their professional role (as well as from other factors).

This framework, while useful, does not tell the whole story, however. We want to focus in more detail on the specific interaction patterns in buying business services.

## The nature of exchange processes in relation to the type of business service

One of the factors describing the purchasing situation between a buyer and seller has a particularly strong effect on the interaction pattern between the customer and the supplier: the *type of service* being exchanged. We will demonstrate that services may be defined in terms of:

- The degree of complexity and the type of problem solution.
- The application, how it is used in the business of the buying company.

Since an essential starting point in this book is that interaction processes (exchanges, adaptations etc.) are primarily aimed at solving problems and making use of emerging opportunities, it is quite natural to emphasize the character of the product being bought. The complexity of the service (simple/complex) and the type of problem solution (standard solution for a low price, advanced or customized solution for a high price etc.) affect the customer's buying behaviour and the interplay between the customer and the supplier.

Even the application, *the way the service is being used* and made valuable by the customer, has an impact. Does the service affect the customer's way of working, will it be part of the service that the customer itself delivers to its customers, is it a general support for the customer's business process or not? These are important conditions that affect the way the interaction with the supplier develops and appears: who is involved, how often, when, what the communication is about etc.

Figure 5.3 depicts the impact that these two aspects have on the shape and content of the interaction pattern.

The complexity and application of the service are not the only aspects that affect the interaction between buyer and supplier, however. There are many more conditions that directly or indirectly have an influence. These include the customer situation in terms of the kind of business and competition it is facing, the nature of the supplier market, the capabilities of the actual supplier and the previous experiences of both parties with each other, the structure of the purchasing organization, the type of purchasing employees and many other aspects. In this chapter, nevertheless, we focus on complexity and application.

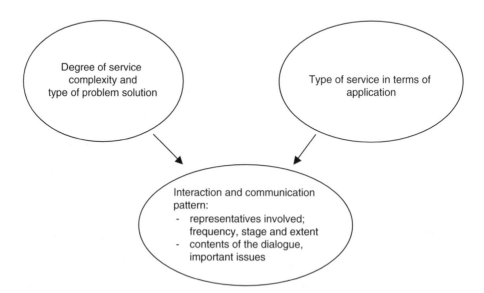

**Figure 5.3** Relationship between the nature of the service as expressed in terms of its application and complexity, and the resulting interaction pattern

## The complexity of the service and the type of problem solution

Important aspects that affect the exchange and adaptation processes and also put specific requirements on the employees involved are:

- Which type of problem solution is the customer looking for?
- Which type of solution can and will the supplier offer?

This can best be illustrated by means of Figure 5.4. The figure defines the following alternatives:

1. Basic function for a low price: the buying company is looking for low prices on a standard service.
2. Better product than standard: the customer requires a better product than the (industry) standard.
3. Basic function with individual adaptation: the customer is looking for low total costs. This implies that the price of the item bought *and* other cost effects of *how* the product is bought and delivered should be taken into consideration. A product that is well adapted to the customer's situation can lower indirect costs. This may involve reduced costs for quality control, invoice handling etc. Here, specific emphasis is placed on the reduction of such indirect costs.
4. A better product with individual adaptation: the customer is looking for a supplier relationship that involves the development of its own business.

In what way do these customer requirements regarding problem solutions affect the demands on the supplier and the demands on the internal purchasing organization?

1. The 'price presser' should meet the customer demands for low prices on a well-defined product (function): the demands on the supplier involve cheap

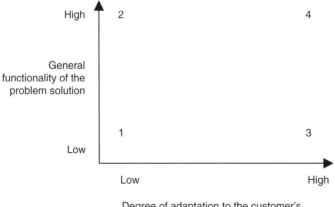

**Figure 5.4** Diagram for the analysis of problem solutions and supplier strategies
*Adapted from*: Håkansson, 1982, p. 386.

but functional resources, the exploitation of economies of scale, limited interfaces to keep costs down etc.

2. The 'product developer' should be at the forefront of product development: efforts with regard to R&D, resources for development including competencies of employees etc. Additionally, such a supplier should identify important development centres to contact and collaborate with. This is what the customer desires when asking for a service and supplier relationship of this kind.

3. The 'customer adaptor' should be able to 'sense' and adapt to the individual customer: a sensitive and attentive market organization, flexible production, adaptability etc. This is what the customer looking for low indirect costs is aiming for.

4. The 'customer developer' is a combination of 2 and 3. The customer that wishes to create business development through supplier collaboration will aim for a relationship that combines the aims and methods of 2 and 3.

Holmlund (1997) has made an attempt to analyse systematically how the type of market offering affects the exchange processes between customer and supplier. These processes are analysed according to the following dimensions: technical, social and economic. Additionally, a characterization is given regarding the expected dominant aspects of the relationship. In Table 5.2, we have redefined the type of offerings (according to the distinctions above), but the argument is in line with Holmlund's discussion. Note that all four variants apply to a simple market offering (e.g. a basic service rather than a professional service). Analogously, we could use a more complex service as a starting point and apply the same arguments.

One conclusion resulting from this analysis is that we can discuss and basically understand (and even predict) what a chosen supplier strategy will imply in terms of the content of exchange processes and their characteristics. This also applies to the way of dealing with the relation itself. This overview provides a starting point for evaluating the demands on the customer's capabilities to deal with the different processes that are required in buying different functional solutions.

## The type of service application

Researchers in the area of industrial marketing have identified systematic differences between different types of products in terms of the interaction pattern (Håkansson, 1982; Hallén et al., 1991). They have based the classification on the type of application, i.e. how the customer uses the good concerned. This method also seems relevant for services (Axelsson, 1987; Jismalm and Linder, 1995). Based on a typology initially developed at a telecommunications operator company, we define four basic types of applications:

- Consumption services.
- Component services.

**Table 5.2** The effects of the type of offering in terms of problem-solving capacity on business relationships

| Type of offering | Technical dimension | Social dimension | Economic dimension | Relation type |
|---|---|---|---|---|
| Simple standard offering | Focus on supplier's production capacity | Quick and simple contacts | Direct costs and price in focus | Cost dominated, unstable relationship |
| Simple adapted standard offering | Focus on the adaptability of the offering, requiring extensive information exchange<br>Trust important | Cross-functional contacts within and between companies | Direct and indirect costs important | Information dominated, more stable |
| Simple but better offering | More technical content than the simple standard offering | More and more qualified personnel involved | Direct costs, price vs value of the better functionality | More developed relationship |
| Simple, better and adapted offering | As above but with the difference that the quality of the personnel involved and the problem solution are a combination of 'better and adapted offerings'. | | | |

*Adapted from:* Holmlund, 1997.

- Transformation services.
- Working method services.

## Consumption services

What characterizes this category is that the services are used within the buying firm without becoming part of its final product. This consumption aspect is typical for so-called MRO (maintenance, repair and operating) items in manufacturing industries, such as lubricants, working shoes, glues, small tools etc. Altogether the category consists of a large variety of items that involve significant administrative efforts: the 'small order' problem. Buying this type of item therefore requires the development of efficient routines.

Consumption services are usually not essential for the firm's core activities. They only constitute support for the customer's business, often as a sort of 'relieving' service (Chapter 2). Consider some examples of these services and how they are managed.

---

**Box 5.5   Examples of consumption services**

**Consumption services at the telecoms operator**
Hotel services, cleaning, security, medical care and insurance were all identified as examples of consumption services. In those cases a highly limited number of people is involved in contacts with the supplier. The services are contracted for on an annual basis, from suppliers that are first evaluated and on the basis of competitive bidding. Important requirements for the suppliers are the ability to offer total solutions, geographic coverage and low total costs. For the long-term relationship, emphasis was also placed on the supplier's 'lending an attentive ear'.

**Weather forecasts**
The Swedish national meteorological institute SMHI is marketing a service called 'weather index' to some 20 companies, mainly within the trade sector. Companies such as IKEA subscribe to a specific service that helps them plan sales and make production more efficient. The index – which can also be delivered in certain customized versions – weighs factors such as hours of sunshine, precipitation and the presence of clouds, and covers a 10-day period. It also indicates the likelihood of a particular kind of weather.

Shopping malls and sports shops want to have an index that indicates relatively bad weather. IKEA prefers really bad weather, because in those circumstances Swedes clearly prefer buying furniture over many other alternative activities. Most of all, the company wants to know what kind of weather it will be so it has some indication of the number of customers to be expected and it can plan its workforce accordingly.

*Source*: *Svenska Dagbladet*, 8 July 1997.

---

These are some examples of consumption (or relieving) services. In these cases the service is targeted at the firm, but it could be targeted at specific individuals within the firm (such as the housekeeping service discussed in Box 2.12).

## Component services

Component services become, *unaltered, part of the offerings to the (final) customer*, and therefore the customer may have specific demands regarding the selection of supplier or component. In its turn, the supplier has to have a good understanding of the customer's product and the ways in which the customer's customer uses the product, together with an understanding of the component itself.

Component services are thus characterized by becoming part of the offering ('package' of core and peripheral services) to the customer's customer. There are essentially two types of component services, standard and special. A standard component is well known and does not need that much interaction by specialists. A special component that also might be quite advanced technologically is likely to go along with a deeper involvement and technical expertise. By using component services, the customer's offering can be differentiated and added value could be created. Therefore it becomes important to clarify to the supplier that the service is part of a package and how the final customer will use it. This is likely to have an impact on the interaction patterns, including the dialogue.

---

**Box 5.6   Examples of component services identified at the telecoms operator**

In the case of installing an exchange system and cables at a new office building, examples of component services are goods transportation and groundwork services. It turns out that the communication pattern between the customer and the suppliers of these component services is quite broad. Many people are in touch with suppliers for the services mentioned. The contacts are deep in nature, as is evident in their high frequency and intensity. Important demands on the suppliers are delivery reliability, and being able and willing to take responsibility for complete 'system solutions' (a number of components that together constitute a complete system). With regard to the long-term development of the relationship investigated, emphasis is placed on 'playing with open cards': customer and supplier should have a trusting and open dialogue.

---

The purchasing behaviour identified here for component services is not surprising. These services are part of the integrated service package that the (final) customer buys. Therefore it becomes important to clarify that the service is part of a context (a component in a package) and how it will be used by the customer.

The component in this example is a standard component. This might explain the broad yet shallow pattern of people interacting with each other. But still, we see that it is vital that the interaction process takes place within the context of the entire product and how that is going to be used in the next step.

## Transformation services

These are characterized by being *modified by the buying firm* and then – in an altered form – going further to the customer's customer. Examples of semimanufactured goods are paper pulp that is processed into paper and steel that is heat-treated and acquires new characteristics. In these situations, it is important that the customer knows how the supplier has treated the material and what is suitable or possible to do with it.

Transformation services are used in a similar way. Examples are information and knowledge. Information can be seen as data that is collected and presented in a certain structured way. Data can consist of numbers, words, sounds and images. Knowledge and capabilities are the result of processing or modifying information, or of the productive use and collection of information. Like similar goods and unlike most services, transformation services can be put into stock. Consumption does not occur at the same moment as production.

---

**Box 5.7   Examples of transformation services identified at the telecoms operator**

Concrete examples are market research, media surveillance and personnel evaluation services. These constitute raw materials that require further processing (analysis) by the customer. It turns out that the communication patterns between the customer and the supplier, in the cases investigated, are relatively limited in terms of breadth. Relatively few people were involved in the purchase of these services. However, the existing contacts are rather deep. Important customer demands are delivery reliability so that the processing of the 'raw material' can take place according to the time plan. Moreover, price is an important element in the dialogue with the supplier. For the development of a long-term relationship, the importance of continuous improvement of the product is emphasized, and this should occur in an open and trusting dialogue.

---

It seems very natural that the firm buying a service that is going to be processed further in its own operation should be as 'ready for treatment' as possible. That is why there is a need for interaction directly between the people supplying the 'raw material' and those who are designated to fulfil the process. Needless to say, there is likely to be a difference in depth and number of specialists involved between an advanced raw material and one that is standard.

## Working method services

A piece of machinery or an installation is used as a tool or instrument for the production of one's own products, e.g. a paper machine. It will strongly affect the production operations of a manufacturing firm. Equipment is also characterized by the fact that after the purchase, it should be used during a long period. Consequently, purchases occur only at very long intervals or perhaps only once. The purchase usually also represents a major investment. Often it takes place in the form of a project with a variety of internal functions involved. A fundamental aspect is that the equipment will affect the customer's way of working, and therefore it is important to *understand how the equipment fits within the production environment in which it will operate.*

Working method services are mainly based on knowledge. The buying firm tries to acquire methods of working from the supplier and subsequently apply these as tools.

---

**Box 5.8  Examples of working method services identified at the telecoms operator**

Concrete examples of services in this firm that are used in this way are education, organization and management consultancy services. These services are bought repeatedly and on a case-by-case basis. This implies that the kind of employees involved may vary, but that the relationship with the supplier becomes more intensive in connection with a specific purchase or ongoing deliveries, which is determined by that part of the company whose methods of working will be affected by the purchase. Important functional demands on this type of services are useability – being useful within the firm's business system – and delivery reliability. Regarding the conditions for long-term collaboration, it is emphasized that the supplier should have the capability to develop and improve its products continuously. They must stay 'in sync' with new developments.

---

An engine needs to fit with other equipment or is likely to alter the role of other equipment in a production process. It has an impact on the entire production structure. Similarly, working method services are likely to have an impact on the ways a business operates. This could involve issues such as how to design certain organizational processes. Therefore it is vital that it fits with other operating patterns, be it existing or new ones (due to the new working method). Again, there is a difference in significance between a minor and not integrated new method and a major change that might have an impact on the entire organization. Such differences should be reflected in the interaction patterns.

An example outside the context of the telecoms operator may help to illustrate this.

---

**Box 5.9  Management consultants who guaranteed the customer a more rational method of working**

One of the best-known international management consultancies accepted an assignment to improve the working methods at a major academic hospital, which should result in annual savings of at least €2.5 million. An extensive mapping of the hospital's routines was carried out and opportunities for improvement were identified. The consultancy firm proposed a fundamentally different way of working and was able to demonstrate that by doing so the expected cost savings could be realized.

The problem, however, turned out to be that the proposal was totally unacceptable to the hospital's personnel. Many important groups of employees turned against the proposals and argued that they were not defensible in medical terms. The proposal was dropped. The service – or the results of it at least – did not fit the business context of the customer.

---

Table 5.3 summarizes how these different types of services may affect the interplay between customer and supplier. For each service type, it indicates the expected contact pattern between the two companies, the most important issues, the way the relationship works and what is creating trustworthiness. It barely needs to be emphasized that this overview involves relatively strong simplifications. We also indicate likely differences depending on whether the service is a qualified or a standard one. It could thus for example be a standard component service or an advanced component service. That aspect is reflected in the matrix.

It could always be argued whether it is meaningful to try to stereotype interaction patterns like this. We all know and we have already pointed to the limitations of trying to explain exchange processes and interaction patterns by just one variable. In practice, from case to case we should expect specific interaction processes to be explained by a combination of influencing variables. What is important is whether the selected factor, in this case the kind of service, is of enough significance to really matter. We think that it is.

Note also that the same service, depending on the way the customer leverages it, can act as a consumption, component, transformation or working method service. A series of seminars by a trainer can be a working method service when it is directly bought by the customer that lets its employees participate, while it is a component service for a training institute outsourcing the content of the seminar but adding marketing, documentation and registration services.

The typology described in this section seems a useful one when trying to understand which type of interaction pattern emerges (and is needed) for the purchase of different types of services in terms of the way they are used. It also provides a useful starting point for analysing which kind of capabilities and internal collaboration is needed within the purchasing function dealing with these purchases.

## Basic services versus problem-solving services – a comment

As discussed earlier, two important aspects on which to evaluate the buyer–seller collaboration regarding a particular product are the way the product or service is being used (as consumable, component, transformable or working method) and the kind of problem solution it embodies (both in terms of the general functionality and the degree of customization, see Figure 5.4). Another aspect, related to these, is whether the service should be regarded as a simple service being bought from a service provider, or whether it should be regarded as a complex, knowledge-based problem solution being bought from a knowledge provider (cf. the discussion in Chapter 2).

Looking at the dimension simple–complex, we can observe that, regardless of the type of service according to the usage classification discussed earlier, the customer may want a supplier that acts as either of the following two sources:

● *An external source of production.* This is a firm that performs a basic function regarding consumption, component, transformation or working method

**Table 5.3** Type of service in terms of application and its effects on business relations

| Type of service | Contact pattern/representatives involved | High priority issues in the dialogues | Relation/trust based on |
|---|---|---|---|
| Consumption services | C: purchasers and internal customers<br>S: marketing representatives | How the service supports various core processes | S's ability to supply the desired service and (if needed) adapt it to the specific situation of C |
| Component services | C: product and market specialists<br>S: specialists regarding final product and supplier product | How the service fits in C's final product<br>Demands of final customer | S's production capacity and quality<br>S's development capabilities (when S is used as external expert) |
| Transformation services | C: production and quality representatives<br>S: production planning and marketing | How the service will be used (transformed) at C and how well it fits in different transformations | S's production capacity and capability to maintain a stable quality<br>S's innovation in production equipment and business development (when S is used as an external expert) |
| Working method services | C: business development representatives and affected customers<br>S: product representatives | How the service is used for changing C's working methods and how it fits with the important aspects of these methods | S's business development and innovation<br>References<br>Collaboration partners |

C: customer; S: supplier

services. The buying company relies on the supplier to perform that task, but that does not imply that the supplier involved has the competence to do something unique.

- *An external expert*. In contrast to the previous type of service supplier, this firm has more than average capabilities and offers added value. The supplier as external expert can be exploited in a more advanced way, which obviously does not come for free.

Looking at the dimension simple–complex in combination with the third, remaining dimension – standard vs adapted – it seems obvious that in general, knowledge-based services, given the definition proposed earlier, have more elements of adaptation, i.e. customized solutions. Basic services can be both standard or customized.

In addition to these general observations, some specific aspects of interaction can be observed when comparing basic, simple services with more complex services.

*Interaction between buyers and providers of basic services*
Some important starting points are that the service is defined as some routine issue that can be repeated identically at numerous times. The service is constructed in such a way that it can be repeated many times and with good precision. Three notable aspects to deal with in the interaction between customer and supplier are the following:

- *The division of labour between the supplier and the customer*: who will perform which activities and how the interaction will be organized. This relates to our discussion on service level agreements later (Chapter 7) and can be seen as a need to construct in a clear way the service(s) that are exchanged.
- *Synchronization between the overall activity structures of both parties*. Since services in general cannot be stored, it is often important to find those intervals during which the supplier's capacity to produce and the customer's need for services are in line with each other. This can be related to our discussion of services as activities and the allocation of those activities, in Chapter 3.
- *The reliability or credibility of the supplier* is to a large extent a matter of its capacity (production ability) to deliver on its promises. For its credibility, however, it is frequently also important to have a documented ability in the design and development of services.

*Interaction between buyers and providers of complex services*
An important starting point for this type of service is that it is being bought by a customer that does not know what the solution is to the problem. In a project-like setting, the supplier has to create – in collaboration with the customer – a problem solution. The aspects discussed above do play a role in this type of relationship as well, albeit less explicitly. Three notable aspects that have a specific influence on the buyer–seller interaction in this type of exchange are the following:

- *The organization of the assignment.* An assignment that involves a broad problem solution puts demands on, among other things, the dialogue between customer and supplier. Even if to a large extent the supplier is the one that creates the problem solution, interaction including communication during the assignment is of great importance to clarify and align the expectations of both parties.
- *The supplier's capability.* Especially in the case of complex, professional services, the customer often wants specific people, identified by the customer, to carry out the assignment. The supplier, however, may want to see the assignment as a relationship between two companies (e.g. in order to have more flexible production planning). These are issues that frequently need to be clarified.
- *The supplier's credibility.* How can a customer dare to trust that the supplier will be able to develop an appropriate problem solution? References from other assignments, image and reputation, methods and procedures are important elements in discussing this issue and with regard to the customer's evaluation, in order to resolve questions regarding credibility.

## Conclusions

In this chapter we have specified some of the aspects of the interaction processes taking place between buyers and sellers of business services, such as the need not only to carry out the purchase of a specific service but also to be able to collaborate with suppliers. It has become clear that, logically speaking, there are certain natural demands for and designs of interaction between customer and supplier as a result of some important aspects of the service being bought. The way the customer uses the service – as a consumption, component, transformation or working method service – has a strong impact on the interaction patterns between buyer and seller. Also the nature of the service itself (standard vs customized) and the type of service in terms of being a basic service process or a knowledge-intensive problem solution have a bearing on this interaction pattern.

It is also clear that there are other factors that are important in understanding both why two parties behave as they do and what it is important to be able to manage in a certain relationship. The history of the relationship, its atmosphere, the current shape of the supplier market and the different characteristics of the counterparts have a clear effect on the relationship. These are also relevant aspects that need to be taken into account.

These observations imply that understanding and being able to manage the interaction with a supplier can be just as important as being able to purchase the desired service. We have also demonstrated that the interaction process can be understood using the approach of the interaction model.

# 6

# The Impact of E-commerce

So far we have discussed a number of important aspects of services. In Chapter 1 we concluded that co-production is a typical feature of services as many of them, to a large extent, are produced and consumed in an interactive process. The division of labour between actors in the market system, who does what and why, was dealt with in Chapter 3. We concluded that in business-to-business (B2B) markets, the interactive processes between suppliers and customers often imply repetitive patterns of activity. Outsourcing or insourcing, partial as well as complete, reflects changes in roles and responsibilities between actors in the supply system. This was dealt with in Chapter 4. Interaction patterns between actors in B2B seems among other things to be dependent on what kind of service is being produced and bought. It is a key aspect that the interplay within and between actors is well fitted to the need for information and knowledge exchange in that relationship. The patterns discussed are not just for fun, but exist because of functionality. There must be a functional division of activities among actors in favour of the best. Such issues were dealt with in Chapter 5.

Information and communication technology (ICT) and its application to e-commerce and e-business are frequently addressed as *the* enabler of great improvements, especially in services production. In this chapter we will approach this 'e-phenomenon' to see what it is and what implications, as an enabler of improved efficiency and effectiveness, it is likely to have for the production and supply of services. The chapter is divided into three parts. First, we look at the potential of e-commerce in general. Secondly, we discuss the implications of ICT for patterns of interaction between firms as well as possible changes of roles and responsibilities along systems of actors, i.e. supply networks. Thirdly, we discuss the implications of ICT for different kinds of services.

## E-commerce: a definition

E-commerce and e-business are related concepts. E-commerce refers to the business exchange between actors involved in B2B or B2C (business-to-consumer) transactions – and other possible combinations. A straightforward definition is: 'All electronically mediated information exchanges between an organization and its external stakeholders' (Chaffey, 2002, p. 5).

Chaffey discusses different nuances of this definition as well as some alternatives, but basically it has to do with electronically mediated exchange processes between actors. E-business is more focused on business models and the kinds of business concepts made possible by exploiting the digital information technology. It is also about developing new procedures and finding new ways of handling specific functions. The same author gives this definition of e-business: 'All electronically mediated information exchange, both within an organization and with external stakeholders supporting the range of business processes' (Chaffey, 2002, p. 8).

We refer to both e-commerce and e-business as they are interrelated phenomena: much of the e-commerce that emerges is done by and/or enabled by firms that have a basic e-business foundation. This means that by e-commerce we refer to genuinely new business functions performed by new kinds of business firms with new business models, as well as to the impact of electronic aspects on traditional business firms and processes.

## Some key benefits of ICT

The possibility of using a digital format instead of analogue technology for telecommunication, or paper-based formats for other kinds of communication, can be traced back to some underlying features. If we try to find the core of this technology, which – when developed into applications – may have considerable impact, we think that much of the generic core relates to some of the following features. One of the most striking aspects is that electronic information, especially when mediated through the Internet, makes it possible to communicate effectively even if the actors involved are in different places as well as at different times. In comparison, physical face-to-face interaction between actors makes it necessary for them to be in the same place at the same time. Other communication channels might work if the parties are in different places but at the same time (telephone) and still others when the parties are in the same place at different times (a written announcement in a shop, for example).

Electronic communication shares this possibility of different places and different times with traditional letters, but there is another feature that comes into focus. A traditional letter is slow. This new medium has great reach and allows penetration of a large population very fast. In this respect it is similar to television and radio broadcasting and daily newspapers. Nevertheless, it is different in a number of ways. Another characteristic is the possibility of re-using and duplicating the same document at almost no cost. Analogue techniques mean that texts need to be copied on a piece of paper and it is difficult to make changes without rewriting, which is costly. The same goes for other products such as CD-Roms and physical products in general.

Pitt *et al.* (1999) argue that these kinds of features mean that for a number of products we see three major effects: the Internet is killing distance, homogenizing time and making location irrelevant. The distance issue is because of the speed of the digital information as well as no extra costs of long-distance transportation of the information. Homogenization of time is because in many cases anyone can get access to anyone else continuously, by visiting the Web. Location becomes irrelevant since where the involved parties physically are does not matter to the same extent – and for many products distance is irrelevant. Furthermore, Rayport and Sviokla (1995) argue that companies that create value with digital assets may be able to re-harvest them in an infinite number of transactions. The 'law of digital assets' – unlike physical assets, digital assets are not used up in their consumption – redefines both scale and scope economies. Even a small actor may achieve low unit costs and in the 'marketspace' – markets without physical limits – businesses can draw on a single set of digital assets to provide value across many different and disparate markets (Rayport and Sviokla, 1995).

Other authors who deal with possible business impacts of the Internet are Malone *et al.* (1987), who identify three effects of information technology, to which Wigand (1997) adds a fourth. All four effects may lead to reduced transaction and coordination costs:

- *The communication effect* – advances in information technology allow for more information to be communicated in the same unit of time, thus reducing transaction costs. It should be pointed out that transaction costs are accumulated at the various stages of a typical supply chain.
- *The (electronic) integration effect* – a tighter electronic linkage between buyer and seller is enabled.
- *The electronic brokerage effect* – an electronic marketplace exists where buyers and sellers come together to compare offerings.
- *The (electronic) strategic networking effect* – information technology enables the design and deliberate strategic deployment of linkages and networks among cooperating firms intended to achieve joint strategic goals to gain competitive advantage.

One could also distinguish between the following four enabling functions of ICT: *information* (being informed via a Web page as well as getting information by an information search), *communication* (dialogue via e-mail and chat), *distribution* (distributing products digitally) and *transaction* (the possibility of making deals via the Internet).

What has been said so far concerns what ICT allows for, so-called generic advantages. In applications, the impact of these could generate advantages that are more or less far-reaching and revolutionary, based on the specific context.

## Enabling techniques

In specific business settings, the first impact of ICT is realized in improved ways of performing old functions. However, it has also contributed to totally new functions in the creation of new products with new values, thereby making previous technologies and products obsolete (cf. De Boer *et al.*, 2002). Quite a number of products have been developed and, in various applications, enable actors to create new functions. Turban *et al.* (2000) provide a useful list of general enabling products available as Web applications:

| | | |
|---|---|---|
| E-malls | Unique Uniform Resource Locator | Static databases |
| Video | EC/financial transactions | Online catalogues |
| Shopping cart software | Direct order procedures | Multimedia |
| Three-dimensional display | Dynamic databases | Telephony |
| File transfer capability | E-mail response and forwarding | Audio |
| Customer tracking | Chat rooms | Forms |
| Animation | Statistics | Security |

This list clearly indicates that many new applications have been developed and are likely to emerge in the future. Furthermore, this make us aware that there are most likely many business processes and models that will be affected.

If we look at a firm in today's society it is likely to operate three different kinds of e-based nets: the Internet, some extranets and its internal intranet.

What general new and exploitable possibilities do the Internet, extranets and intranets create? Turban *et al.* (2000) provide some lists that are also useful in this respect. As we are going to discuss some other similar overviews we limit ourselves to mentioning a few. An extranet could enhance communication and contribute to improved marketing, sales and customer support, support productive collaboration between work groups, enhance business by improving the value added, help reduce costs by reducing errors, reducing travel and meetings as well as administrative and operational costs. Furthermore, it could improve information delivery by ease of maintenance and implementation and elimination of paper publishing and mailing costs.

An intranet could support internal communication by providing interactive communication such as chatting, audio- and video-conferences, but also document distribution and workflow and Web-based download and routing of documents. It could also improve the creation and utilization of databases by providing Web-based databases and search engines and directories to assist in keyword-based searches. All these generic functions of an intranet provide for a large number of applications, for example enhanced knowledge sharing,

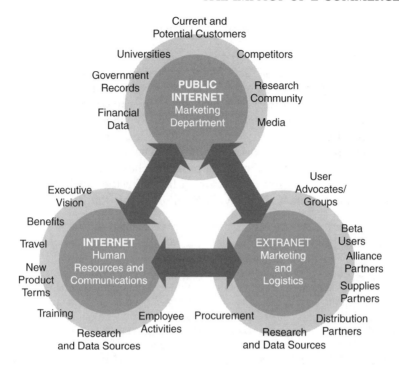

**Figure 6.1** Internet, extranets and intranets: connected parts of a firm's e-strategy
*Source*: Hanson, 2000, p. 86.

enhanced group decision and business processes, empowerment, software distribution, document management, training, project management etc.

Via the Internet, firms and individuals can access a multitude of information. Via extranets companies can operate as a group to synchronize their business. By using intranets companies can, in their internal operations, communicate and build databases and many other useful applications. In addition, firms are not limited to information in text format but can also use voice, pictures etc. Later in this chapter we come back to the kinds of implications that this technology is likely to have for business, especially the purchase and supply of services.

## The potential of e-commerce

It seems to be quite a common understanding that firms in general only exploit a fraction of the potential of e-commerce. They keep on doing things in the same way as before the introduction of the digital format. Instead of making a specific document on paper and sending it by a letter or fax, it is now typed in a digital format. But nothing has, in such cases, been done to redefine the processes and practices as such. Other firms take the new technology as their point of departure, redesign their procedures in accordance with what the technology allows, and thereby get more powerful effects on corporate capabilities.

## General approaches to e-commerce and e-business

Different approaches to IT and business in terms of the extent to which firms exploit the new possibilities have been discussed by, among many others, Venkatraman (1994). He uses Figure 6.2 as a reference point.

The evolutionary steps correspond very well to the minor adaptations where the use of IT is limited to a new technology being used to better carry out old processes and functions. The revolutionary steps include redesigning entire processes and create new business models based on the 'e'. The impact of ICT on business practices is of course dependent on the approaches chosen. In cases where a firm or an entire industry has chosen to develop in line with the revolutionary mode, a much more dramatic impact is likely. Some illustrations follow.

---

**Box 6.1 The invoice**

A simple, but nevertheless important step is to type out and send invoices in digital format as e-invoices instead of as written, paper-based documents. An investigation of what happened with an incoming invoice in a typical big manufacturing firm showed that it was treated at approximately 30 different stations. At one station it was checked for quality and quantity, at another it was checked for that specific unit's deliveries and so forth. The estimated time it took to deal with the invoice as well as to pass it around was substantial. It was considered impossible to 'close the loop' in fewer than 30 days. It cost, for the entire loop, between €50 and 100 in terms of time spent on each station. An e-invoice could reach all actors who need to see it instantly. It could be delivered in seconds, with almost no costs for writing, copying, enveloping, sending and receiving activities etc. Possible deviations from actual deliveries and specifications could be noticed by all units simultaneously – it need not be sequenced. The process could be fulfilled in a very short cycle and at far lower cost.

---

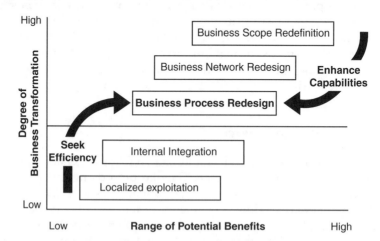

**Figure 6.2**  Different degrees of IT exploitation

*Source:* Venkatraman, 1994, p. 85.

---

**Box 6.2   Transportation services made available through the Internet**

In transportation the use of capacity is key. The fleet of transport vehicles should be filled up with material as much as possible; the vehicles should not transport air. One way to achieve this is to combine transport work for complementary customers: if one customer needs transport from A to B the complementary customer might need transport from B to A and at a time and volume that fit in with the first customer's wishes. ICT has facilitated such coordination. But, maybe even more interestingly, it has also improved spot-market opportunities. Buyers and sellers of transport services can use the Web and see what empty spaces there are on vehicles going to and leaving a certain place. If time, route and space match, it is a very interesting deal for both parties. Without the transaction in question the vehicle would be likely to transport air, and that is not profitable. These two mechanisms, better synchronization of regular tours and better knowledge about temporary transport needs, have contributed to improvements in the usage of vehicle fleets in most countries where ICT is actively in operation. It could have a major impact on the profitability of firms, as well as on the strategies of buying transportation services (cf. Andersson and Norrman, 2002).

---

**Box 6.3   Call centres: a simple service made a strategic capability**

Call centres are units within firms that handle complaints and other questions, most of all from customers. Traditionally this involved units located close to the local operations with which customers interact, complemented by a minor central unit to handle policies and very specific issues. Today, it is quite normal for there to be a minor unit locally and a major unit centrally. That centre could be located in quite a remote area, in order to benefit from a stable and cheap workforce. The key is that all complaints and all other communications in a certain range are directed to that centre, which facilitates a uniform way of dealing with the issues. This has been made possible by new technology.

That is not the whole story, however. Call centres of this kind have turned out to be not just a new way of handling these issues. They have in a number of cases turned out to be a strategic resource, as they can create databases with accumulated experience from the field. By data-mining techniques, the company can learn far more about its business and its customers than before and thereby turn a function from merely being passive and making excuses to customers into a genuinely strategic one. As a service operation and a service concept, it also means that the customer could get benefits from a more knowledgeable supplier.

---

These illustrations demonstrate that adaptation and exploitation of ICT could imply minor changes as well as revolutionary ones. But it is also evident that what might appear to be a minor change at the introductory stage could be the first step in a much more far-reaching journey. There are also other ways to discuss increased utilization of ICT. Bickerton *et al.* (1999) have divided it into three groups:

- *Publishing*, which means that the Internet is used for presentation of reports, product catalogues etc.

- *Collaboration and interaction*, which means complaint handling, e-invoicing, newsgroups and conferences, customer support etc.
- *Transaction*, involving such possibilities as direct links to back-office systems, online ordering and quotation systems.

The choices depend on a number of circumstances but the distinctions between them demonstrate that there are many possibilities and a potentially great impact of the 'e'. It is also evident that collaboration and transaction give room for improvements in ongoing relationships. Bickerton *et al.* (1999) argue that these strategies are more or less a matter of sequence: firms start with publishing and move on to collaboration and then transaction. But there are many choices involved and firms' strategies and adopting habits could vary a great deal. However, it is not self-evident that all companies in all contexts go for the most far-reaching among the possible techniques.

An interesting overview of potential improvements from utilizing e-market opportunities that are well in line with these illustrations has been put forward by Andrew *et al.* (2000). The authors present the matrix in Table 6.1.

The first major group, a value shift that primarily shuffles activities and costs from one actor to another, is of lesser interest to us. The second category, the activities that create genuinely new value, are more interesting and challenging. Many of the identified sources of value and drivers are focused on lowering costs (transaction, inventory, costs in use etc.), while some focus on ICT-enabled new product development. This aspect is not really brought into the matrix but should be stressed. It is not only a matter of lowering cost but also of providing new functionality. ICT could help suppliers offer new and better products by providing more functionality, higher as well as more consistent quality and so on. Some of these possibilities are illustrated in the rest of the chapter.

This is an interesting overview of possible sources and drivers of value creation. It adds accuracy to the possibilities indicated above. There are other, complementary kinds of overview. Some authors look more closely at specific business models made possible by the 'e' and the likely potential degree of improvement when they are in operation.

## The potential of different techniques and practices

One way to discuss the potential of IT has been presented by Timmers (1998). He has identified nine business models and discusses the potential improvements made possible by each of them on a scale with two axes. The business models identified are the following:

- E-shop (Web marketing of a company or a shop, a model for seeking demand).
- E-procurement (additional inlets, seeking suppliers).
- E-auction (electronic bidding with no need for prior movements of goods or parties).
- E-mall (a collection of e-shops, aggregators, industry sector marketplaces).

**Table 6.1** Value shift and value creation through e-commerce

|  | Sources of value | Driver |
|---|---|---|
| *Value shift activities* | Aggregation | Achieved results by consolidating volume |
| Activities that take value from one party and transfer it to another ('zero-sum game') | Process automation Transparency/ auctions | Decreased maverick buying Increased competition among suppliers |
| *Value creation activities* | Lower marketing and sales costs | Lower costs to reach and serve consumers |
| Activities that create new value through improved efficiency or productivity ('win–win' scenario) | Lower transaction costs | Fewer ordering errors Streamlined approval process Lower supplier evaluation costs Streamlined accounts-payable and receivable process |
|  | Lower costs in use | Access to superior products Customization of inputs and after-sales service raise quality and yield input |
|  | Lower inventory costs | More efficient supply chain reduces need for inventory Less obsolescence, less rework |
|  | Lower cycle time | Collaborative design and project management improves products, reduces redesign and speeds time to market |
|  | Improved asset utilization | Increased scale through reorganization of the value chain Higher labour productivity Better capacity planning and utilization |

*Source*: Andrew *et al.*, 2000, p. 10.

- Third-party marketplace (a common marketing front end and transaction support to multiple businesses).
- Virtual community (focuses on added value of communication between members).
- Value chain service provider (supports part of the value chain, e.g. logistics, payments).
- Value chain integrator (added value by integrating multiple steps of the value chain).
- Collaboration platform (e.g. collaborative design).
- Information broker (trust provider, business information consultancy).

For each of these business models, Timmers discusses possible advantages offered to users as well as some critical factors underlying its possible success. He goes on to position all these in the matrix in Figure 6.3.

The simpler the usage, the less impact. An e-shop is a way to get an address and a window with some information as well as the possibility of settling deals on the Internet. It is easily achieved but in general has little impact on the business in itself. E-procurement is somewhat more advanced and has more potential, according to Timmers. The existence of virtual marketplaces like e-auctions and information brokerages has more potential and means (at least for e-auctions) more complexity. The most demanding but also the greatest possibility for making a difference is, according to Timmers, the use of IT to integrate complete supply chains or, in the terminology of Gadde and Håkansson (2001), supply networks. In between, we find virtual marketplaces and a number of other techniques and practices. We cannot deal with all of these, the pros and cons of them and/or the problems associated with trying to exploit each of them, but it is interesting to see this overview as well as the indicated potential impact. Quite a lot still remains to be experienced and demonstrated.

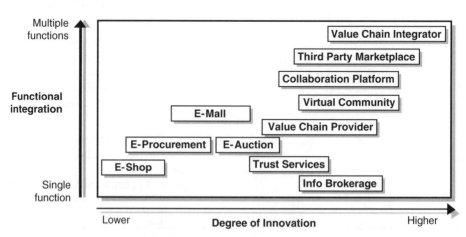

**Figure 6.3** Positioning different business models to exploit the new technology and the potential of each

*Source:* Timmers, 1998, p. 7.

Some very basic questions remain as to the extent to which ICT will enable the realization of potential business improvements and under what circumstances.

---

**Box 6.4   Freesourcing – creating an integrated supply system**

Freesourcing is a company established to develop software and apply it to create new distribution channels of material and components to the construction industry. The business concept is to help in synchronizing business between companies in the construction industry and their suppliers. It is basically a vertical marketplace in which suppliers of certain materials are available. It is also a concept aimed at minimizing the logistics involved and it has to a great extent been developed in cooperation with the transport company Schenker BTL. A customer using this system can, when considering how to, from whom and what to purchase, immediately see what is available at which suppliers, when, in what ways and under what conditions. But it is not an open virtual marketplace; instead it is a limited group of actors that together benefit from better synchronization. The system offers better and more prompt information, joint standardized documents, faster and cheaper logistics as well as new sources of supply. There is an estimated two-digit expected saving that, together with the improved service, creates the attractiveness of the concept along with the opportunity to change a traditionally rigid system.

---

**Box 6.5   The Senate – a new channel for competence development**

The Senate is a virtual marketplace for education services and consultations. Companies that join pay a monthly fee that varies according to the number of users to get access to the information available on the website. The company provides knowledge in a number of areas such as marketing and sales, purchasing and supply, law, ethics, accounting and so forth. Each area consists of text material along with video-recorded seminars and mini-lectures. They are upgraded regularly and there are news functions, e.g. reporting on an interesting book or seminar, in addition to the general information. In addition, the customers could put questions, standard or more complex, to the editors (who are in most cases well-known academics). The answers to these questions are prepared individually by one of the editors or someone authorized by the editor. These services are paid for according to negotiated fees.

What the customers get is prompt delivery of knowledge, individual support (consulting) and continual updates on important trends within specific areas of knowledge. The users could reach many of these services at any time and get quick access to specific services.

---

As companies gain more experience and as researchers study different phenomena related to the 'e', we will know more about the potential and the impact of different contexts. Interesting experiences have been reported in the use of electronic marketplaces (e-hubs). They can be used as open markets welcoming all actors who qualify as suppliers and buyers, or used exclusively for a strictly select group of actors. In the latter case the reasons could be to make more integrated, synchronized operations possible. From Figure 6.3, we can see that the economic potential as judged by Timmers should be higher for those firms applying an integrated approach.

Another important distinction is between vertical and horizontal marketplaces. Vertical marketplaces are segmented towards a specific industry and display and make available goods and services that are relevant to that industry. Horizontal marketplaces generally have a wider assortment with a greater reach in terms of industries. Some interesting problems relating to creating electronic marketplaces have been noted by Kaplan and Sawhney (2000). One of the problems that has been reported is the 'chicken and egg' issue. No one wants to enter such a marketplace if specific other actors are not there too. Likewise, changing from an established channel to a new one, with new actors involved, could be a very dramatic move for a company, especially in B2B where trust and mutual expectations are built up over time and represent heavy investments. To alter such relationships and adopt a new actor with a new technology could often be accompanied by high risk. This is very much in line with the general experiences of introducing new products and procedures. It is not just a matter of developing them; it is more difficult, in many cases, to get them accepted by the actors in the market (Håkansson, 1987; Axelsson, 1996a, Chapter 13).

Freesourcing (see Box 6.4) has experienced many of these kinds of problems. Its way of getting around them was by coordinated action, being in dialogue with and simultaneously bringing along more than one significant actor. It brought along entire chains of actors that were already working together. It thereby became coordinated action. Nevertheless, there have been many traditional rigidities to overcome in the system. In the case of the Senate (see Box 6.5), it also had to make a choice of the target groups. Should it specialize in a certain industry and/or a certain category of people or specific companies to approach and thereby design the business system around? Its choice was to offer its services to managers at top levels in a broad range of industries as well as a broad sweep of functional areas. These choices had a great impact on the kind of services offered as well as on the marketing activities and the technology developed.

## Basic forms of e-procurement

De Boer *et al.* (2002) argue that when it comes to practices within e-procurement broadly defined as 'the use of the Internet in purchasing', including intranet and extranet applications, one can distinguish six practices that are better established than most others:

- E-MRO.
- Web-based ERP.
- E-sourcing.
- E-tendering.

- E-reverse auctioning.
- E-informing.

The authors argue that e-MRO as well as Web-based ERP refer to the process of creating and approving purchasing requisitions, placing purchase orders and receiving goods and services ordered, by using a software system based on Internet technology. In the case of e-MRO, the goods and services ordered are maintenance, repair and operation (MRO) supplies (i.e. non-product related). The supporting software (an ordering catalogue system) is used by all employees of an organization. But in the case of Web-based ERP (enterprise resource planning), the goods and services ordered are product related. Usually only the employees of the purchasing department (or the planning department) use the supporting software (the Web-based ERP system).

E-sourcing refers to the process of identifying new suppliers for a specific category of purchasing requirements, using Internet technology (usually the Internet itself). By identifying new suppliers a purchaser can increase its competitiveness in the tendering process.

E-tendering concerns the process of sending RFIs (requests for information) and RFPs (requests for proposals) to suppliers and receiving their responses using Internet technology. E-tendering could also include the analysis and comparison of responses. It does, however, not include closing the deal with a supplier. It automates a large part of the tactical purchasing process, without focusing on the specific content of that process.

E-reverse auctioning is the opposite of a traditional auction. The auction operates with an upward price mechanism (an English auction with several bids) or a downward price mechanism (a Dutch auction with one bid only). In practice, an auction enables a supplier to sell (surplus) goods and services to a number of known or unknown buying organizations. During a relatively short time frame the buying organizations involved submit bids for the goods and services that are auctioned. A reverse (English) auction is the opposite: a customer auctions its *need* for goods or services to a number of known or unknown suppliers. E-reverse auctioning is the Internet technology-based equivalent of a reverse auction. Usually e-reverse auctioning focuses on the price of the goods and services auctioned (Teich *et al.*, 1999).

Unlike the previous forms, e-informing is a form of electronic procurement that is not directly associated with a step in the basic purchasing cycle, like contracting or ordering. It is the process of gathering and distributing purchasing information both from and to internal and external parties, using Internet technology. For example, publishing purchasing management information on an extranet that can be accessed by internal clients and suppliers is a way of e-informing.

None of these six practices, however, looks very much into ongoing business relationships and the possibilities of improving everyday exchanges between buyer and seller. As the 'e' basically is about improved ways of handling information and transactions, many improvements should be made available in such contexts. This has also clearly been indicated in Figure 6.3. Such issues will be more in focus in the following section.

## E-commerce and the interaction patterns between actors

We have emphasized that interaction between a customer and a supplier is (or should be) functionally determined. The interaction follows from the kind of service that is exchanged, the previous experiences of doing business between the parties and other aspects of the context. It is often a matter of *ex post*, patterns that have developed by experience, but it could also be *ex ante*, something structurally decided: this is the way to deal with this supplier or customer. Interaction patterns are a matter of interplay between people, they are about exchanging information and they also include a social exchange. This latter aspect has much to do with the development of trust, something that to a great extent comes along with social exchange and performance in line with expectations.

What about the possible impact of ICT on interaction patterns? There have been studies of information exchange, e.g. between buyers and steel producers in manufacturing industry, indicating to what extent the exchange is via personal contacts or via telephone, letter or fax (Håkansson, 1979). A follow-up to that study has been carried out, focusing on a broader range of businesses (Leek *et al.*, 2000). In this study a number of buyers as well as sellers express their estimates of and attitudes to the kind of issues that are dealt with through each kind of communication channel. It is evident that e-mail has changed a lot and to a great extent has replaced telephone and fax contacts – and to some degree also personal, face-to-face contacts. There are some obvious reasons for this, the most obvious that it is convenient. But e-mail entails and exploits some of the generic characteristics of digital information. The sender and the receiver do not need to be in the same place at the same time and one can re-use the text in an e-mail, something that is not possible to the same extent with the other channels. There are more advantages of this sort.

If we look at the replacement of face-to-face contacts, it seems as if more of the basic communication aspects are dealt with in relation to distance. But there are still many key questions, not least in the early stages of emerging business relationships, that need to be handled face to face. The possibility of using all five senses at the same time is in some cases hard to replace and it seems as if the parties more quickly reach the point when they really need to meet physically. Still, video-conferencing and other channels are likely to substitute for a substantial share of previous face-to-face contacts. However, the content of the information is not likely to have changed very much and basically the same issues need to be solved. Likewise, in the study referred to, extranets as a channel had not yet been put into use to any great extent even though this was expected to change in the future.

The 'e' has already had and is likely to have an even greater impact on the interaction processes that go on between customers and suppliers in B2B contexts. But it is a new tool for communicating the same information that has always been necessary. We have indicated some of the rationale for this and we will give an illustration of what IT enables when it comes to interaction between the two parties.

> **Box 6.6   Key account management in a bank**
>
> This bank has since long tried to coordinate its activities towards some of its customers, big multinational corporations. Coordinating this relationship has not been easy, as the two parties involve a number of geographic places and times, have different problems and need different services. However, the new software gives much better support than before. If all people involved with this customer report their activities to the system they can easily get to know other activities and initiatives, ongoing and planned. If the London office has dealt with some of the customer's problems, all the rest of the people involved might know that if the access to that specific information is not restricted somehow. This facilitates the activities of the key account manager, the person responsible for the entire relationship. It is easy to reverse the entire context to purchasing, by merely identifying with the customer in this case.

This illustration clearly demonstrates and underpins our argument that ICT has an impact on business potential as well as interaction patterns between buyers and sellers. But we have also indicated that the new possibilities are not realized just because the technology enables it. There are many other things that need to be in place. In discussing electronic marketplaces, for example, we have indicated that there is a need for trust between the parties both when it comes to open portals (hubs) as well as applying the technology to integrated hubs. In the first instance the parties need to trust that what they order really will be delivered according to specification; how could such this aspect be guaranteed? In the second case the parties involved integrate their operations more strongly than before, invest time and money in the new concept and become more dependent and locked into the relationship. Both cases call, in different ways and for different reasons, for trust in the other party. This is not a new phenomenon, trust has always been an essential part of all business relationships. But with new technology substantial changes are made possible and thereby the trust issue is likely to be frequently raised. When a business is carrying on according to standard procedures there is no need to question the relationship, it is a taken-for-granted, everyday situation.

It is thus evident that the 'e' has the potential to influence any business relationship or supply network in a multitude of ways. More illustrations will be presented in the next section.

## E-commerce and the impact of patterns of division of labour along supply chains

New, e-based business models and techniques, some of which are illustrated above, will change the allocation patterns of services (Chapters 3 and 4) as well as changing (excluding, replacing, adapting) specific activities and activity chains. They will also make certain actors disappear, some to enter the marketplace and still others to change their roles. Already the IT-enabling systems are in themselves different kinds of supply chains.

In Chapter 3 we described a number of services produced and the activity patterns that actually created those services. Many of the illustrations, in fact, were examples of changed patterns and, furthermore, most of them were enabled by ICT. This is not surprising, since ICT has already had and is in the future likely to have even more of an impact on the division of labour in supply systems in a multitude of ways. A frequently discussed notion is the possibility of disintermediating traditional distribution structures by utilising e-commerce (Wigand, 1997). This means that in many cases better possibilities for purchasing directly from the producer have emerged and been put to use. This, in turn, means that previous intermediaries have been left out. Another frequently noted effect is that of re-intermediation, which means that old intermediaries or other actors have been replaced by new ones performing a different but necessary function. Naturally IT has created new roles, not only in individual cases (specific firms) but for structurally based phenomena. Such changes include the following.

---

**Box 6.7: Information specialists due to separation of physical, financial and information flows**

Traditionally it has been more or less self-evident that the flow of information follows the physical and financial flows in market channels. Today we frequently experience a separation of these flows. In many fields we can see for example information specialists, who have as their core competence knowledge of good solutions to different problems. It could be firms advising other firms on suitable media for advertising, choice of the best insurance offering, or the optimal security system for a company. This is about selling knowledge; the services that follow from such recommendations are produced by other firms.

---

This example illustrates the emergence of new actors with new roles in established supply systems including market channels. The most significant effects of the 'e' might be on the structure of market channels. ICT represents, to a large extent, a new channel for distribution. It changes the distribution of goods, but it might be even more challenging when it comes to the distribution of some specific services. Furthermore, it also has an impact on existing and enduring channels as well as on existing and enduring actors, as existing channels and actors can benefit from the new technique without being replaced by anything entirely novel.

Examples of changed patterns and roles between actors in supply systems include the following.

---

**Box 6.8: Rank Xerox London**

Similar to many other companies who install equipment at their customers' sites, Rank Xerox has a complementary business, repairing and servicing the copying machines and other equipment that has been bought by customers. The traditional procedure is that the service technician receives the next day's tasks at the end of the day. In early morning he or she drives to the local warehouse to fetch the components that are likely to be needed in the field during the day. This is time consuming: it takes time to reach the warehouse, to pick out the materials needed and to get out into the 'field' in the London traffic.

Now the technician orders the components he or she needs via e-mail from a central store. They are picked there in the late afternoon and evening and transported during the night by UPS (or a similar operator) to the technician's home. As a result, the technician can immediately go out into the field and start the servicing. This makes it possible to reach a much higher 'invoice-able time'. The service that Rank Xerox buys might cost something extra even though there are vital savings in concentrating all components into a central stock in comparison with a number of local ones. Nevertheless, it compensates for these costs with the benefits of being able to sell more services (more time per technician) to customers. Again, this is made possible by the use of IT and the development of new kinds of business concepts among suppliers (the UPS operation).

## Box 6.9  Recurrent global allocation of activities using ICT

One of the major international consultancy firms has organized its 'production' in a different way with the help of ICT. The consultants often do interviews with respondents at the client's location or elsewhere. The interviews are recorded on tape and then an extensive and expensive task is undertaken to transcribe the contents of the interviews to make future analysis easier.

The new element is that the notes of these tapes are no longer written through the consultancy's own (expensive) assistant capacity. With help from a global courier company, the recorded tapes are sent to the Philippines to be transcribed by lower-paid, English-speaking personnel, and the consultancy firm receives the notes delivered the next day by e-mail. This has consequences for the activity structures and resources involved, both for the customer and for the supplier. Recordings that were never previously transcribed due to estimated usage and cost can now be documented and the notes of tapes that have been transcribed can now be produced both more quickly and at a lower cost (Van Weele and Rozemeyer, 1996).

In all kinds of business structures there are always a number of ongoing processes. These could be processes of coordinating and synchronizing activities, resources and actors that should be done in a timely way and functionally fitted to other activities (cf. Chapter 3). There are also processes of prioritizing, directing and managing, when actors try to get their way and influence the activities that they and others perform. Such processes are always being conducted with varying intensity in connected systems, not least in market structures functioning like networks (Håkansson and Eriksson, 1993).

In logistics there are some very important concepts that are closely related to these processes. One concept is *pooling*, which means that components and activities are brought to (or connected at) certain places. Related to this is *docking*, where more or less prepared systems of products (functions) are merged at certain locations (merge in transit, cross-docking points). Related questions are the following: Where are suitable places to pool things? What functions should be merged where and when? *Customizing* is a third important concept: at what stages should the products and/or assortments be differentiated to fit a certain customer or category of customers? Related to this concept is, in turn, *postponing*, when customization of an offering is done closer to the point of sale than usual. It is not always possible to produce to customer-specified orders, but through postponing techniques the suppliers do not have to look ahead too far. The Hewlett-Packard example described in Box 3.12 is an example.

Changes also occur among actors: who should be involved, who should take responsibility for what etc. We have mentioned vendor-managed inventories as one recent practice that has been enabled by ICT, but there are many other possibilities. Likewise, we saw in the case of the consultancy firm that needed transcripts of recorded interviews that new actors and a different division of labour turned out to be efficient. Again, this was not an attractive alternative before the development of the relevant communication technology.

If we look back at the cases above we find some illustrations demonstrating that the answers to the questions inherent in these concepts have changed. Instead of pooling many products locally, in the individual store, and from there customizing them, many firms tend to pool and customize at a central stock instead. Instead of merging the components with the service technician at a local storing place, this is done far away and moved directly to the technician's flat or house. These are basically different answers to the coordination–synchronization issue.

ICT is a generic technology that has an impact on almost all possible businesses. This means that it has enabled many of the new concepts and practices of which we have given some examples. It also means that it has contributed to new prerequisites and new answers to old questions. All the questions illustrated by the concepts from logistics (pooling, merging, customizing, postponing etc.) were used by Cox and Goodman as long ago as 1956 in their study of a house-building project in Philadelphia, US. The answers that were 'right' then, taking into account the then existing technologies of house-building, transportation and information handling, are 'wrong' today. This is due to changes in all these areas, but the basic questions are still the 'right' ones.

As ICT has such a scope we find in many networks that established procedures are challenged, as are the actors performing them. This means not only that specific individual business practices change, like the ones illustrated in our examples. The 'e' causes changes in power structures and the relative importance of specific resources and skills as well.

## E-commerce and its likely impact on different kinds of services

This book is about the purchasing of services. We have made it clear that most customer offerings as well as requests from customers consist of combinations of tangible goods and mainly intangible services. We have also demonstrated that a great variety of services exists (Chapter 2). One interesting question related to this is: what kinds of services are influenced the most by e-commerce and why?

## Digital vs non-digital services

Digital services are possible to express in a digital format and to present as a package. Abrahamsson and Brege (2002) introduce two distinctions: whether the service is in a B2C or a B2B context and whether it is entirely digital, which means that it is also possible to distribute it digitally. This is demonstrated in Figure 6.4.

The authors use this frame of reference to discuss the market offerings' dependency on physical logistics and, from that, their potential for improving business. They argue that when the customers are consumers and when the offering is dependent on physical logistics – which is the case for many IT-based business concepts – the potential for improved business is relatively low. It is basically a substitute form of traditional mail order but can, of course, give rise to important rationalization effects. On the other hand, when there is a B2B context and the products are digital, Abrahamsson and Brege argue that the potential is very high. The distribution of products is much easier, faster and cheaper. As B2B is normally repetitive and involves a lot of dialogue as well as exchange of documents, interaction patterns change and many everyday improvements are made possible. This is why quadrant 1 in Figure 6.4 gives a higher potential for improvements than quadrant 2, even though the same basic reasoning applies to both situations. The attractiveness of quadrant 3 is also quite high as the products are digital and can be distributed in a much more efficient way than before.

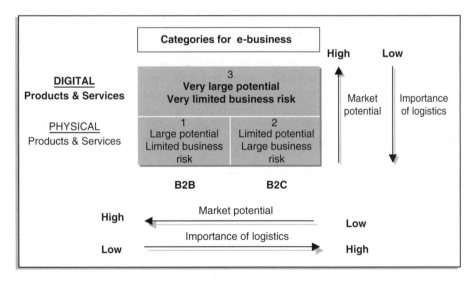

**Figure 6.4** A matrix for discussing different customer offerings in terms of dependency of physical logistics and potential for business improvement

*Source:* Abrahamsson and Brege, 2002.

For different kinds of services produced and exchanged in B2B, this means that the 'e' should be of interest to most services, but especially those that could be expressed in digital formats. There seems to be a very strong trend in today's business to make products and processes explicit in order to prepare for digitalization. It seems also to be possible to make a surprisingly large share of services more digital. There are examples of legal services that always have been considered very dependent on human interaction but that have been possible to make digital to a certain degree on a range of issues. It is clear, however, that many services could not become entirely digital. This has, in relation to knowledge management, been discussed as a difference between codifying versus personalizing strategies (Hansen *et al.*, 1999). The authors argue that for some knowledge it is necessary to have dialogue face to face, while others are better suited to codifying procedures. Nevertheless, even in those cases ICT is likely to bring important possibilities for changes and improvements.

## Other classifications: short-term vs long-term and simple vs complex

Let us return to some of our classifications of services in Chapter 2, where we discussed them in terms of long vs short term, standard and simple vs complex and creative and so on. It is difficult to say what kinds of services, according to such a classification, would be affected the most by ICT and in what ways. Fundamentally this comes back to the same reasoning as above on the potential of ICT in searching for new suppliers vs its role in contributing to changes within ongoing relationships in dyads of two or in entire chains of activity structures or supply networks. ICT could facilitate the search for and identification of new prospects and help in making alternative suppliers and alternative offerings more transparent. In ongoing relationships it could foster the redesign of exchange processes, rationalize and increase quality, as has been demonstrated in earlier sections.

It is also likely that many standardized and non-creative services could more easily be transferred into digital formats. Creative and non-standardized services will be more difficult to digitalize, or codify, as they build on the skills of individuals with often a high degree of tacit knowledge (Nonaka and Takeuchi, 1995). Furthermore, the outcome depends on how individuals, bringing their more or less tacit knowledge, manage to forge solutions in interactive processes. Nevertheless, ICT could in many ways enable and support such assignments as well.

## Further classifications and the likely impact of ICT

There are some alternative classifications to the ones we used in Chapter 2 that might better apply to this specific theme. One is the differentiation between hard and soft services (Erramili, 1989) where the hard services are possible to package. Frequently mentioned examples are computer programs and functions stored on a CD-Rom or similar services that can be both stored and digitalized. Soft services are more dependent on the social interplay between individuals and are thus much more difficult to digitalize. ICT technology can still to a certain extent replace physical, face-to-face interaction in many applications, for example by interacting with another person on a video screen. This is the case for some educational, counselling and medical services, for instance. In this context the argument above concerning non-standardized and creative services should apply fairly well.

Another alternative classification better suited to this theme is the one proposed by Zeithaml (1981). She distinguishes between services that are high in search qualities, experience qualities and credence qualities. This means that some services can be searched for and judged by information from a market. Price and similar characteristics are tangible and determined prior to purchase. Some services, in contrast, can only be judged and evaluated after the customer has experienced them. Examples of factors that it is not that easy to evaluate prior to purchase are satisfaction, speed and reliability. Yet others are primarily judged and evaluated according to the credibility of the service provider. Qualities such the extent of the provider's professionalism and knowledge may only be known a long time after the purchase.

This classification has attracted researchers addressing the area of ICT. In a discussion of different kinds of services and the degrees of information asymmetry between buyers and sellers, Nayyar (1990) found that information asymmetry is greater for services that have considerable experience and credence qualities than for services with search qualities. Asymmetry means that one party (the supplier) has better information about the true quality of a service. Wymbs (2000, p. 471) argues that 'based on this, we would expect firms using information technology to first attack information asymmetries related to "search" characteristics like car and insurance policy sales. Electronic attacks on information asymmetry components associated with experience and credence will be more difficult but are possible, e.g. doctors and pharmacies on-line having to successfully attack both "experience" and "credence" characteristics.'

Essig and Arnold (2001) have also referred to this classification in a conceptual discussion of the possible effects of electronic procurement on supply chain management. This seems to be a more fruitful classification for discussing the impact on services of ICT. It is nevertheless evident that the outcome of this discussion is closely related to our previous discussion of standardized–non-standardized as well as creative and non-creative services. The creative and non-standardized ones are more likely to be high in credence qualities. In each case the judgement resides on the possibility of digitalizing the service in question in a meaningful way.

In Chapter 5 we also use a classification of services based on the ways in which the service is applied by the buyer: whether it is a consumption, component, transformation or working method service. One could argue that making service components is facilitated by digital technology. It is often possible to digitalize parts of a service package. From this it follows that it is likely that the possibility of creating and combining different service packages, built up by service components, will be facilitated by ICT. It might also be possible to identify an impact of ICT on the other types of services (consumption, transformation and working method), although we think that the classification from Chapter 5 has more merit in the discussion there.

## Barriers to exploiting e-technology

After having presented such a positive picture of the possible impact and improvements due to IT, we should also take an objective look at the other side of this phenomenon. The potential does not come without effort and there might be substantial barriers to overcome that are worth emphasizing. Otherwise, we would give a skewed impression of the impact of the 'e'. We first discuss this in general terms and then consider trust as one specifically important barrier (or enabler).

### Barriers in general

If we first look at the purchasing department, it needs not only to possess the new technology and to have employees who are able to utilize it, there is also a need for an improvement in conceptual thinking in order to be able to 'see' possibilities and create new solutions. If we then proceed to the relationship with the supplier, the two parties not only need to have the technology and the skills to use the new technology, but in order to realize many of the new possibilities they also need to have established trust and be willing to experiment. Whether this barrier is a serious one depends not only on attitudes but also on other relationships in which the supplier is involved. To start doing business in a different way with one customer might cause trouble in the supplier's relationships with other customers or other parties.

From a broader perspective we are also likely to face barriers on a system, market or network level. In a specific industry there might be numerous systems and practices and in order to take full advantage of a certain technology it is important that all actors adapt to the same system. If no one dominating design exists (Utterback, 1994, pp. 23–56), this is likely to provide severe barriers to the exploitation of new technology. On this level there are also numerous institutional barriers such as rules of conduct and laws to apply in business when old concepts no longer apply. One barrier of specific importance, as always when basic conditions change, is trust.

### Trust as a barrier or enabler

It is important for the purchasing function to be aware of the great power of having trust between parties. It is widely held that trust is something that is built over time, often a long time. In contrast, it can be destroyed very rapidly (Håkansson, 1982). An important implication is, therefore, that it is not advisable to change purchasing strategy too often. The actor who works in a relation-oriented way one year only to change to a transaction-oriented purchasing strategy the year after must expect a deterioration in certain dimensions of trust. If this actor wants to change back again within a couple of years, strong action is required. It is also often held that trust is earned more on the basis of one's actions rather than on one's words. Another important aspect is consistency, that other parties know what they can expect from the company.

Sako (1997, p. 32) postulates five important aspects or forms of trust. One party in a relationship can trust the other in certain areas, but not in others. The five aspects are as follows:

### Contractual trust

This kind of trust, or in fact the lack of trust, is built on the fact that everything is regulated and contractually regulated. This form of trust is always an important ingredient in the relationship if one of the parties vehemently argues: 'We prefer to have everything explicitly dealt with in our contract with this business partner.'

### Competence trust

This expresses one party's trust in the other's ability – competence – to solve potential problems. Trust according to this dimension is low if statements apply such as: 'The advice we get from this actor is not always the best.'

### Goodwill trust

This is a matter of one party trusting in the other's willingness and ability to 'be there' and do something out of the ordinary if an unexpected event happens. Trust on this dimension is high if statements apply such as: 'We can trust this actor to help us when needed, more than the contractual obligations force it to.'

### Trust in terms of being just and fair

One of the parties sees the other as fair and just if it will agree with the following statement: 'We can depend on this actor always to treat us fairly and correctly.'

### Business opportunism

The level of business opportunism, i.e. one party's inclination to only have its own gains in mind, can be high or low. This is an important aspect of trust. Trust is lower if there is reason to agree with the following statement: 'Given the chance, our partner will try to gain an advantage to the detriment of our company.'

An interesting point in Sako's reasoning is that the concept of trust becomes more diversified and clarified. This creates the possibility, when assessing the atmosphere in a relationship (see Chapter 5), of there being a high level of trust in certain of the dimensions discussed and a low level in others. Hence, there is a better basis for a realistic assessment of where the parties are, how different courses of action are likely to be received and also how trust could be developed most appropriately.

The general need for trust in business transactions is often put forward as one explanation for the rather slow development of various portals or e-hubs, which are virtual marketplaces. The general experience seems to be that it is primarily standardized items that are bought via so-called open hubs. The more advanced ones demand a more trustful relationship. This is in essence the same as saying that products that, in Zeithaml's (1981) terminology, are high in search qualities could be bought from open e-hubs without much prior experience of the chosen partner. Those that are high in experience and credence qualities put much higher demands on trust in both the marketplace (the hub) and the partner. This makes trust such an important barrier to and – when trust is established – enabler of e-commerce.

## Conclusion

Fundamentally, ICT provides ways of drastically reducing different categories of transaction and communication costs. It influences the interplay and the patterns of interaction between buyer and seller. It also has the potential to influence the division of labour between actors in supply chains as well as the efficiency and effectiveness of the operation of such systems. Furthermore, it does not only contribute to cost cutting but also to creating new values and new service functions that we have not experienced before.

The benefits of various forms of electronic procurement (EP) seem largely undisputed (Smeltzer and Ruzicka, 2000; Croom, 2000). Still, as argued by De Boer *et al.* (2002), a clear theoretical basis seems to be lacking for specifying conditions under which different EP forms are appropriate in different purchasing and organizational settings (see e.g. Emiliani, 2000; Min and Galle, 1999).

When it comes to the potential inherent in specific services, no matter in what context, those that could be expressed in digital format and thus be delivered over the Internet involve the greatest potential. If the service also involves some kind of atoms (physical things; Negroponte, 1995) that need to be moved, the potential is restricted by the physical logistics involved.

ICT is also likely to have an impact on such issues as:

● How to specify services, as the digital format fosters the process of making them explicit (Chapter 7).
● The selection process as well as the evaluation model of possible partners (suppliers), as one important prerequisite for effective collaboration may be the partners' capabilities in ICT (Chapter 8).
● Possible pricing strategies, as experiences of specific services from different application areas can more easily be mapped (Chapter 9).
● Different ways of buying services in terms of transactional vs relational approaches (Chapter 10). Both approaches could benefit from ICT, but it could also influence the balance of preference between approaches.

These latter kinds of impacts of ICT are addressed as integrated aspects in the following chapters.

# Part III

## Application: The Process of Buying Business Services

# 7

# Specifying Business Services

In the typical textbook, the purchasing process is described as a sequence of steps initiated or triggered by a conscious need that has arisen at the customer. After that, a number of steps are taken that result in a purchasing decision and the acquisition of a product. In the current chapter, we want to focus more on the beginning of the purchasing process: the specification phase. In the subsequent two chapters we look at the choice of suppliers (Chapter 8) and contracting (Chapter 9).

Specifying needs and wants when buying services can be a demanding task, especially in the light of some of the service characteristics we mentioned earlier (Chapter 1): intangibility and the close integration of production and consumption. In this chapter, we will take a closer look at such issues.

## Purchasing as a rational decision process

A customer's purchasing process can be seen from two different time perspectives: a short-term perspective that looks at individual purchases, and a long-term perspective that deals with purchasing strategy. Purchasing behaviour regarding individual purchases is usually described as a decision process with several consecutive steps. One of the first descriptions of the industrial buying

**Figure 7.1** Purchasing process and related definitions
*Adapted from*: Van Weele, 2000.

process was developed by Robinson *et al.* (1967) and consisted of eight buying phases:

1. Problem recognition.
2. General need description.
3. Product specification.
4. Supplier search.
5. Proposal solicitation.
6. Supplier selection.
7. Order-routine specification.
8. Performance review.

A more condensed version of the industrial buying process is illustrated in Figure 7.1.

This is a simplified model of a typical decision process for a certain purchase. There is a pre-purchase process within the firm that involves internal customers. From that follows specifying the requirements for the specific service, for supplier quality and so on. The process ends with a performance review or after-care and evaluation. An illustration of this type of model is the following set of guidelines for buying a recruitment service.

---

**Box 7.1    Recommended approach to buying a recruitment service**

The editors of a Swedish human resource management magazine interviewed a large number of buyers and sellers of recruiting services as offered by headhunters or executive search consultants (*Personal and Ledarskap*, 1997). On the basis of those interviews, the magazine presented a number of rules for those considering hiring such services. The guidelines assume that this is a new situation for the buyer and that he or she has no established relationships with this type of service provider. These are the (slightly condensed) guidelines:

1. Find out which consultants operate in your industry and at the level at which you are looking for candidates. Check the appropriate guides and catalogues [examples given].
2. If you are using an executive search consultant and you are not satisfied with this way of working, you can contact the ethical committee of the Association of Executive Search Consultants [a professional association in Sweden, which works with development, competence and ethical issues in this area]. Remember that a number of consultants have their own ethical guidelines and have a very good reputation, even if they are not a member of the Association.

3. Contact people in your own network to get advice and suggestions. However, do not put too much weight on individual comments on specific consultants or companies. What may work for your colleague may not work for you and vice versa.
4. Consider whether you want a consultant that only specializes in searching or one that offers different additional services, such selection, outplacement and general management consulting.
5. Ask the consultant you have in mind for references. Even in this sector, it is possible.
6. Ask the consultant to tell you what he (or she) thinks about carrying out the assignment. Does he have an international network? Does he have assistance in searching activities? Does he have an extensive database?
7. Spend time and effort on the design of the job profile.
8. Find out whether the consultant has the necessary depth and breadth: a large contact network and knowledge about your industry. When the consultant does not know your industry well, there is a risk that he will only touch the surface since he does not understand the issues deep down in the organization.
9. Spend time in getting to know the consultant. The assignment will be a large investment for both parties. Assure yourself that the consultant that you meet and trust will also be the one doing the actual job. Discuss the terms of payment right at the beginning.
10. Decide who is going to inform the successful and not-successful candidates, the client or the consultant.

Various factors affect the course of the purchasing process. One key factor is the previous experience of the buyer with buying the product involved: is it a 'straight rebuy', a 'modified rebuy' or a 'new task' buying situation (Robinson *et al.*, 1967). In the case of a straight rebuy, fewer people will be involved and the several steps in the purchasing process will be executed more compactly and efficiently than in the case of buying a new task. Other factors are the difficulties in quantitatively and qualitatively measuring and defining the needs, the complexity of the problem solution, the experience that the customer and supplier have with the specific problem solution and so on (Håkansson and Wootz, 1975).

Underlying the more or less extensive buying processes is the decision maker's perceived uncertainty. A new purchase situation in combination with a complex problem solution creates higher uncertainty. This is reflected in the interaction and dialogue between the parties concerned, but also in the organization and membership of the purchasing decision-making unit or *buying center* (Webster and Wind, 1972). This is also reflected in different risk-reducing strategies. Mitchell (1995) identifies 17 separate strategies, while Mitchell and McGoldrick (1995) found that most managerial studies only consider five risk-reducing strategies: information search, brand loyalty, quantitative analysis, multiple sourcing and group decision making.

The special characteristics of services that we defined in Chapter 1 obviously also affect the different stages of the purchasing process. The definition of the function and quality of the service, which internal units will be affected by or involved in the purchasing process and the evaluations of different suppliers' capabilities are all examples of issues that may be handled in a way that is specific to services (and the nature of the specific service and the specific situation). It has to be noted, however, that the guidelines given in the illustration above regard one specific service transaction, a specific recruitment activity. How the purchasing process is managed is also affected (among other things) by the previous relationship that the recruiting company has with the consultant. This will also affect the opportunities for future recruitment projects. It can be imagined that a company that has a good relationship with a recruitment consultancy has a certain priority regarding the most interesting candidates. It is also likely that the evaluation of a supplier is dealt with totally differently when the supplier is already known to the customer, compared to a situation when this will be the first transaction between the two parties.

Of the various steps in the purchasing process, we will now take a a closer look at the specification stage – or, in the terms used by Robinson *et al.* (1967), the steps of *problem recognition, general need description* and *product specification*.

## Service level agreements: a way of specifying business services

Service level agreements (SLAs) are a method of specifying or defining services (Hiles, 1993). After an agreement has been reached, the services should be delivered and the assignment completed. This is, or should be, the natural sequence, although it is not uncommon for services to be delivered without there being an explicit agreement between the customer and the supplier. In those cases, the parties should identify and clarify afterwards which conditions should apply and what has been achieved.

The answers to what should be achieved and how are obviously dependent on the type of service involved, what is important to the customer and what is possible for the supplier. In most situations, there are some basic aspects that are key indicators of the effectiveness and functionality of the service and are therefore important to identify. Consider the following examples.

---

**Box 7.2   Examples of clarifications and specifications in SLAs**

- Availability, i.e. the service has a certain quality in terms of its use or accessibility.
- Execution characteristics, for example in terms of speed (the supplier being able to deliver within a certain number of days, hours, minutes, seconds – whatever is appropriate).
- Numbers per unit of time, for example the number of people trained in a certain programme, the number of people visiting a booth at a trade fair, the number of people contacted per day by a telemarketing firm.
- Performance per page or correction. In the case of translations or proofing, for example, it may be relevant to specify the performance quantitatively or qualitatively. Qualitatively, the performance may vary between 'grammatically correct' to 'elegant language customized to target group'. Quantitatively, specifying the number of pages is quite normal, but it may also involve the number of corrections in a certain amount of text or per hour.

Hiles (1993) presents a general SLA checklist indicating what an SLA may include. Because the SLA method can be used for all sorts of services, the checklist is rather generic. Here are some of its main elements:

- Basic contract: goal, date, period, parties.
- Definition of the service. Explanation and goals: groups for which the service should be available.
- Important specifications:
  a) The coverage and levels of service (number of working days, peak workloads, availability etc.)
  b) The actual service: specifying each service element (input and output). For example, the service package 'IT support' may include:
     - the kind of services being included (e.g. the kind of software and hardware being covered), different levels of support, problem-solving goals: repair times ('time to fix'), precision, effectiveness, upgrade procedures.
     - supply, installation, maintenance, related peripheral equipment, software maintenance, security, backups etc.
  c) Manpower and other resources that will be available during the different stages of the service.
  d) Reaction times.
  e) Precision.
  f) Availability, e.g. for problem solving.

This only gives a rough idea of the type of conditions that may be specified in an SLA. It can serve as a tool for specifying the desired quality of a purchased service. Obviously, an SLA needs to be adapted to the specific situation.

Apart from SLAs, it may be useful to consider some more fundamental alternative methods of specifying services.

## Methods for specifying business services

The quality of a service as perceived by the customer is highly dependent on the result of the customer's comparison between the experienced service and the expected one. Earlier we noted that it can be difficult for both the customer and the supplier to define the exact contents of a service (and to communicate this content). Even when, in an SLA for example, it is specified who is responsible for which function and activities, it might give little indication of the quality of execution of these functions and activities. Nevertheless, the quality and content normally need to be defined reasonably precisely.

Broadly speaking there are four methods of defining the content of a service. These methods could be a great help in completing an SLA.

A service specification could primarily focus on:

- Input, i.e. the resources that should be spent (by the supplier, for example expressed in personhours, and by the customer, for example in terms of the

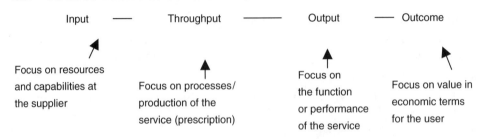

**Figure 7.2** Four methods for specifying business services

involvement in and commitment to the interaction that is needed during the process). It could also specify the quality of these resources.
- Process/throughput, i.e. how the goal or assignment should be fulfilled (the production of the service).
- Output, i.e. the expected results or function.
- Outcome, i.e. the value of the service, in monetary terms.

These four specification methods emphasize different aspects of the service and service provider. They could be organized as a flow chart in accordance with Figure 7.2.

It should be noted that in each specific business deal we could expect a combination of focuses, but we could also expect different kinds of services to be dominated by one of the four methods. We will come back to this issue.

Let us first have a closer look at each of the four methods and what they imply. We start with the process/throughput-oriented approach, followed by output, outcome and input respectively.

## Process-oriented or throughput-prescriptive service specifications

This type of definition implies that the customer very precisely defines the activities it wants to be performed and which minimum quality levels should be fulfilled in order for the service to meet the expected quality outcome. This is closely related to a definition aimed at defining the processes (activities) that the customer wants the supplier to perform.

---

**Box 7.3  Examples of process-oriented or throughput-prescriptive service specifications**

**Telemarketing service**
A telemarketing company receives an order from a client to contact 300 respondents within a certain target group. These respondents should answer ten questions with a limited number of alternative answers. When a respondent is not available, two repeated attempts should be made.

In terms of quality, the way the interviews are conducted is very important and in this respect it is often only possible to specify minimum levels, such as suggestions for how the interview should be done. The ability of the interviewers to 'get a grip' on people, 'see' and pursue interesting aspects during the interview plays a role in both the response frequency and the quality of the information collected, but is an aspect that is hard to define in a activity-based contract.

**Cleaning service**
A cleaning service can also be specified in this way. The customer discusses with the supplier in great detail which surfaces should be vacuum cleaned, dried, dusted etc. This is often determined by the type of surface – wood, concrete, carpeting – and its size. The contract may also specify how often the cleaning should be done and with which precision, which tools and chemicals should be used, and when and for how long it should take place.

**Document handling services**
The service of handling a document that is no longer to be archived can in some cases demand a sophisticated process. In some contexts, there may be a need for disposal of the documents to take place in such a way that no unauthorized personnel have access to the documents. Sometimes the contract specifies the destruction of documents in a certain way.

This method of defining the service requires not only that the customer knows its needs and is able to express them, but also that it is able to indicate which activities need to be performed (and how) in order for the desired function to be delivered.

## Output-oriented service specifications

There are two main variants of this principle:

- To meet the functional demands put on the service, the customer may choose to let the supplier translate the demands into activities. The customer buys a function and only defines the output.
- The supplier together with the customer tries to clarify what is needed in terms of activities and resources, in order for the desired functional qualities to be delivered. In this alternative, input, processes and output are all defined. But although the customer may know what it wants, it may often be difficult to exactly specify the output requirements.

Consider the following illustrations.

**Box 7.4   Examples of output-oriented service specifications**

**Specifying snow- and ice-free roads throughout the year**
The Swedish National Road Authority wants to buy 'snow and ice-free roads all year round' from its contractors. But this needs to be specified further: when should there be snow ploughing or sprinkling (with salt), in which temperature and snowfall conditions,

at which speed and with which routing sequence? In recent years, techniques such as photographs and videos have increasingly been used to facilitate more precision in clarification and communication between the road authorities and the contractors.

**Specifying innovativeness**
In a research project that should result in a new book, the assignment was roughly formulated as 'something very interesting with innovative features, on competence development from the perspective of firms'. What would this mean? The first step was to survey the existing literature and the main questions that had been raised in debate in this area. Where there any gaps? A second step was to try different approaches: 'If you approach the problem from this perspective, what happens then?' An essential element was testing the thoughts in dialogue with the client and showing step by step the development of the project. In this way, the expectations and the actual contents of the initial specifications of the assignment were further clarified.

This way of defining functional demands requires that the customer really knows which needs it has (which function it wants to be performed) and that these needs, from the beginning or in a joint process, can be translated into requirements for results from the supplier.

## Outcome-oriented or result-prescriptive service specifications

This method is a variant of the previous two, indicating what the service provided should accomplish. It is a matter of defining what the service makes possible after it is executed (the service as an *enabler*; Normann and Ramirez, 1994). Some examples may again provide a better understanding of how this method can be used.

### Box 7.5   Examples of outcome-oriented or result-prescriptive service specifications

**The outcome of an education service**
Purchasing an education or training service can be based on the customer indicating which activities should be performed, such as the number of teaching hours, exercises to be done etc. This type of definition is process oriented. Alternatively, the service can be defined output-wise in such a way that after the course participants should be able to perform certain activities, such as writing grammatically correct English business letters, or working with a wordprocessing, spreadsheet or communication software program, and change between them without problems.

  If the education service is to be defined on the basis of the results the service will enable, the definition of requirements focuses on what these new abilities may accomplish (e.g. type a correct letter in three minutes), i.e. in which way they will be used in the business. The following step is then to try to define the value of these new abilities for the customer. Consequently, defining a service in terms of prescribed results makes it important not only to clarify which assignments the employees should be able to perform, but also what the benefits of that for the company will be. How will the company, for example, be able to improve its ways of working and what does this mean in different situations?

### The function and results of a consultancy service

One management consultancy service is interim management, or 'management for hire'. This means that a managerial service is bought for a specific period of time, e.g. for a year, to temporarily fill a position or to steer a company through a difficult change process. The person concerned (the consultant) should lead the business during this period. In the assignment, there may be a specific statement to achieve a turnaround in terms of creating profits again.

The service can be defined by the client in a throughput-prescriptive way, meaning that the consultant is confronted with an action list of a number of steps. The service can also be output oriented, meaning that the consultant may act as he or she pleases as long as the final results are according to plan. The outcome-oriented version would imply in this case that the demands on profitability are rather precise, e.g. in terms of a specific profit margin.

### A 'mass calls' service enabling the creation of value

Many telecoms operators and call centres have developed services that can be called 'mass calls'. This means that the customer buying this service can take thousands of calls simultaneously. This creates interesting possibilities.

Television and radio programme producers, for example, have been able to create a new type of programme on a more interactive basis. One example could be soap operas in which the action (the story) creates a specific situation, e.g. a crisis between husband and wife. The question could then be: should the wife leave her husband or not? The television audience can call and vote, with each call costing a fixed amount of money. After a few minutes or before the next episode, the votes are calculated and the choice of the majority is put into effect. Another example is a film on television, where the audience can call in and choose between three different movies they want to see, which is then – almost instantly – broadcast.

The value of this type of service can in many cases be calculated relatively easy. When the number of people watching or the number of people likely to call is known, it mainly becomes an issue of 'price elasticity'. This results in a calculation of the expected monetary value of the service, which may have little relationship to the actual costs of producing it. For telecoms operators, the service meant that they had to learn about the production of TV and radio programmes and become acquainted with scriptwriters so that these people would know about the possibilities of the new service. With this service, the telecoms operator does not only develop its own service offering, but also that of its customers.

This third method of specifying services, as illustrated in the last example, is particularly interesting. It is only with this method that the value of the service for the customer is really defined. Some consultants argue that we will see an increasing focus on this kind of method in the future. Because of that, an increasing number of companies in a growing variety of sectors, buyers as well as sellers, are expected to try to find methods of specifying the value of their offerings in a defined application, e.g. for an individual customer (Anderson and Narus, 1998).

Simply stated, the main difference between the three methods we have discussed so far is that in the first method the customer defines 'what the service consists of' (process oriented). The second method defines 'how the service should work' (output oriented), and in the third method one defines 'what the service should accomplish' (outcome oriented). Let us now consider the fourth and final method of defining services.

## Input-oriented or resource-prescriptive service specifications

The fourth method can be described as *competence* procurement (sometimes called 'consultancy' purchases). There are two main varieties: purchasing extra capacity and purchasing specialist competencies.

The 'extra capacity' variety implies that the customer purchases a specific type and amount of human resources for a certain job, in order to meet a certain workload. The resources concerned do not have unique characteristics, but can be seen as 'available labour capacity' (sometimes referred to as 'body shopping').

In terms of the methods for defining this type of service, those mentioned earlier can work rather well. Most often, however, the service is specified in terms of inputs (competence) plus process or output. In the first case, a number of people are 'bought' for a certain time period. In the latter case (inputs + process) the contract is arranged in such a way that the consultant works (as long or as hard as necessary) to meet certain functional demands.

---

**Box 7.6   Technicians who had lost their self-confidence**

The new CEO of a major manufacturing company was surprised when he learned about the budget for hiring technical consultants. He thought that this budget was very high, while the company actually had a large group of internal engineers. 'What kind of consultancy do we buy and what kind of engineering do we do ourselves?' he asked his assistants. The answer was that the consultants were obviously used as the experts they were and that the internal engineers did the more routine jobs. As soon as a problem was beyond the existing knowledge and capabilities of the company's employees, a consultant was brought in.

The new CEO thought this was wrong. This meant that the employees did not learn anything new and that they lost their self-respect. 'This needs to be changed. I think we should do it exactly the other way around,' he suggested. 'We should use the consultants for the routine assignments – as long they have no unique capability from which we want to learn. In this way, we have more time to deal with the more advanced issues ourselves and we create more long-term learning. By doing that, we also become less dependent on these consultants.'

---

Buying 'specialist competencies' is different. The typical situation for this method is that the customer needs assistance of one or several *experts*. The customer may know which needs it has and which type of expert – perhaps even exactly which firm or person – is right for the job.

However, the situation is not always that simple. There are many situations in which neither the customer nor the supplier is well positioned to define precisely which service and which service quality is required. In those cases, the customer buys a relatively ill-defined service, or rather the efforts of one or several people during a certain time period. The expectation is that this resource will be able to create a valuable asset. In this case, the emphasis during the negotiations will be on the input, i.e. which resources and in which volumes. Consider the following two illustrations.

---

**Box 7.7   How to improve? Ask a 'resource person'**

A relatively new manager of a production plant thought that the purchasing function of the company did not work too well and was old-fashioned. The manager could not pinpoint what would need to be done differently, but asked a consultant for advice. 'I do not know what our problems are, but I am convinced that you will be able to identify important areas for improvement,' said the manager and he asked for a first diagnosis.

A marketing manager in a consumer goods firm did not know how the methods of working within the company could be developed and what 'really' needed to be done. Just like the plant manager, he asked a consultant: 'Since you can "sense" so many of the situations, environments and problems we have here, would you be able to spend a week or so in our business and then give us some ideas of what we can and should do?'

---

In both examples, the customer starts from the assumption that neither he nor the consultant knows what are the important problems. The customer assumes that the consultant knows a lot about the general area and also has considerable knowledge of how other companies act. It is exactly these resources (competencies) of which the customer buys a number of 'time units'. Consider a third illustration.

---

**Box 7.8   The photographer who needed to capture a feeling**

The Executive MBA programme at Uppsala University (Sweden) needed a new brochure. The brochure is one of its 'faces' to the outside world. It needs to send a simple and clear signal to the reader of what the programme and the university are all about. Some important functional requirements relate to the dimensions of the brochure, the number of pages, the type and amount of content in terms of text and images, colour vs black-and-white pages, type of paper etc.

The programme managers agreed that it should be a very informative brochure that should communicate a certain feeling of 'depth'. 'A brochure with some weight, indicating a content-filled and demanding education' was the brief. At the same time, the brochure should look nice and make a professional impression, because the programme is rather expensive and is mainly targeted at managers in companies and other professional organizations. The photographs should communicate a feeling of tradition (Uppsala University was established in 1477), of being up-to-date (the newest management insights), of joy and enjoyment, but not of some sort of general 'fun' – and all of this in one brochure!

The assignment for the photographer was designed to capture these feelings, this emotion. An alternative would have been, if the programme managers had been confident to say how it should be done, to fulfil these demands by specifying the number of pictures, the type of shots in terms of angle and light etc. However, they chose to give the photographer a more open mandate. It was not primarily a set of pictures that were bought, but rather the photographer's time and expected creative capabilities. This photographer is known as one of the very best artistic photographers in the world, with a list of references including highly prestigious publishers as well as museums.

After the project was carried out, during which the photographer and the programme manager were in continuous contact, the university was pleased with the results. There were pictures of objects and situations, taken from angles that the programme managers could never have thought of, but that were nevertheless 'right'. They recognized the answer to their demands when they saw the results.

Clearly, these latter examples deal with contracting a certain (highly skilled) capability. It is not so much the time period for which the resource is contracted, but rather which qualities the expert has. The customer buys time from an expert or specialist and hopes (for good reason) that this will enable the expert to create something of a desired value for the customer.

This concludes our discussion of the four different alternative specification methods. We now want to take a brief look at some of the factors that affect the choice between these different alternatives.

## Different ways of specifying services put different demands on the buying company's purchasing competence

The four methods of specifying a service create different conditions for the interaction between the parties involved. For the buying company, there are some differences regarding the emphasis on defining different aspects before, during or after the purchasing process. Definitions that use process-oriented methods usually focus more on the services actually bought. Input-oriented specifications focus mainly on the supplier. The output- and outcome-oriented methods clearly focus on the results of the services.

In the first method (process oriented) the buyer itself takes a greater responsibility for the quality of the service by placing a much more detailed order, defined in terms of activities. In the second case (output oriented), it becomes essential to define the functional demands so that both (all) parties involved interpret these demands in a similar way. In some cases this may be very simple, while in other situations it may be more diffuse, depending on such matters as whether the functional demands are measurable or not. The third method (outcome oriented) sets similar demands, possibly even at a higher level. The fourth method (input oriented) is more open and leaves some room for interaction between the buyer and seller. It relies primarily on the parties having a certain competence that will result in a qualitatively satisfactory result.

## Different ways of defining services lead to different responsibilities for buyers and sellers

The different methods also imply different demarcations of responsibilities between the respective parties. Who takes care of what? And how will these responsibilities be coordinated and harmonized? A comparison between two previous examples can illustrate these differences.

---

**Box 7.9   Communication and coordination of responsibilities**

**Telemarketing**
The telemarketing service described earlier is clear regarding the different activities and responsibilities. When the activities described are performed, the service has been completed and delivered.

**The book and training project**
Other services are not that clear-cut. The book project mentioned earlier, which should result in 'something new and interesting in a certain area', is definitely more diffuse. The service is difficult to communicate and responsibilities are more difficult to separate. One way of preventing misunderstandings and future disappointments is by having the supplier carry out subsequent 'fine-tuning' with the client.

---

After these discussions and those in Chapter 2, it will be obvious that services can be categorized in many different ways and that there are big differences between different types of services. It is also clear that services can be defined according to different methods, sometimes very precisely.

It is important to note that the agreements on the service itself, its design and functionality, do not necessarily imply that the agreed performance will also be realized. This notion leads us to consider some fundamental issues of service quality.

## Business service quality

As we have already discussed in detail, what needs to be specified varies from service to service, from customer–supplier relationship to customer–supplier relationship and from situation to situation. It is essential for both the customer and the supplier to succeed in clarifying their respective expectations and responsibilities.

Generally speaking, the definitions of how the service should work to fulfil the contract are divided into two groups or situations:

● Definitions and specifications of performance quality when everything goes according to plan. This applies independently whether it is a long-term or a short-term service, a simple or a complex one etc. (Chapter 2). The demands relate to the service itself and some main aspects, such the availability and acceptability, i.e. to which degree the service should function optimally during a certain period and which deviations may be accepted.
● Definitions and specifications of performance quality when there are problems.

Later in this chapter we will discuss these two situations in more detail. First, we need to consider what constitutes quality and customer satisfaction.

## Customer satisfaction

Grönroos (2000) nicely demonstrates the importance of expectations in a discussion of quality as being the difference between expected and experienced service. This is illustrated in Figure 7.3.

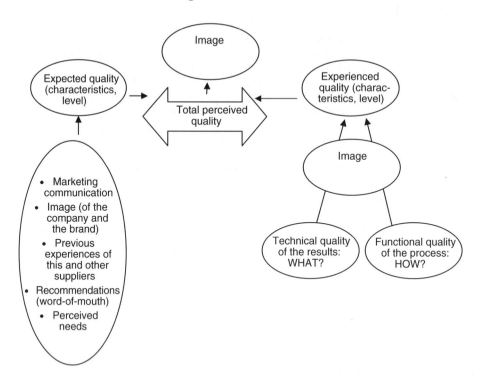

**Figure 7.3** Perceived quality as a match between expected and experienced quality
*Source*: Grönroos, 2000, p. 67.

According to Grönroos, therefore, quality is defined by the customer, with experienced quality being a function of expected and realized service delivery. The result can be that the customer's expectations are:

- exceeded;
- met;
- met within reasonable limits; or
- not met.

In essence, quality can be described starting from the two words 'What?' and 'How?'. Grönroos relates these respectively to *technical* and *functional* quality. Technical quality concerns the hard and soft aspects of the core function itself: what needs to function, the need that should be fulfilled or the problem(s) that should be solved. Functional quality concerns the process aspects of the problem solution, which often are very important (see Figure 1.1). This can involve, for example, the way communication works between the different parties involved.

The expectations of the customer, in their turn, are the result of a very complex process. The customer may have previous experience of buying similar services from the same or another supplier. In its marketing efforts, the supplier may have promised more than it can accomplish in reality. The customer may have obtained recommendations from others that have created certain expectations of the service and the supplier's capabilities.

A customer who does not feel that the provided (experienced) service is on a par with what it expected will react differently than the customer whose expectations are met or even exceeded. In other words, it is not so much about the actual quality – whether the service is good or bad – but rather about the relationship between expected and experienced delivery. The result can have dramatic effects.

An interesting way of illustrating this tension is shown by Heskett *et al.* (1994), who discuss the degree of customer loyalty as an effect of the degree of satisfaction (see Figure 7.4).

Research at Xerox has shown that the relationship between customer satisfaction and customer loyalty is not a straight line but rather more a curve. Other research has found other curves that can be U-shaped, nearly straight lines or inverted-U shapes. This means that the general relationship is not so easy to determine. There are services with which the customer is very satisfied, without becoming very loyal to them and their supplier, and others with which the customer can be very disappointed but still be loyal to them and their supplier. Everything depends on the situation, for example what the customer's alternatives are (when there is no alternative the dissatisfied customer remains loyal, and when there are many alternatives even a very satisfied customer can become disloyal).

The basis for the satisfaction of the buying firms' representatives should obviously be that the services provided to them function well, that they are in accordance with or even exceed the customer's expectations. As we have indicated earlier, the company's ability to communicate – before, during and after the production of the service – is also an important complement to the

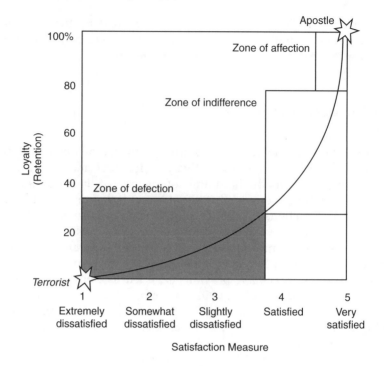

**Figure 7.4**  Perceived quality at different levels
*Source*: Heskett *et al.*, 1991 (as in Lovelock *et al.*, 1999, p. 640).

service delivery itself, which can affect the expectations and perceptions of experienced quality. Figure 7.4 illustrates the meaning of the concepts 'terrorist' and 'apostle'. A customer that is enthusiastic – more than satisfied – may serve as an enlightened apostle to the benefit of the selling company and proclaim to its environment the benefits of the service provider. A strongly dissatisfied customer, a terrorist, may cause equally strong negative effects.

The fact that the customer's expectations and the respective responsibilities of both parties may vary from situation to situation should not hinder the parties from trying to clarify the aspects (criteria, dimensions) that can be important. This is not only a task for the selling party, but also a purchasing issue. Grönroos (1990) reports on a study that analysed what customers generally would value most and what, therefore, would have a high impact on their perception of quality. In that context, the following factors seemed to be of a strong importance:

● Professional abilities – both the employees and the company as a whole are competent in relation to their tasks (responsibilities).
● Attitudes and behaviour.
● Availability and flexibility.
● Reliability.

- Recovery – the ability to correct something that has gone wrong.
- Reputation and credibility – this creates expectations and trust in the supplier.

Which of these aspects is most important depends again on the specific situation, such as the type of service production, who the customers are, and the type of market in terms of competitive offerings. However, as a general overview these dimensions give a feeling for what can be important (compare also the discussion on SLA elements). They also seem reasonable given that a large share of service production involves human interaction, in which there are often important elements of psychology, e.g. the construction of expectations, the desire to be treated with a certain respect and so on.

## Business service quality: the what and the how

We have already indicated that the basis for the perception of service quality lies in the congruence of expectations and realizations of the quality of the service's substance (technical quality), and in the delivery process before, during and after the service (functional quality).

One way of emphasizing this argument is to distinguish some principal aspects of services. Several attempts have been made in the literature and Gummeson (1987) provides an interesting discussion of three main dimensions that capture many relevant aspects of service quality:

1. *Design quality* of the service and the service production:
   - During normal times: design of the whole service.
   - During deviations: routines for e.g. repair and recovery.
2. *Production quality*:
   - During normal times: daily routines.
   - During deviations: adaptability to new situations.
3. *Delivery quality*:
   - During normal times: the interactive moments, normal 'encounters' on different levels, collaboration and interaction processes.
   - During deviations: adaptability to new situations, the 'moment of truth'.

These three main dimensions probably capture the most important aspects of what – from a customer perspective – defines quality and where possible quality defects may arise. This distinction may be used, among other elements, to group all the complaints and defects regarding the service(s) of a particular supplier. The following step may be to try to find the source of the individual defects: in the design, production or delivery ('process') of the service. Such a procedure may be complemented by involving the buying firm in diagnosing the supplier's possible quality problems, if only to prevent it from directly choosing another supplier. One way of preventing and preparing to handle certain deviations, both for the selling and the buying firm, would be to deal systematically with sources of potential problems.

Berry and Parasuraman (1991) have developed an alternative approach that is especially useful for identifying and localizing quality defects. This is an often-quoted model that gives support to an equally systematic approach. The 'gap model' identifies the following sources for quality defects:

- Misunderstanding of the actual demands of the customer.
- Defects in the specification of the quality. Customer demands have not correctly been translated.
- Defects in the service delivery. The quality specifications have not been met by the services that are produced and delivered.
- Market communication gaps. What has been promised in the marketing efforts is not met by what is delivered later.
- Gap between the customer's expected and experienced quality.

If the customer realizes that the supplier's service is not well designed, or if the process quality has some defects, the customer can decide to choose another supplier or opt to work on these defects in collaboration with the existing supplier. Such defects could be due to the ways in which interaction processes are handled (Chapter 5). They could also be due to the functional (technical) qualities of the service involved, as well as to the specific physical and/or virtual environment – the 'servicescape' (Bitner, 1992) – where the service interactions take place. But even when normal production and predictable deviations are defined (for example, a helpdesk function always deals with deviations but most are predictable), there will be situations that fall outside the boundaries. These situations are especially interesting.

## Quality deviations: when routines no longer work

Deviations beyond the predictable and routine are especially interesting and demanding. How such deviations are dealt with has a strong impact on the whole relationship. The customer who has chosen a supplier that proves to be very capable of solving a difficult assignment in a good way will probably intensify its relationship with that supplier. There are also studies indicating that certain aspects, in addition to the supplier's ability to deal with the deviation itself, are especially important. According to one study quoted by Grönroos (1990), the most important actions, from the perspective of the customer, in the case of deviations are:

- Be contacted at the moment promised.
- Get an explanation of why the problem occurred.
- Get information on contact people (telephone numbers, e-mail etc.).
- Be contacted as soon as a problem occurs.
- Possibility of contacting a person with managerial responsibility.
- Get information on how long it will take to solve the problem.
- Be offered possible alternatives when the problem cannot be solved.
- Be treated as a 'human' and not as an account number.

- Be informed on how to avoid the problem in the future.
- Get situation reports when the problem cannot be solved directly.

Which is the most important of these different actions depends on the specific situation: the type of service, the customer's situation, the market, the alternatives in terms of the offerings of other suppliers and their capabilities etc. It is, however, important to note that these ten issues all deal to a high degree with communication: customers want to be informed of what is happening and their expectations of what will happen should be taken seriously.

This is also a reminder for the buyer to make sure that the selected supplier has well-developed recovery strategies (Hart *et al.*, 1990; Grönroos, 2000, pp. 112–21). This is especially important in services as the service provider usually cannot build security by storing its products.

There are many different ways to reduce the frustration that may arise when deviations occur. One method is to predict the problem and prevent it. Another important method is communication. A third, more specific way is for the parties to create instruments (routines, ways of working, technologies) that give the customer an insight into the supplier's work. Consider the following illustration that emphasizes these latter two methods: informing and/or supporting the customer to inform itself.

---

**Box 7.10   Increased customer satisfaction by troubleshooting and greater transparency of the supplier's processes**

At Swedish telecom operator Telia, a project has been executed focusing on clarifying routines for troubleshooting and for enabling the customer to follow the troubleshooting efforts more closely. In Telia's case, the availability of the services provided is a crucial indicator of how the service is performing. Availability is high, more often over than under 99 per cent. Nevertheless, it is argued that if something does happen: 'The 99 per cent is of no use: an affected customer is a 100 per cent dissatisfied customer' (Kvarnemo, 1997, p. 10). However, by means of effective troubleshooting one has the opportunity of regaining customers' confidence.

**Problems that may arise**
Large private companies buy telecommunication services from the business unit Telia Megacom. Troubleshooting is aimed at three types of problems: defects in customer-owned equipment; defects in a subscribed service, where the defect is connected to an individual subscription; defects in Telia-owned equipment that is used for delivering the service (the network), not connected to an individual subscription. Troubleshooting, in all three cases, involves bringing back equipment/services to its original condition.

The first group of defects are usually covered by separate service agreements. In some cases, repairs are carried out and ordered and paid for on each individual occasion. For the second group, there are service agreements that complement the basic service agreement. Repairs are obviously included in the basic subscription, but the customer may require a higher service level, for example a faster solution. This can be arranged in a separate service agreement. For the third group of defects, there are no separate service agreements with the customer.

## A development project

A development project has been undertaken to create a robust description model of the troubleshooting process within Telia, in relation to its Megacom customers. The aim of the model is that it can be used as a frame of reference in the customer–supplier dialogue. The project also aimed to find practical suggestions for making the activities in the troubleshooting process visible ('transparent') for the customer. An important goal in doing this was to increase the experienced quality of the service involved (Kvarnemo, 1997).

The starting point was the following. When a customer notifies a problem to Telia Megacom, the first step is to investigate the source of the problem and hand the issue over to the unit involved. In this way, a problem can migrate across several units before the actual troubleshooting starts. Even at the customer, several units may have been involved before the problem was communicated to Telia. Figure 7.5 presents a description of this process.

The figure shows a suggested main route based on the buyer–seller relationships that apply within the Telia group. In practice, there is a host of alternative paths, hence Figure 7.5 gives a rather simplified picture (at least for some parts of the process).

In the figure there are a number of handovers between units and therefore a number of interfaces where the units meet. These may be changed. The customer, in some cases, can determine what the problem is and thereby skip some of the steps, and if necessary the helpdesk may directly contact the unit with the required competence. By demonstrating, in the dialogue with the customer's buying function, what the process looks like, the supplier increases the transparency and the perceived quality of the troubleshooting operation, and thereby of its overall service process. Furthermore, there are alternative paths and the possibility of other divisions of responsibilities to increase understanding, for example enabling the customer to follow the process actively. In this way the expectations and experiences of quality may be affected and this has a consequent impact on the degree of customer satisfaction.

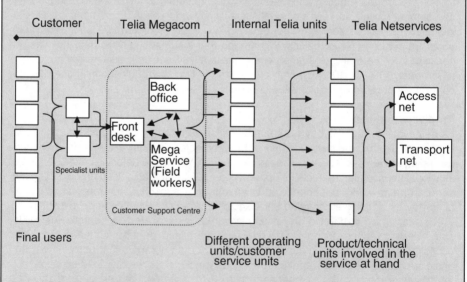

**Figure 7.5** Problem-solving process

*Based on*: Kvarnemo, 1997.

In this case the supplier has created a clear and well-understood process for troubleshooting. This assists in communicating convincing and understandable competencies to deal with unexpected events. In addition, a documented list of problems and repairs in the past, within the current business relationship or in others, can be an important factor for the buying firm in evaluating alternative suppliers. In essence, this demonstrates a key concept in service management: the line of visibility (Grönroos, 2000, p. 321; Lovelock *et al.*, 1999, Chapter 3). The more insight there is into the supplier's operation, the more accurate the customer's expectation will be. Additionally, a clear line of visibility puts pressure on the service supplier, as it will be aware that the customer can see more of its operations (the equivalent of 'open kitchen cooking').

## Service level agreements dealing with deviations

The agreement on what the service should accomplish in normal times is, as previously discussed, an important element of the contents of an SLA. Against the background of the discussion above, it is also important to try to indicate in an SLA what will happen when the unexpected occurs. Here are two examples.

---

**Box 7.11   Expecting the unexpected**

**Repair services: reaction times are crucial**
Repairs of production equipment (including computers) can be a very time-critical service. One way of describing the demands and meeting customer expectations is to set out how quickly a service repair representative should be on location to start working on a defect. An additional element may be that within another period of time, say two hours, any required specialists should be on location to provide further special assistance.

**Customer collaboration is often required to meet certain promises**
Telecommunication service providers often demand (in their standard contracts) that on request they can have access to customer premises all year round, even after office hours. In this way they are able to meet certain service levels, such as in the case of an emergency repair. Without this support ('co-production') from the customer, they cannot give such promises.

---

The specifications can involve demands on the results of the repair/recovery service itself, but also demands on the behaviour (including availability or readiness) of the actors involved.

The important aspects, the 'substance', of the basic service and the methods of dealing with deviations vary from service to service and may also differ from customer to customer.

## Service quality assurance

As buyers, firms often demand that their suppliers should be certified according to some specific norm, such as the quality standard ISO 9000. Such a certificate implies that the supplier can demonstrate that it has the required capabilities to develop, produce and deliver a certain range of products, and that it has well-defined procedures for dealing with the necessary processes required to achieve the targeted results.

For a company that goes through such a certification process, this may be a very demanding yet rewarding experience. It helps in evaluating and documenting the current processes and thereby creates some incentives for development and improvement. In this context, it is of special importance that certification helps the company in indicating, with reasonable stability and predictability, when, how and in which way it will meet its promises. By developing routines for normal work as well as problem situations, the employees concerned know how to deal with whatever happens. This does not imply a guarantee that things will always work the way they should. What is guaranteed is that the company has routines and capabilities in place. Nor does this imply a guarantee that the company is highly qualified or effective. Most often, a certificate is or should be seen as a platform, starting from which continuous, more or less intensive quality improvement efforts have to be made.

Having said this, it is obvious that there is a number of traps into which the unwary may easily fall, as the following illustration demonstrates.

---

**Box 7.12   What does the guarantee guarantee?**

A purchasing manager observes an interesting problem in relation to buying consultancy services: 'There are two types of suppliers from which we can buy consultancy services: the traditional consultancy firms and temporary labour firms such as Manpower and others. An essential difference between the two is that the traditional consultancy firms offer an integrated activity; the consultant is part of the firm's product. The company carries out product development, which means it can solve certain types of customer problems. The temporary labour firm is more a broker of human resources. If that firm is certified, it does not need to imply more than that it has documented, sound routines to monitor the workers to which it has access and where these are employed at a given time. Certification of a traditional consultancy firm involves more 'moments' (checkpoints) and is therefore, qualitatively speaking, different from the other type of firm. This is true despite the fact that both may be certified according to the same standard.'

---

The conclusion is that it is important for the buying firm to know what type of activities are actually being certified.

Despite all the positive aspects described above, there is a risk of certification having a negative effect. In some cases it has led to the creation and formulation of routines in a context where everything was already working well, because that kind of behaviour was part of the company culture; it was 'in the walls'. After the routines have become official, the employees no longer take the naturally appropriate measures, but instead become 'paralysed' by the manuals and procedures. In other cases, it has resulted in 'homogeneous' attitudes and behaviours, which are often positive but which sometimes can also be negative because essential discussions no longer take place. The dynamics created by differences in opinions and behaviour have subsided due to the homogeneity.

The crucial message here, however, is that much of what we have identified as purchasing problems in the case of services involved uncertainties that can be reduced when the supplier has gone through some form of certification process. Among these is the difficulty of knowing, as a customer, what you will get because the service is not there before it is ordered, it is created interactively.

Assuring the quality of a service is not only a matter of certification or defining, for example, which activities need to be performed, how much time these are allowed to take and what the customer's general expectations are. In most cases, there are other essential, *quality-defining* factors.

## Service quality assurance: analysis of critical components

One method of specifying the expected functional substance of a service thus becomes a matter of identifying the most critical resources with regard to the quality of the service and the tasks of the supplier. It involves analysing the critical 'components'. But what are these components, how do they become manifest and how can they be identified? This obviously varies from situation to situation, but below are some examples of common functional key ratios and critical components in different sectors.

---

**Box 7.13   Important key ratios and critical components in different sectors**

**General functional requirements**
In the transport sector, the share of transportation capacity actually being used in relation to the maximum capacity is a key ratio. An analogous key ratio is 'occupancy rates' for different types of accommodation, such as hotels. These ratios indicate the supplier's use of capacity, which lies at the basis of the product offering to the customer.

In other contexts there are other ratios. The ratio 'availability' was discussed in the Telia Megacom example. How available a service is, for example during the 24 hours of a day, is relevant in areas such as electricity distribution and financial services (e.g. the opportunity to trade shares in the middle of the night, or arrange other urgent financial matters). The number of stock-outs is an important indicator for trade companies. The customer wants to be sure that the products in demand are available when needed, always or 95 per cent of the time, and with certain time restrictions on how quickly a supplier should react in the other 5 per cent.

Results per unit of time, for example surface area cleaned per hour, are interesting functional specifications in other situations. An alternative may be price per square meter cleaned. In the context of music production and sales of advertising space, for example on television, audience shares and duration of attendance are important ratios. For a trade fair or a rental agency in a shopping mall, visiting frequency or amount of people walking by a certain location, possibly divided into different categories of people, are some of the common key ratios.

**Functional requirements in the case of deviations**
In comparing different companies, functional key ratios that may be applicable in the context of deviations vary even more than the general ones. For some companies and services, the activities may be extremely time sensitive. An essential functional requirement then becomes how much time it takes after notifying a problem until the supplier is at the location and has managed, by itself or by involving someone else, to correct the problem (either at the location or at a distance).

It may also be a matter of specifying the intervals within which a service may be allowed to vary, such as minimum and maximum temperatures, humidity conditions etc. regarding certain inventory management services. As another example, it can involve access to advice or consultancy to a certain level and within certain time intervals.

These illustrations demonstrate that there are certain important functional aspects of all services, but that some are extremely critical. These may be examples of what can be the subject of an SLA. In some cases, the critical factors may be easily identified and specified. In other cases, they can be identified but they are difficult to specify. And finally, in a third group of cases they may even be difficult to identify.

## Service quality assurance: more than specification setting

In this chapter we have focused on the early stages of the buying process for business services: the specification phase. Earlier, we emphasized that there is life after the contract, i.e. after the specification and selection phase. For the customer, getting the service at the desired quality levels is as dependent on managing this post-contract time as it is on setting appropriate specifications and selection criteria.

Competencies for and understanding of management or collaboration between companies is a key issue. This is an aspect noted by Bryntse (2000), with reference among others to Ranson and Stewart (1994). The capability to handle the interaction and cooperation with suppliers are in reality probably more important than the ability to make decisions and to carry out negotiations and set specifications, e.g. through SLAs. Ranson and Stewart (1994) express this as follows:

> The area in which one can exert its influence becomes bigger than just some decision moments. Influencing another actor does not follow predetermined ways, but is rather done through 'openings' (moments) for influencing possibilities, because they are dependent on the collaboration.

How the daily cooperation between the customer and the supplier is handled, what variations there are and what determines the structure of this cooperation has already been partly discussed in Chapter 5, and we will return to it in more general terms in Chapter 10. What is appropriate to emphasize at this point is that the *relationship* between the customer and the supplier is important, both as an aspect that precedes decision processes and as a crucial condition for the practical collaboration that follows after specifying the service and selecting a supplier.

## Conclusions

So far, important elements in our discussion of buying business services have been:

- *The elements of services*: services consist of activities and service production can be described using the concepts of activities, resources and actors (see Chapter 3).
- *The context in which the services are produced and consumed*: this can be seen as an aspect of the customer–supplier relationship (see Chapter 5).
- *Specification*: this can occur by means of prescribing input, process, output or outcome. Quality is a matter of expectation vs realization, for which it is very important to be able to specify, interact and communicate (see this chapter).

In Chapter 8, we will discuss in more detail how service suppliers can be selected and evaluated.

# 8

# Selecting and Evaluating Business Service Providers

## The importance of supplier selection and evaluation

When defining the title of this chapter it occurred to us that the word *evaluating* should precede the word *selecting*: first you evaluate possible candidates and then you select from among them. That seemed to be the self-evident and natural sequence. A second thought was, however, that it could be equally relevant to put it the way we have done now. After you have chosen a supplier and started trying it, you need to evaluate its performance – as well as the relationship as such. Thus evaluation of suppliers should, in our view, be considered a continuous process. We acknowledge, however, that in the case of highly important choices a more careful evaluation should apply *before* the choice is made. We are referring to situations when the company is about to choose a new supplier or deciding to continue to work with just a few of many previous suppliers.

   If the choice of a specific supplier will lead to strong technological bonds and/or have other effects that will severely limit the possibility of change in the future, the choice is critical. This is the case because the cost of change rises and the time frame to reach a desired change increases. A choice of a supplier for a long time horizon, say a number of years, is naturally a much more strategic choice than choosing a supplier of a standard product on a single occasion. The choice could thus also be critical due to the product, the function, that the supplier is expected to provide. If it is an important product, i.e. involving high technical risk and/or great economic value, the choice is of great significance. This means that the choice and evaluation processes need to be put in their context; the design of the processes and their execution are contingent on each other.

Another important point of departure is to consider whether it is a new relationship or an existing one. In the first case, the two parties have no previous experience of cooperation, which normally increases the uncertainty. In cases where the two parties do have extensive experience of cooperation, the point of departure for the evaluation and selection process is very different. Then the representatives of the buying firm do not have to trust only external sources and other parties' experiences. They can also rely on their own experiences and the history of the relationship: what has happened before? Do we as a customer seem to be accorded a high priority by this supplier?

Analysing a supplier is equivalent to analysing a corporation. You don't analyse a corporation without some point of departure, be it the company as a profit-generating unit or a gender-policy unit or something else. The specific aspect in our case is that the supplier/corporation should be analysed as a provider to the buying firm and its needs and requirements. The criteria that will have to be applied should therefore differ from a corporate evaluation in general. The criteria should also differ among different suppliers based on the roles they are likely to play in the customer's sourcing pattern. In our opinion, many firms tend to apply the same evaluation model in the same way, regardless of the situation. They do not see the need to collect a great deal of information, check for validity and analyse it in detail before choosing a supplier of a standard item, characterized by low risk and low cost in a one-time transaction, where there are plenty of alternatives.

We also think that many firms are too eager to apply their selection criteria without first having generated the information necessary and built up a knowledge base about the supplier against which to apply the criteria. They evaluate and judge without having good and sufficient information. We will therefore first introduce a model for structuring and capturing the necessary data and knowledge, and then proceed to models of evaluation. We discuss these topics under the assumption that we are going to make a vital choice and therefore require a critical evaluation.

## A model for data capture

We divide this section into four different but tightly related parts. First, we argue that in order to gain a reasonable understanding of a supplier, it is important to stand back and consider the kind of business that the supplier is in: what does it do? There are many similarities between all business ventures, but also great dissimilarities. In order to evaluate any company, we need to have some kind of general understanding of the business as such.

Secondly, we take the view that there is a great need to look at the basic processes of the firm. This implies considering somewhat more closely what the firm does and how it carries out the basic processes of its business.

Thirdly, we argue that carrying out such processes will involve a variety of resources and that it is important to get an idea of what kinds of resources are needed, as well as what kind of control the firm has over the resources needed. We thus refer to Wernerfelt (1984) and Grant (1996). Related to this issue is our fourth step, the need to indicate the kind of position the supplier has in important resource areas. If it has a strong position in critical resource areas, this is likely to be beneficial for the future.

## Business system: the first step

All firms have to come up with an answer to the following questions: 'For whom?', 'What?', 'How?', and 'Supported by whom?'. This amounts to an overview of its business system. The first question has to do with aspects such as the groups of customers to approach and what problems and needs the firm is going to address. The more accurate the answer, the better the understanding of what it takes to meet those needs. And if we consider ourselves as the customer addressed by the supplier, we should look at the supplier's understanding of the customer's situation.

The second question deals with the market offering. What is it that the supplier offers to its customers? What does its product look like: its functions (technical solution, other features), its appearance, the values associated with it and so on. It has also got to do with the contribution (value) of the product and the overall offering (price, terms of payment etc.). Again, if we consider our firm as a customer to this supplier and as a buyer of its offering, it is of interest to see how these attributes fit with the firm's needs and the role of the product in the supplier's operation: is it prioritized, how is it developing?

The third question, the how, covers a variety of aspects. It is the firm's entire 'organized system' in terms of resources, organizational logic, systems, routines etc. This will be discussed at length later in this chapter. What is most important is to see that the corporation, when considered as a (possible) supplier, has adequate *capability*. An important aspect of this capability is the firm's value system. If the firm, according to its own opinion, is doing something of the utmost importance, the likelihood of a prevalent strong value system increases. This is clearly demonstrated by Collins and Porras's (1994) discussion of companies that have survived for a long time.

The fourth question is an extension of the third. An important part of most companies' capability is their *external resources*, including all their suppliers. When evaluating a supplier, we think that this should be an essential part of that evaluation: which are the most important partners, what kind of position does our (possible) supplier have among actors in its surrounding system of resource providers? This position should facilitate the necessary mobilization of various resources.

## Processes: the second step

Any firm needs to carry out activities, be they physical or mental. In any firm, actors are likely to carry out a great number of activities that together make up important processes. When evaluating a supplier, it will be fruitful to identify some of the most important and general processes that all companies have to perform. We distinguish the following basic processes: operative (inbound, production and outbound), administrative/organizing, strategic and development processes. These can be presented as in Figure 8.1.

The reason behind this is that all corporations are likely to have to acquire resources, fulfil activities that add value, transmit and make this value available for their customers (marketing). In addition to this, we know that all these activities have to be organized somehow and that the process of value creation should have some kind of short- and long-term direction (strategic processes). We also know that most firms will have to change, to adapt their activities to changing circumstances and also to create change to be innovative, in order to survive in the long run. Let us have a look at each of these basic but fundamental processes.

Operative (flow-based) processes from resource acquisition via production to marketing, distribution and sales are to a great extent the essence of what the firm does. They could, in practice, be expressed as follows:

> The firm acquires raw materials X and Y from suppliers A, B and C. This input is then processed in Z steps by personnel in production with specific skills in O and P and supported by production equipment Q. This is, after on average R days of storage, transferred to customers.

Such a description could equally well start from the customers, what their desires are and the ways in which the operative activities take care of these demands.

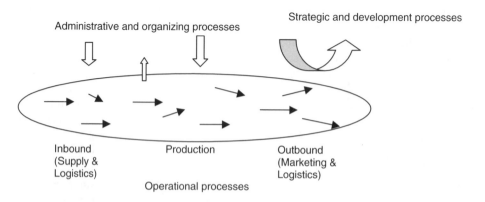

Figure 8.1  Basic processes in firms

The above illustration may primarily give an impression of a typical manufacturing firm, but in our opinion all firms, even consultants, have production. Research, conceptual development, analysis – it is all production. Non-manufacturing firms also need to acquire a variety of resources: information, marketing, publishing, accounting etc. They also need to find and deal with customers. Of course, there are great differences between a sawmill, an accounting firm, a logistics operation and so on as far as the characteristics of these processes are concerned. But our understanding of their operations will always benefit from a thorough description of these processes.

If we are to judge whether a (possible) supplier should be considered good or bad we also need to make some kind of evaluation of its performance of these processes. Is everything in good order, can representatives from the supplier describe what they are doing, does it look as if they are conducting the processes according to best practice? If yes, how could we keep monitoring this? If no, what difference does it make? The description provides us with systematic information that should facilitate such evaluations. Let us look at an illustration in order to clarify this.

---

**Box 8.1   The activities of a car rental operation**

Inter Rent Europe Car is a well-known car rental provider. When faced with tough price competition some years ago, the management team started to reconsider the entire operations of the firm. Most customers of such services regarded all car rental operators as identical. They all offered modern cars, pick-up at one place and return at another, a choice between different payment options such as a fixed price for unlimited mileage or payment by the mile etc. A question asked at Inter Rent was how it could distinguish itself from others. Preferably, this should be through something that is difficult to copy.

An effort to trace the operative processes was begun to see how activities were performed and connected, and whether there was a possibility of identifying ways to improve and – as a result – to be able to offer some more value. One of the most important processes, from a customer's point of view, was the transaction cycle. The first activity is when a customer makes contact with a representative from the car rental firm. What actions take place then? There could be issues such as available options on car sizes, prices etc. Is there anything that creates problems in that sequence or could be done in a different way? The second activity is having the car delivered and there are choices for that part of the service. The same questions were asked. What actions take place, what could go wrong, what could be done differently? The third activity is the actual usage of the car, the intensive consumption process. The same questions applied. The fourth activity is delivering the car back to the rental firm somewhere, being able to leave the keys and get out of that place. Finally there is an invoicing and payment activity, to which the same questions again apply.

This is a brief description of some of the operative processes in this business. It could be extended to other complementary activities as well as other processes, such as development, organization etc. In this case Inter Rent found out what went wrong at various times. A customer could, for example, experience problems with the car. A related question was in what ways the rental firm could offer anything to guarantee that customers really would reach their destination. Something else that caused complaints was handing over the car keys to the customer, which at times took too long. Furthermore, the invoice for the service caused frustration. People had rented the car according to one payment schedule but realized later that a different payment option would have been preferable, and as a result became frustrated.

This mapping procedure laid the ground for the development of some guarantees. 'Reach the destination' – if the customer was delayed more than 45 minutes from the time when they called for support from the car rental firm, at any time of day, the entire service would be for free. 'No trouble' – if the customer has not got the keys and an appropriate description of where to find the car within five minutes of reaching Inter Rent's desk, for example at an airport, the entire service is for free. In addition, if the customer has complaints about the invoice and it is not settled within 48 hours, the entire service is also for free.

These guarantees forced the company to carefully investigate its basic processes to see what activities, resources and internal and external actors needed to be changed in order to be able to meet these challenges. To guarantee the 45 minutes demanded a partner, a security firm with service available 24 hours, seven days a week, as well as taxi couriers and some other parties. The other guarantees also demanded many changes. But the concept turned out to be successful and difficult for competitors to copy for one reason: Inter Rent has the advantage of owning all its cars and employing all its personnel. The fleet of cars was therefore better controlled and personnel better trained.

*Source*: Lectures by Hans-Åke Sand, CEO Inter Rent Europe Car Sweden.

Administrative and organizing processes are also important. The ways in which an operation is organized, how activities are grouped, distributed and managed, says a lot about the company's performance. Here we need to look at the basic structure, the organizational design, but also processes and routines, as well as leadership and management practices. We know that organizing is contextual; the best solution for one firm might be far from the best for another firm. After having portrayed what are considered to be relevant aspects of such processes, the customer is likely to have at its disposal a point of departure for the evaluation of these processes.

Strategic and development processes – the firm's long-term orientation, what it aims to be good at – are crucial. Whether there is a strong direction, whether the firm has a track record of being determined, whether it has ongoing research programmes and so on should be important information in an evaluation of its future. This also includes the ways in which it develops its personnel (recruitment, training, education, on-the-job learning, career paths etc.) and what kinds of innovation processes are carried out. Other relevant aspects are whether there are important cooperative ventures with customers or suppliers, whether there are strictly internal projects, whether the firm invests a lot or just a minor part of its resources including time in development. An evaluation should identify what kind of strategic direction and development processes are vital for a firm such as this, look at the processes carried out and evaluate whether practice at the firm is poor, good or excellent.

Merely describing these processes in the early phases of a supplier evaluation is a valuable exercise. Customer firms performing this analysis will have to solve the puzzle and thereby create an understanding of the supplier in question and its processes. They are also likely to develop their own understanding of the various kinds of businesses that they will consider. This is very much the same argument as that put forward by proponents of quality assurance programmes.

One more important aspect is that the evaluations need to be conducted with a broad horizon. They need to be able to judge whether a certain practice is good or not. This is a strong argument for involving a *team* of evaluators in this process. Needless to say, the evaluators should have the relevant competencies and apply good practices themselves.

## Resources: the third step

The processes discussed above all mean that activities are going to be performed. But in order to carry out activities there is a need for resources (including knowledge). Different kinds of activities call for different kinds of resources.

We distinguish between four groups of resources:

- *Financial resources.* In order to carry out some activities the resources needed have to be financed in some way. It is, for example, easier for a company with good access to financial resources to keep ambitious development programmes running.
- *Material resources* such as production equipment, office and factory facilities as well as other physical production items (raw material, physical components etc.). It is self-evident that such resources are vital in many operations. Even most services firms need some (often a large amount of) physical resources to fulfil their mission (think, for example, of the vehicle fleet of a logistics service provider).
- *Human resources.* People are often said to be a firm's most valuable resources. It is always individuals who interpret and act, be it with varying degrees of support from other physical resources. In most operations we could distinguish between operative, specialist and management categories, but every operation has its specific pattern of human resources.
- *Immaterial resources* are increasingly being recognized. We distinguish between three main categories, *knowledge, relationships* and *brand/image*. Knowledge could either be primarily inherent in the human resources (*who* knows 'how', 'what' and 'who'), but it could also be a part of the so-called structural capital. The firm, as an entity, has learned about practices and procedures: 'what works in our company'. It has also a reservoir of past experiences, lists of references, construction drawings and many other sources of corporate knowledge. Relationships could, just like knowledge, be considered both as a company asset and an asset belonging to individuals. If a company has served its customers well, if it has developed a structure of suppliers and/or other actors, it has built up a base of important capabilities. Individuals have played a role in this, either primarily as a representative of the firm or

primarily as an individual (as a private person). More and deeper contacts provide the individual and the firm with better opportunities. This is probably an important asset to most firms. The third immaterial resource is the firm's image or brand, including product brands. The brand is the result of customers or other actors integrating with and collecting experiences from that firm over time. Integrating means that the firm's brand is created and built up via experience of the products (the offerings), the organization, the people and the symbols (Aaker and Joachimsthaler, 2000). As the brand represents a promise and also an insurance regarding what to expect in contacts with the firm, this is in many cases a critical asset. Fundamentally, it has to do with credibility.

These four categories of resources and knowledge as well as the combination of them look different to all firms depending on what activities and business they are in. In order to evaluate a (possible) supplier it should be a good idea to try to identify not only what activities that supplier carries out, but also what resources and knowledge are needed and which are critical.

The next step is to consider the supplier's access to those resources and, in doing so, to create an understanding of the core competence of the firm. That core competence could either be based on one or more specific resources, for example some unique knowledge, or more often on a combination of resources and aspects of knowledge. Again, in order to evaluate the various resources, the team of evaluators needs to possess adequate competence.

## Supplier position: the fourth step

What is normally brought into focus when the position of a supplier is estimated is its financial position. Mostly these analyses focus on solidity and liquidity. The first measure is an indicator of the firm's ability to withstand losses. The second is an indicator of the firm's short-term access to cash.

We would like to add another aspect of the firm's position in terms of financial resources, namely its owners: the larger constellation of which the firm is a part. We could add other aspects such as established relationships with banks and other capital providers, but that is still only one resource area.

The firm's positions in customer markets, as well as different (complementary) resource markets, need to be taken into account as well. Market share is often considered an important measure of the firm's position in customer markets. We could add the structure of its customer base and its position in certain networks. If the firm has a central position, if it is one that many other firms refer to, respect and follow, this is an important indicator of its position and capabilities. Likewise, if the firm has superior access to some critical resources, raw material, technology, or knowledge of a certain kind, this is also an indicator of strength.

Taken together, such an overview of positions should provide the basis for a discussion around aspects that are normally part of a SWOT analysis: What seem to be the strengths, weaknesses, future opportunities and threats of/to this supplier?

Only when all this is done are we ready to proceed to some kind of company-specific evaluation model.

## Evaluation models

What we have done so far is to suggest a model for data capture, meaning that in order to evaluate and judge we need not just data, but data organized in a certain way and covering relevant aspects. The model we have suggested has been applied in practice and it seems to have helped people move away from merely expressing more or less well-grounded beliefs and attitudes.

One test we did was to let two groups, each of three people, make their evaluation. One group provided the study, collected the data and wrote a report. The other group just read the report. What was good was that both groups came very close when they made their evaluation covering ten important aspects. We think that the proposed pattern of description helped a great deal in providing a firm basis for evaluation.

Here we are going to take our next step, the judgement phase. There are a number of available models and ways to go about this process.

## Elements in evaluation models

Someone who asks a company representative about their 'model' for supplier evaluation is likely to find that there are great variations as to how systematic these models are and which factors are included. To provide some kind of average model, we present an extract from a survey of firms aiming at investigating what they value about their suppliers. The respondents were asked to consider the importance of the following elements:

- Product quality.
- Specific characteristics of the product.
- The quality level of services related to the core products.
- Supply costs.
- Supply/delivery times.
- Stability in supplies.
- Price levels.
- Ability to participate and contribute in product development.
- Ability to flexibly adapt to changing demands, e.g. cancellation of orders.
- Geographic location.
- Technological standards.
- ISO certification.

These elements could be grouped into three caterories:

- The product and its attributes (e.g. price, quality).

- The performance of the supplier (e.g. delivery reliability, flexibility, communication between supplier and customer).
- The underlying capabilities of the supplier.

This could be considered a collection of typical factors to include in a supplier evaluation model.

## Types of evaluation models

Supplier evaluation models can be described and categorized based on two main aspects:

- The use of quantitative versus quantitative measures.
- The level of detail, e.g. whether or not scores for different areas of evaluation are weighed together.

With regard to the use of qualitative versus quantitative measures, a distinction is usually made between *vendor rating* and *supplier audit* models. Vendor rating mainly uses quantitative measures, whereas supplier audits rely to a large extent on more qualitative measures. The underlying reason for this difference is that vendor rating is used for evaluating the performance of the supplier and its product (see the distinction made earlier), whereas supplier audits are more geared towards measuring the capabilities of suppliers. Audits are primarily used for determining a supplier's 'suitability' for *future* collaboration, whereas ratings are much more focused on the past (Van Weele, 2000). For a further discussion of the differences between supplier audits and vendor rating, see Table 8.1.

Regarding the level of detail of supplier evaluation methods, one can distinguish three main approaches in terms of weighing different performance scores. These different approaches mainly pertain to vendor rating; supplier

**Table 8.1**  Differences between supplier audit and vendor rating

| Supplier audit | Vendor rating |
| --- | --- |
| Qualitative | Quantitative |
| Future | Historical orientation |
| New + current suppliers | Only current |
| Selected, important suppliers | Most suppliers |
| Broad scope | Limited, few aspects |
| Time consuming | Standard data |
| In cooperation with supplier | By manufacturer only |

*Adapted from*: Van Weele, 2000.

audits normally do not use any (formal) form of weighing different performance scores.

### Categorical plans

This is a simple, non-weighted method that relies on the buyer keeping a record (vendor rating card) on the good and bad features of its (major) suppliers. The buyer can for example score the supplier each month and discover trends. Categorical plans may well appeal to smaller organizations because of the simplicity of the system – little training is needed to operate these plans and data collection is not very resource intensive – and because they are cheap to operate.

### Weighted point method

The objective of this method is to arrive at an overall rating figure regarding a supplier's total performance. The overall rating is equal to the weighted average of the partial scores for the criteria considered. For such an overall rating, a consistent method of scoring performance is required to facilitate data collection and compilation. The main advantage of the weighted point method is its transparency – there is only one rating figure to consider.

### Total cost of ownership (TCO) method

An alternative to the weighted point method that offers more sophistication in measuring supplier performance is the TCO method, which is essentially gaining insight into the total cost associated with a certain component (or service) from a specific supplier. The advantage connected to this method is that the results are expressed in monetary terms, which makes the costs and benefits of supplier (non-)performance very 'tangible'. However, apart from the fact that not all performance-related aspects may be so easy to monetarize, the great disadvantage is that it does take a great deal of time and effort to collect and maintain the underlying (cost) data; selective application appears to be a solution. A compromise between the weighted point method and the TCO method is the so-called 'value-based' TCO method, where a weighted point method is used to calculate a supplier's performance on delivery, quality etc. That score is then used to multiply the price quoted by the supplier, in order to achieve a sort of TCO index. This method requires less data collection (Ellram, 1995).

A problem with the various weighted methods is that they may result in a mechanistic procedure, which could be misleading. The model gives a strong impression of accuracy, something that could lead to ignorance of the complex and multidimensional relationships that exist within and between every module. These weighted models could give the interpreter a false feeling of security. The strengths are that such models are rather straightforward and the outcomes are, consequently, relatively easy to draw conclusions from. An example of a relatively advanced way of using weighted point evaluation models is described in Box 8.2.

---

**Box 8.2  Supplier evaluation at NCC**

Nordic Construction Company (NCC) has developed a model in which the supplier is evaluated according to nine areas. Among these are the company as such, the products and solutions offered, the supply performance of the company, the development capability of the supplier and the degree of priority that the supplier gives to NCC.

These areas are first ranked in order of importance. For some suppliers, in some businesses, development capability is very important. For others this is not as important. Each performance area is ranked on a scale from 1 to 3, where 3 represents 'extremely important' and 1 represents 'normal basic prerequisites'. After that, each area is graded on a 1 to 5 scale to position the specific supplier's performance or capability. Consequently, a supplier that is the best possible in an area that is considered extremely important will get 15 points in such an area. The scores on all nine areas are summed to reach a total score.

NCC applies a system where a very good supplier should reach a certain percentage of the potential sum. Acceptable and non-acceptable suppliers are separated at a lower level. After the results are summarized, an overall check follows: does this total score look reasonable? Even though the company is good enough when judged from the total score it could be too weak in a specific area, and therefore still not qualify. The scores are used as a tool to support evaluation. The basic idea is that the evaluation sheet and scores do not represent the entire value of an evaluation process. The learning by all actors involved – internal and external – is equally important.

---

## Not just a technique but an organized procedure

There are ways of overcoming some of the problems mentioned. One is, as has been discussed, to complement the quantitative model with qualitative judgements and thereby add some 'softness' to it. Another prerequisite is to invest in careful data collection according to some kind of systematic underlying model, like the model of data capture suggested above. There are also complementary ways. Let us illustrate this by NCC's thinking about its model.

---

**Box 8.3  Use the model as a point of departure for internal and external discussions**

'You should not look too closely at the final figure,' says Klas Frisk, vice-president of purchasing at NCC. 'You should consider it as one of the points of departure for your internal discussions, in order to clarify the points of view of people related to the supplier. Incidentally, that's why you should always carry out the evaluation by a team of people covering different fields of expertise.' The team's efforts could also be designed in different ways. One is for them to sit down together and step by step carry out the evaluation. An alternative is that each of them individually first goes through the evaluation and then begins a process of comparison to reach a joint standpoint. A further alternative in this phase is to base the final judgement on an average of the individual team members' opinions.

A second important aspect is dialogue with the supplier. 'Ideally, you should do your own evaluation, ask the supplier to do a self-analysis, and then meet to compare and discuss with them: why do you consider yourself world-class in logistics when we think you are mediocre? Such a process is a great opportunity for learning on both sides,' Frisk concludes.

We very much agree with the perspective taken in the NCC case. It is often not the calculation in itself that is the vital thing. The important issue is to lay the ground for future improvements on both sides. Using an instrument like the one suggested creates a good opportunity for such processes. Of course, there are situations when the judgement itself is more important, and even then this is still a relevant model. Nevertheless, we think it is important to address the process, not merely the evaluation model as such.

## Evaluating an established supplier relationship

In the model presented in Box 8.2 some performance measures are included. There is also one aspect, NCC priority, which could be interpreted as the likelihood that a potential supplier would give a high priority to the new customer.

The evaluation will obviously become more valid and relevant when it concerns suppliers in ongoing relationships. In such cases, we would like to suggest a second and complementary model of data capture that is not about evaluating the supplier as such, but about evaluating the relationship between the buying firm and the supplier. This should include the kind of aspects that can be judged before it would be possible to put a figure on variables such as performance and priority.

*Supplier relationship checklist*
1. What does this supplier supply to us?
   ● Standard product, a product specifically adapted to our needs or a general unique quality difficult to copy?
   ● Which needs does this supplier fulfil for us? Which needs do we fulfil for the supplier? Why do we buy from this supplier? What are the unique selling points of this supplier in comparison with other possible sources?

The answers to these questions mean that the basic functions of the exchange processes are considered.

2. The importance of the supplier to us, quantitatively as well as qualitatively.
   ● Percentage of our total purchasing volume? Percentage of our purchases of this function? Changes in percentage during the year?
   ● Is the supplier economically valuable (profitable) for us? Does the supplier give us valuable knowledge, contacts, possibilities for development and

improved market positions? What inferences could we draw from this in terms of our dependency on this supplier?

3. Our importance to the supplier, quantitatively as well as qualitatively.
   - Percentage of the supplier's total sales volume? Percentage of the supplier's sales volume of this product? Changes during the year?
   - Do we provide anything 'extra' in addition to payment for deliveries to this supplier? Are we as a customer important to this supplier? What conclusions could we draw from that in terms of expected priority?

4. What do the contact patterns look like between our firm and this supplier?
   - Who are the contact persons? What is the frequency of contacts? Which are important issues in the dialogues?
   - Is this a functional way of operating this relationship, or would other contact patterns or other frequencies provide better functionality?

5. What about the atmosphere, including the mutual expectations of this relationship?
   - What is the history of the relationship? How long has the relationship been going on? What have been the most important events – good and bad – and how do they affect today's businesses? Who have been the key individuals in this relationship?
   - How stable is this relationship? What technical, social, economic, legal, administrative etc. bonds are there between the firms? How influential are they? Are the parties embedded in other relationships that are likely to influence this? In what ways?
   - What do we want to do with this relationship? Do we want to change the content, i.e. its functionality? If so, in what ways? Do we want to change our own organization and thereby organize this relationship differently? What does the supplier want to do? Which issues does the supplier put forward in our contacts with its people?

6. What is the profitability of this relationship?
   - The value of the relationship has two aspects. First we have the core function (the core product). In addition we have important but secondary functions such as development cooperation, providing valuable information and knowledge, acting as a reference and a bridge to other businesses. What could be translated into money and what values are to be considered additional?
   - The costs of the relationship also have two aspects. First, there are the costs of paying for the product, the price. Secondly, there are other costs such as handling and contract costs in order to take care of the relationship over time. How much time is spent on this relationship? What is the value (alternative use) of those costs?
   - It is reasonable to ask oneself what such an equation, the pluses and minuses, looks like for each of the company's key suppliers. What is the profitability of the relationship? How has it developed during later years? What do we believe about the future of this relationship?

These points seem to cover enough aspects to provide a basis for evaluating the importance of the relationship as well as the performance of the supplier. We have pointed to the importance of adopting a contextual view on evaluation procedures. More specifically, we have also argued for the need to adapt the degree of extensiveness and the criteria to apply to each specific case. We have also emphasized the difference between evaluating the supplier as such and evaluating the relationship between the buyer and seller when that is applicable (if there is any existing relationship to evaluate).

## Tracking models for continuous follow-up

The more comprehensive model, illustrated by the NCC version, is well adapted to occasions when a major change is at stake. It could also fit well with major revisions, once a year or at some other suitable interval. In the meantime, in ongoing relationships, there still is a need for follow-up.

This would include monitoring delivery statistics, quality performance, price development and other aspects of the everyday operations in a buyer–supplier relationship. This is what is usually called vendor rating. During recent years, such follow-up has become greatly facilitated thanks to the development of new tools and methods related to IT, such as ERP systems, e-procurement and so on (see Chapter 6). It is about registering activities, collecting information in databases and the possibility of having easy access to and convenient ways of analysing these data. To some extent this could also be considered to be supplier evaluation.

In addition to such continuous follow-up there is often a need for discussion in the form of development meetings with the supplier. In all strategic supplier relationships where there is a substantial amount of business and where each party has far-reaching commitments, NCC for example demands from its supplier that there should be an annual meeting. These meetings should involve supplier top management, in addition to the people who operate the relationship day to day and those who are in charge of it. On the buyer's side, the annual meeting should also include operative personnel, the purchasing manager and the purchasing director as well as a top line manager (sometimes the CEO). That group of people should take their time to evaluate the relationship, addressing questions such as: have the intentions been met, have there been any specific problems or achievements during this period, is it a healthy relationship etc.

It could also address aspects such as the organization of the relationship and the interface between the two parties. Does the supplier make the right kind of capability available to the customer, in the right ways and at the right moments, and vice versa? Such efforts could be relevant, for example, in cases where the supply base is reduced. The idea of organizing the meetings this way, with such a spread of people, is to make the process powerful. This is also an important kind of supplier evaluation.

So far, we have discussed supplier evaluation both on a regular basis and related to major decisions. We have also differentiated between a situation where the two parties have experience in a joint relationship and one where they have not. However, we haven't really addressed one very critical issue. It is not always self-evident that there will be a deal or a relationship, even though the supplier meets all possible requirements. A deal or a relationship does not only have to do with capabilities but also with motivation, the *willingness* of both parties to cooperate. That is why we need to address the question: 'What could make two parties come together for a business deal and/or develop a business relationship?'

## Prerequisites for a relationship: a matter of fit

The question 'Who could work with whom?' has been addressed in the literature. When cooperating in dyadic relationships – and also in groups of more than two – it is evidently important that the resources that the two or more actors control complement and match each other. In essence, there seems to be a need for the parties to possess complementary resources of some kind (Håkansson, 1982). However, there are more aspects that need to match. Laage-Hellman (1997) provides a list of five sources of good or bad fit:

- *Functional complementarity* means that the parties complement each other in terms of resources: one actor has some knowledge or other capability that the other is missing.
- *Strategic fit* means that the parties are heading in complementary future directions.
- *Organizational fit* means that the parties fit well together because of their organizational designs that facilitate cooperation. This also comprises, for example, the social fit between the individuals involved.
- *Business philosophy fit* implies that the parties have more or less the same values for conducting business. Should the relationship be opportunistic or truly cooperative? Should it involve joint developments and a search for synergies? Should it be short term or long term etc.?
- *Timing fit* – as all actors are involved in a number of activity processes the timing of new activities and/or cooperative ventures is critical. The parties might be unable to achieve a fit due to imbalances in their timing.

Lorange and Roos (1992) add to this by stating that all cooperation must be founded on overlapping motives in order to be successful. Axelsson (1998), reviewing Laage-Hellman (1997), also emphasizes the element of willingness. It is often the case that if two or more partners really decide that they want to cooperate, they will find some areas in which cooperation can take place.

In addition to this, timing is especially worth highlighting. It is often impossible for one party to manage the other as each actor is normally involved in a number of activities. To some extent, one actor could try to move faster and/or be prepared to act at a later time, but normally there are limits to such adaptation. Uncontrollable processes could, at best, be delayed, frozen or fixed, and thereby time and the timing process could be managed to a limited extent. The conclusion is that the four other forms of fit are necessary but not sufficient.

A cooperative venture also needs to appear during a suitable time period ('window of opportunity').

We have already mentioned that resources and knowledge could contribute to functional complementarity. We have also pointed to various kinds of resources (financial, material, manpower, technologies, procedures etc.). In addition, it is worthwhile distinguishing between various kinds of knowledge.

Knowledge can relate to different kinds of technologies: electronics, mechanics, biotechnology etc. It could also be knowledge regarding business processes: how to carry out a supplier evaluation, how to operate the value chain, how to organize to be able to manage a strategic relationship, how to learn from mistakes in order to avoid making the same mistake over and over again and so on. One way to differentiate between different *forms* of knowledge is the following taxonomy (Axelsson, 1998):

- Routines and work methods.
- Laboratory or research-based knowledge.
- Ability to learn and develop.
- Individually based knowledge.

It is evident that the fit between the resources and knowledge of the various partners forms an important prerequisite for functional complementarity.

## Specific aspects to consider when the supplier is a service provider

The discussion of supplier evaluation has, so far, not specifically addressed service firms. What we have suggested is a general approach, applicable to all kinds of suppliers. The specifics of service firms are built into the model of data capture, as it suggests a careful description of the important processes and the resources needed to carry out those processes. If the processes are special when services are at stake and if some kinds of resources are especially critical for certain service firms, that should be taken care of in this description and analysis process.

Chapters 1 and 2, on the characteristics of services and service firms, contained quite extensive discussion of the issues that could be more significant in service operations than in traditional manufacturing, which mainly have to do with the intangibility of services. This also concerns the kind of service as such; traditional, simple services from service firms differ from problem-solving services from professional firms. We are not going to repeat those arguments here. However, let us conclude that if the product to be bought is highly dependent on the interplay between the buyer and seller, it is likely that it will be necessary to look more closely at the supplier – the interaction partner – than at the product (the service) as such. In that sense, supplier evaluation should be brought more into focus when buying services than when purchasing traditional goods. The important message is that the model of evaluation and the criteria applied need to be adapted to the kind of operation that is performed by the supplier and, to some extent, that products produced with a high degree of interaction should put a great deal of emphasis on the interacting parties.

## Conclusions

We have suggested a model for supplier evaluation that has some specific features. Before an evaluation can be made there is a need for data systematized in specific ways. We suggest a model for data capture that consists of four main steps, to lay the basis for an evaluation of a supplier before a major decision such as beginning to buy (some substantial products) from that firm. We also suggest a complementary model for data capture to be used in cases where the two parties have done business before, i.e. an ongoing relationship. We also point to the fact that in addition to such, more comprehensive evaluations there is a need for continuous, everyday evaluations. Some ways to carry out such evaluations were discussed. We also presented an example of a comprehensive model.

The basic message is that evaluation models need to be adapted to the specific situation at hand. The general model could be the same but the weight of different criteria, the level of detail of the analysis and the ways in which the evaluation process is carried out need to be adapted. Our model has a built-in mechanism that makes such adaptation natural, as it recommends a careful investigation of the important processes to be carried out by the supplier and an equally careful analysis of the resources required to do that. We also argue that specific features of services and service operations put specific demands on the evaluation of service suppliers. Such specific aspects can easily be captured by the proposed model.

# 9

# Contracting Business Service Providers: Pricing, Negotiations and Payment

In order for a transaction to be completed, pricing by the supplier and the customer's willingness to pay have to be congruent. In this chapter, we discuss some basic principles for cost evaluation, pricing, negotiations and different principles for payment.

## Pricing principles

In principle, there are three starting points for determining prices:

- The production costs – what it costs to produce and deliver the service.
- The alternatives the customer has – the choices it has or the market situation.
- The value of the specific service for the specific customer.

This may not sound complicated but in fact it is far from simple. Let us illustrate this point with some examples from training and lecturing services.

## Box 9.1 Pricing problems

### The training service

A training service was being purchased in a local community via open bidding. The community received a number of bids and selected the one that the people responsible argued to be the best. This implied that the community did not select the lowest bidder. The selected supplier offered the training service for a price nearly 50 per cent higher than the lowest bid. The local newspaper found out about this and published an article claiming that 'the community has thrown away taxpayers' money'. Representatives of the community defended themselves by saying that the lowest bidder was unknown to them, while the selected one had carried out similar assignments before with very positive results. Unlike the lowest bidder, this supplier was 'a sure bet'.

### The guru who was misled

One of the world's leading management gurus had made an arrangement with a conference bureau regarding a speech. The content, length and timing of the speech had been agreed, as well as the number of attendees, a maximum of 250. Based on these conditions, the parties had settled on a fee.

When the day of the 'production of the service' had arrived and the guru was in attendance, a problem arose. It turned out that interest in the speech had been so high that the organizer had been able to double the number of attendees. In many respects this was quite positive, but the guru was not happy with it. He refused to go on stage if his fee was not doubled first. His negotiation position was excellent at this point and he could get his way. But the issue led to a situation where both parties were very upset and both also felt they had every right to be so.

What was right and what was wrong in these examples? That is hard to say. There are many different methods for determining a price (see e.g. Kotler, 2000). The three main principles mentioned earlier are the most important. They can be seen as complementary as they will be given different weights in different situations, which is illustrated in Figure 9.1. Where the price will end up depends to a large extent on the strengths of these three factors in any specific situation.

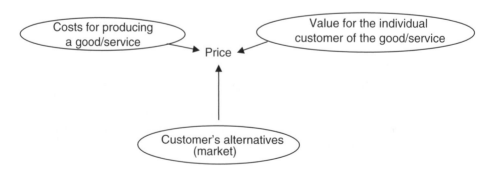

**Figure 9.1** Three forces that determine price

## Cost-based pricing

In the long run, price will be close to production costs for a service in those cases where the alternatives for the customer are sufficient, i.e. there are a number of alternative suppliers or solutions available on the market. In the short run, price may even lie below production costs. But how can these production costs be calculated?

## Full costs

Some underlying methods for determining full costs are the following:

- Analyse which activities have to be performed in order for the service (assignment) to be carried out. This may include cost calculations, transport, travel, contacts and meetings (compare the checklist for activity analysis in Chapter 3).
- Evaluate which actors (internal and external) and/or which other resources – e.g. different types of production equipment – must be used (exploited) and to which extent. Who is doing what? How much time and energy are spent on the different activities? (Compare the checklist for actor analysis in Chapter 3.)
- Evaluate the use of resources for performing these activities and the costs of these resources. What is, for example, a reasonable price per hour for a service repairman, a consultant, a lawyer, an artist? What is a reasonable price per day for the use of earth-moving equipment, an automatic postage machine, or a computer with unique software for specialized calculations? (Compare the checklist for resource analysis in Chapter 3.)

If we know from the second type of analysis that the assignment is human resource-intensive and requires the efforts of a highly qualified person during 40 hours and 400 hours of support, one way of calculating the production costs can be to allocate the costs of these persons to the customer. However, the costs for the resources that these people will need to use for performing their assignments also have to be taken into consideration. These may include costs for access to offices, computers, transportation etc.

An alternative example can be a less human resource-intensive service. In that case, it may be more reasonable to use another measure as the main basis for calculation, such as the capacity of a certain piece of production equipment (a mixer, a robot etc.). The costs for using this capacity should be calculated, taking into consideration purchase and replacement costs, operations costs and the like. After this, one has to determine how much of the total capacity will be used by the specific assignment under consideration. In cost-based pricing, this becomes an important starting point for evaluating costs, and thereby price.

These are some of the fundamental aspects that a purchaser will normally try to evaluate. They provide some indication of how much it is reasonable to pay for a certain service, without considering the supply and demand situation or the value of the service (in use) to the customer.

> **Box 9.2   What does it cost and what do we get?**
>
> An illustration of this point can be a company that has to choose between two suppliers of fund management services. One supplier takes as payment 1 per cent of the value of the combined shares, bonds etc., while the other takes 0.5 per cent. If the customer can assume that the services are equal, that both suppliers offer equally qualified fund managers, the choice between the two suppliers is not a major problem. But how can it determine whether that is the case – how should the customer act in these circumstances?
>
> There are many different ways. One way can be to determine how the two fund managers have performed in the past. However, this may not be a guarantee for the future. Another way is to try to determine their working methods. If one supplier has only half as many qualified analysts as the other, with comparable volumes, the price differences as discussed earlier would be explainable in the case of cost-based pricing.

This example shows that there is sufficient cause for a purchaser of a (heterogeneous) service to consider not only the price of the offering, but also the quality and the conditions that may be critical for achieving a specific level of quality. In such cases, it becomes essential for the customer to attempt to evaluate what is reasonable competence, both quantitatively and qualitatively, for producing a certain service. The analyst resources have a price and, hopefully, a value.

## Calculation principles for the full costs of services: traditional allocation methods or activity-based costing (ABC)

What has been described above are the basic principles of so-called full costing. All costs that can be traced back to a specific product should be allocated to it. Within these basic principles, however, there are several alternative methods to choose from. Traditional accounting methods have been based on the consumption of resources, primarily the use of materials and direct labour, which can be directly related to a specific product. Other costs that can only be related indirectly to a certain product, such as administrative activities, service, sales, purchasing activities etc., have been treated as common processes and have been allocated to individual products with the help of some general accounting schemes.

As a result of the fact that indirect costs in many industries have been increasing steadily, and sometimes have even become dominant, this type of accounting method has lost its relevance in many different situations. An answer to these problems has been so-called activity-based costing (ABC) and accounting (Kaplan and Norton, 1992). According to this method, the accountants try to follow more closely which activities – of all different kinds – are being carried out to produce a specific product or to handle a specific customer or supplier relationship. In this way, the choice of calculation method has consequences for price setting, especially in those cases where prices are primarily cost based.

## Full costs vs marginal costs as the starting point for cost-based pricing

Among well-established costing methods, in addition to full costing, there is also the so-called marginal costs method. As explained before, according to the first method the firm tries to evaluate the full costs of the product, i.e. what it costs to produce. This is a long-term principle; the selling firm cannot, for a long time, sell its products at a price below full costs.

The other method is marginal costing. According to this method, it can be beneficial to the firm in some cases to sell a product at a price lower than the full costs, but higher than the costs that are added by the specific sale (marginal costs). Consider the following illustration.

---

**Box 9.3   Surplus can sometimes be sold at cheaper than full cost**

The global telecommunications network is not being used equally. For example, during European working hours it is night in large parts of North America. At that point there is over-capacity in the telecommunications network that can be purchased cheaply from US operators. Telecommunications brokers have been established to help buyers make the best choice for a specific time of day. Each transaction that results in positive marginal revenue is interesting for the selling operator. Another, comparable way of using this excess capacity is, for example, the delayed distribution of fax messages. The operator stores the message and sends it at a time when network utilization is lower, making it cheaper in the end.

---

## Market-based pricing

In the case of market-based pricing, the supplier starts with the price that the market is expected to be willing to pay. Sometimes this may mean that the price is much higher than production costs and sometimes it may be lower. This is determined by market conditions. The following example illustrates this issue.

---

**Box 9.4   Large price differences raised questions regarding the specification and price of the service**

The purchase of a consultancy service led the customer organization to reconsider its ways of working. In the same request for quotations, the customer received offers in the range of €50 000–200 000 for the same job. The customer thought this was wrong in principle. To some extent, it must be dependent on how the supplier interprets the market situation. The customer is now considering including, in addition to other bidding information, a price indication in its requests for quotations.

---

According to the market-based pricing principle, the market mechanism, in the form of the customer's range of alternatives, will determine the price level. The price of the products varies, based among other elements on the volumes offered by the producers of the products and the extent of demand for the product. This relationship is easily illustrated with traditional supply and demand curves, as in Figure 9.2.

The supply curve illustrates the notion that the higher the market price for a product, the higher the volume offered by the suppliers. The demand curve illustrates that the higher the price, the less volume will be bought by the customers in the market. Equilibrium price and equilibrium volume are achieved at point P, Q.

Many factors can change the shape of these curves: new technology that makes it possible to produce at lower unit prices; more intensive competition that pushes more efficient production and thereby changes the supply curve; accumulated supplier stocks that affect supply and lower prices per unit for a certain time; changed preferences among consumers that may affect the demand curve either in a positive or negative way. These events illustrate the normal relationships between price, supply and demand. However, there are situations where demand is growing as prices increase (so-called 'snob goods').

These economic relationships imply that volume rebates are quite common. This means that the more the customer buys, the lower is the price per unit. For these reasons, it is often interesting for the customer to collate its purchasing requirements and carry out negotiations based on these combined volumes. The logic of volume rebates normally applies, but not always. Here are two examples of other, but still logical ways of thinking.

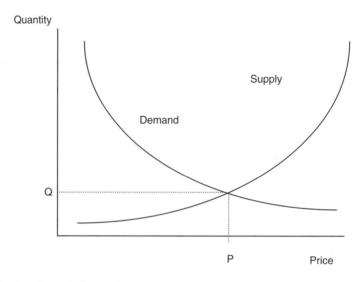

**Figure 9.2**  Supply and demand curves

**Box 9.5   The volume rebate that never came (1)**

Every second year, a particular European MBA programme buys a seminar abroad for its students at a top management school in the US. Included in the purchase order are requirements regarding the desired lecturers but also regarding the location of the lectures, the school's centre for all executive training that is beautifully situated by a lake with superb facilities. The European MBA programme leaders have a deal on a special 'university price', which is lower than the US school normally charges corporate clients.

The European group usually consists of 35 people and a price is determined per person for participating in all the seminars and lectures. The volume rebate that never came occurred when one year the group consisted of 65 rather than 35 people. The Europeans' point of view was that the price per person should therefore be lowered; obviously, the costs of the lecturers and so on were fixed and would be lower per person than with a smaller group. This was impossible. The US school's educational programmes are much sought after by business. When the European group consisted of only 35 people, the US school refrained from filling a classroom of that size with participants from American companies. It would miss out on the alternative and higher revenue that such a group would generate. When the European group consisted of 65 people, a larger classroom was needed and the host school would therefore miss out on an even higher amount of revenue from the more profitable alternative usage. The volume rebate never came.

**Box 9.6   The volume rebate that never came (2)**

After the merger of two previously competing firms, one small and one larger, the context for their common future was being analysed. One of the areas under consideration was purchasing and one of the elements being compared between the two companies were the purchasing conditions from a specific supplier. It turned out that the smaller company, also the smaller customer, had clearly better conditions than the larger one. How was this possible? How could the supplier explain this and how could the tarnished trust in this supplier be re-established?

The explanation was that the supplier applied full-costing methods for its basic production capacity. Prices for large sales orders had been calculated in this way. The smaller quantities, which came 'on top' of these basic volumes, could be dealt with in another way. Their prices were calculated to provide positive marginal revenues to cover the general costs or even to generate a (small) profit.

These examples show that what is logically right often has to be analysed against the background of a more detailed investigation of the specific conditions that apply in any individual case.

Von Schéele (1996) argues that there is reason to believe that the characteristics of many services – they cannot be stored, are intangible and are therefore difficult to find and compare – mean that access and time have especially strong effects on the shape of their demand and supply curves. Von Schéele writes:

As the customer has relatively little knowledge of how the service can answer his needs, he places strong emphasis on cost and time aspects. The customer has opinions on how long a service may take to be performed, when the service should be ready and when the work on the service should start. The customer even puts emphasis on the total price, as he often has a budget that sets restrictions for solving the specific problem. Finally, the customer often talks in terms of price per hour, price per week or price per month.

Von Schéele concludes that organizations and networks are always limited in what they can deliver in terms of time. A lost hour never comes back, it can never be stored (Von Schéele, 1996, p. 20).

The fact that services often cannot be stored and that the customer does not have complete information on all the possible offerings in the market has two important implications for demand and supply curves as specifically applied to services, as shown in Figure 9.3.

The customer's demand for a specific service is represented by the demand curves D1 and D2. Both curves describe a trade-off between price and moment of service delivery. D1 describes a curve that corresponds to a customer utility lower than D2. Customers always are more or less ignorant about the details of the service, but are clear about two things:

● They can accept price variations between P1 and P2 (per hour).
● They can accept that the service is delivered at a moment between T1 and T2, but neither earlier nor later.

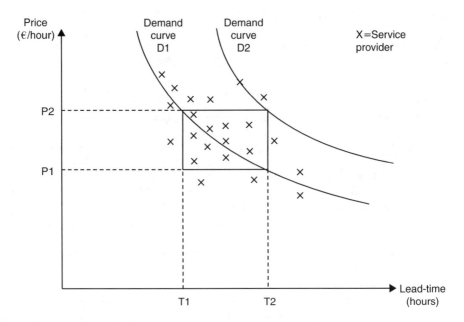

**Figure 9.3** Purchasing box and supply cluster for a specific service
*Adapted from*: Von Schéele, 1996, p. 21.

In the figure the service offerings are described from the customer's perspective. There is a small rectangle, the purchasing box, which describes what most customers 'see' and what they accept. Von Schéele concludes: 'Within this rectangle, most of the transactions for this service will occur, for the given price per hour and at the given delivery time.' For various reasons, the customer has decided to neglect a large part of the market's service offering. Obviously, the customer neglects those services that do not meet its requirements in terms of price and time of delivery. Additionally, the customer cannot survey the whole market; it only sees part of it. The factors that affect the customer's ability to see determine to a large extent its evaluation of the availability of suppliers.

One consequence of this line of reasoning is that the customer is able to demand different service profiles, within the purchase box, in terms of the two variables:

- Cheap and fast (P1, T1). This is a service for which the quality requirements are presumably not that high. What is important is that the service can be delivered quickly, that it meets basic standards and that the price is low.
- Expensive and fast (P2, T1). This is a common situation, where the customer needs the service quickly, for various reasons. This may include maintenance of a piece of production equipment or similar. For such delivery speed, the customer is willing to pay a premium price.
- Expensive and slow (P2, T2). This is probably a less attractive service. Normally speed is preferred, but in some cases a service that fits into the customer's existing activity structures may be attractive for various reasons. It may also be the case that the expensive service has certain quality advantages that motivate a higher price.
- Cheap and slow (P1, T2). This is a more common situation. In exchange for a slower delivery, the customer retains a premium in the form of a lower price. For the supplier, this implies increased flexibility and possibilities for improved resource usage.

Consider the following examples of 'cheap and slow' services.

---

**Box 9.7  The prices of advertising agencies and car repair shops are time based**

Two bids were received for the production of an advertising brochure. It turned out that it made a big difference whether the agency had four months or four weeks to work on it. Similar experiences occur in the purchase of car repair services.

The explanation in both cases is that producers will make up for their losses resulting from the lower price by improved usage of their resources.

---

Generally speaking, the market context is always important in determining price. In the case of intensive competition, where the customer has many comparable alternatives, this factor will clearly affect the price of the service. It is, however, interesting to observe that this factor has an exceptionally frequent and strong impact on the purchase of services, given that many services cannot be stored.

## Value-based pricing

For new products, individually adapted products and in those cases where there are not that many alternative suppliers, a natural starting point for determining price is the value of the good or service for the customer. Consider the following examples.

---

**Box 9.8    What is the value of a consultant's efforts?**

On assignment to a large industrial customer, a consultant carried out an overview of the firm's logistic system, including the number of warehouses, distribution methods and stock sizes. The analysis led to the conclusion that the customer stood to gain a great deal from changing its practices in a number of ways. The annual savings were calculated at some €3.5 million.

The assignment took the consultant five days to carry out. What would be a fair price? Would it be a fair share of the customer's expected gains of the new measures (the value of the service), a traditional daily fee of €1000–2000 or the costs of the consultant to his or her employer?

---

**Box 9.9    Buying a programme format**

What is the value of a programme idea, for example one's own variant of *Wheel of Fortune* or *Big Brother*? Some actor has a patent (intellectual property right) on this programme idea, or 'format' as it is commonly called.

All the principles discussed so far (cost based, market based, value based) could be applied. However, costs as a basis for pricing seem less relevant. The market principle implies that the rights to the format are auctioned. The party that pays most, within a certain geographic (broadcasting) region, gets the right to use the format there. But value-based pricing also seems reasonable and relevant because, among other things, the price that the customer is willing to offer will reflect to a large extent the value that the customer thinks the format will hold for its business. This in turn may be very dependent on the customer's specific situation. How many viewers does the channel have? What profile do these viewers have and how can the new format affect the channel's market share? How can the channel exploit exactly this idea – are there special celebrities that it can attract as hosts and on what conditions? These are just some examples of aspects that can affect the value of the right to exploit the format in a specific situation.

## Box 9.10    What is the value of a mobile telecommunications licence?

In various countries, authorities have offered telecoms operators the possibility of bidding for a licence to operate third-generation mobile telecommunication networks. The main question is: what is the value of such a licence?

The answer depends on many factors. How large is the relevant population (market)? What structure – in terms of age, wealth, communication preferences – does the population have? Are there strong loyalties between certain population groups and other operators, or is there a possibility of gaining market share? Does the firm have an interesting concept for winning market share? What are the experiences in other places, and what are the firm's opportunities for combining all its strengths to win in this market?

Depending on the answers to these and many other questions, there is a strong possibility that the licence will have a different value for different operators. In such auctions, it is the market that decides who gets the licence, but it is always the individual operator that evaluates the value of the licence according to its own situation – and that is an important starting point before making any final offer.

## Box 9.11    The value of educational services

A firm producing packaging within the paper and pulp industry was considering buying the service of 'high-school education for all 100 employees in the fields of physics, chemistry and English'. If this were to be realized, all operators would have high-school competence in these three areas. What does the service cost and what is it worth to the firm?

The answer was that the costs were easy to calculate. An offer from the local high school was received and that part of the costs was then quite clear. Additionally, the education would be carried out during working hours and free time. The loss of productive labour and the economic costs of this were also relatively easy to calculate. But what were the benefits? The company managers realized that if all employees were to have the desired competence, they would be able to identify possible production breakdowns earlier because they would have a better understanding of the underlying mechanisms. This was assumed to reduce production breakdowns by 5 per cent. The value of this could be calculated easily as the costs of breakdowns in this industry are well known. Similarly, the service was expected to enable further production rationalizations of approximately 1 per cent. This could also be expressed easily in monetary terms.

Other effects were more indirect. How would the motivation of employees be affected? How were other important aspects likely to be affected, such as the realization of environmental objectives, internal collaboration and so on? At this company, the manager responsible for competence development tried to identify all direct and indirect effects and to attribute some economic value to them whenever that seemed possible and relevant, noting and clarifying both costs and benefits.

These examples are special in the sense that they deal with services that are relatively abstract. The example in Box 9.12 is somewhat more concrete. In order to expand on these value-related issues, we describe, in some detail, a generic method for determining the value of a service for a given customer.

---

**Box 9.12   Calculating the value of a logistics consultancy service**

Logistics is not merely a matter of moving a parcel from one place to another; there are many aspects to consider. One is how to define what is to be transported – is it a parcel or a pallet? The answer decides what space will have to be allocated to the goods in transport. There are numerous similar aspects, not to mention what kind of transport is relevant and which specific operators to choose.

A particular consultancy firm has specialized in designing the structure of logistics for its customers. When its consultants do this they analyse the logistical activities that have been carried out at that company during the year that has just passed. They consider all choices and estimate their cost consequences. After that they design their alternative(s), demonstrate the functionality of these and estimate the costs. The basic functionality has to be equal or better than what was realized with the previous year's practices. The customer is asked whether it expects a similar distribution pattern in its operations in the coming year. If there are expected deviations the consultant will take this into account. The next step is, based on historical data, to present the case to the customer. If the consultant has developed a better alternative and the customer decides to utilize it, the net savings are shared equally between the two. If not, the consultant receives nothing. In some cases the fee stretches out to a second year and then the consultant receives one quarter of the savings and the rest is kept by the customer.

---

## Evaluating a service: a method of value analysis

One way to determine the value of an offering, in an individual case (transaction, customer) and in an individual business, is to go through the steps described below (cf. Anderson and Narus, 1999):

1. A natural starting point for a value analysis is to determine the functional aspects of an actual or possible offering (a product with certain conditions):
   - A logical first step would be to list, as completely as possible, all possible direct effects that the offering will have both in terms of benefits (value) and costs. This is a crucial step that often requires a great deal of creative thinking. Costs and benefits can include direct effects on energy consumption, human resources, time at the supplier and/or the customer etc.
   - The offering can, however, also have more indirect effects in relation to the actual transaction and parties involved, e.g. effects on the customer's customer, working environment, competitive strength, long-term market position etc. These effects also have to be mapped in detail, so that as many effects as possible can be evaluated. This step is just as creative and demanding as the previous one. One common experience in this kind of value analysis is that it is definitely easier to see and identify costs that can be reduced than values that can be created.
2. Step two is trying to attach economic values to these plus and minus factors. It is especially important to do the following:

- Clarify the assumptions on which the attributed values are based. If, for example, time savings by or at the customer or the supplier are an important element in the service offering, this time should be expressed in units. But the important point to clarify in this context is the value of the time savings and the assumptions on which the attributed value is based. This may include, for example, an assumption that surplus human resources can be taken out of the company so that their costs disappear, or that the surplus can be used in a similarly valuable activity. Otherwise, the time savings will have no economic effects.

- It is also important to try to evaluate how sensitive the calculations are to changes in these assumptions. If only 50 per cent of surplus personnel can be deployed for alternative purposes, what are the consequences? If the travelling time of employees is reduced, what does this mean? Is travel time idle, or can it be used to make telephone calls, think or do something else that is productive? The latter implies that parties should realize that travel time savings do not result in 100 per cent increased value.

3. Step three is to sort out the other direct or indirect effects that are difficult to evaluate economically. These may be 'aesthetic' experiences or 'peace of mind' associated with a particular (e.g. branded) offering, but also more tangible factors that are still difficult to value, such as effects on personal health and well-being. It is important to list those issues that cannot be attributed with any economic value in a meaningful way, so that they are included in the final evaluation. It is also important in this context to consider the potential long-term and dynamic effects of an offering. What could happen in the future as a consequence of what is being evaluated? Are conditions created for a future important resource development?

4. A fourth significant step is to try to increase understanding of why the effects listed so far occur to that specific extent, and in that way specifically for that company. What is it in our business that means that exactly these effects occur in the way they do? Increased awareness of these factors increases understanding. At the same time, it helps the company to evaluate more systematically the potential of changing both positive and negative effects by trying to alter the basic conditions. What are our main 'core' conditions? What does it mean if we change some of the conditions that affect our work now? This step resembles the analysis that the supplier normally carries out to understand which effects occur to what extent at various customers and why. When the supplier understands this and is able to build a system of offerings based on the characteristics of these different customers, it has taken another step in becoming a value engineer.

5. A fifth step is to create, internally at the buyer but perhaps also at the supplier, increased awareness of which type of functional solutions could imply an even greater improvement for the company. This creates the foundation for continued learning and development. If many employees know the most important actions for improving the business, they can more easily identify improvement opportunities and formulate needs, wishes and requirements for suppliers.

Companies that operate according to a logic such as this one have good possibilities for applying value-based pricing. As customers, they can endeavour to rely not on achieving the 'right' market-based price, but instead on looking for the individual, firm-specific solutions that the supplier can offer. These companies can also dare to invest in the development of capabilities (competence) to create – together with suppliers – important improvements to common functions that in many cases can take a long time to realize and an even longer time to calculate economically.

At the same time, it is important to note that the principle of value for the customer is not always applicable to pricing in practice. For example, it may be possible for a certain service to have a high value for a particular customer, implying a high price. But the customer's financial situation could mean that this does not have any impact; the customer just cannot pay the high price. It is also important for the supplier to realize that customers can get together and make comparisons. An identical service can have a highly different value for two customers depending on the context in which the service will be used. Even in such situations, significant problems (in terms of trust and trustworthiness) are likely to arise if it turns out that one customer pays much more than the other for an identical service. Such problems need to be anticipated and dealt with effectively. This impact of the market mechanism on a purely value-based analysis has to be handled one way or the other.

## Interrelations between the three price elements

The three price elements discussed previously – the costs of producing a service, the market situation in terms of availability and demand, and value to the customer – are all important variables that, depending on the context, affect prices to a greater or lesser extent.

## What is objectively the right price?

Obviously, the actual price level will be set according to the specific situation at hand. But what is the right price? An interesting example in terms of the basic principles involved is a conflict between the Swedish organization STIM and three commercial TV channels, which has been dealt with by the Swedish National Competition Authority and the regional court of Stockholm.

In Sweden, and internationally in collaboration with its local sister organizations, STIM has the task of overseeing and controlling the right to compensation of composers, writers, musicians and artists in the case of copyrighted music. But what should those using this music pay?

> **Box 9.13   STIM and the broadcasting companies: what is the right price for copyrighted music?**
>
> The basic rule regarding compensation for provision (to provide the possibility for exploitation) and exploitation (how much this possibility is used and how) is that

royalties will be paid. Usually this is based on a percentage of the revenues that the exploiter will receive. The basic principle, therefore, is a blueprint based on the results of the exploitation or the exploiter. This blueprint should be at a reasonable level compared to the utility that the work has provided (compare this with performance-based compensation).

In this specific case this has been the basic principle and it also applies from an international perspective. However, TV broadcasting companies have argued, supported by the Swedish National Competition Authority, that the relationship between their economic results and the exploitation of music is far too indirect to be used as a satisfying principle to calculate compensation. They have suggested that a new principle should be introduced.

The Competition Authority announced that such a principle should take into account the actual exploitation by the exploiters, potential target groups (how big an audience has access to the channel concerned) and the costs for STIM to administer the activities (monitor exploitation, collect payments etc.) and that it should be competition neutral. The latter implied that in this specific situation commercial channels were not to be negatively affected relative to the state-owned channels and vice versa, and that the commercial channels were all to be treated equally. Additionally, compensation should be at a reasonable level from an international perspective, since STIM also monitors the rights of foreign intellectual property right (IPR) holders while its partners monitor the rights of Swedish IPR holders internationally.

In essence, therefore, the court had to pay attention to all three starting points for price setting simultaneously: costs, market factors and value. The legal case was especially important because STIM has a dominant position (monopoly) and such companies have, according to antitrust legislation, a specific responsibility to behave impeccably. But what is the right price? Does it exist?

Some of the questions raised when analysing this in more detail are the following:

- What value should be assigned to the provision activities, for example in relation to the maximum potential audience that a channel can reach?
- What value should be assigned to the various forms of music? Should popular music be compensated just as much as opera music? Should instrumental music be treated as equal to vocal music?
- What value should be assigned to the different ways of enjoying or exploiting music? Should prices be the same for background music to a test image as for a live broadcast with moving images of the artists?
- What value should be assigned to the actual exploitation? Should a channel that has a higher share of music content in its broadcasts pay a higher price than those that have a lower share?
- What value should be assigned to actual audiences? When a channel broadcasts a great deal of music but the audience is limited, should the channel pay less?
- To what extent should compensation levels in other countries be taken into account and how could the different principles for calculating compensation be made comparable – and is this important?

In its verdict and proposal for solving the dispute, the court chose to base the compensation on the main principle of consumption. The main unit that should be used for determining compensation would be consumption in terms of minutes watched/listened. STIM's administration costs were, in this context, negligible, and an unambiguous market price – in the form of an alternative to a royalty arrangement –

could not be identified. This implied that a channel that broadcasts a great deal of music pays more than a channel that broadcasts only a little, assuming that both audiences are more or less the same. It implies also that the channel that has 100 per cent coverage of the market pays twice as much as the one that has 50 per cent, assuming that both audiences on average watch/listen to the channel equally often. The potential audience is taken into account indirectly because the basic principle (of actual consumption) automatically discounts this, but it is not weighted as strongly as STIM had desired – despite the fact that the principle of provision weighs quite heavily within intellectual property right law. The distribution of compensation between the different forms of music was not an issue in this part of the market, but when STIM distributes the compensation collected it takes such other variables into account, according to its own rules.

The level of compensation, the price per minute, was determined in accordance with a model applied in Denmark and calibrated to international price levels.

Was this the right price? Was this the right method for price setting? These questions are difficult to answer, as in many other situations. Price is always a combination of a number of factors. In this specific case, in a monopoly situation, market forces were not given the room for manoeuvre that they may have in other situations. Moreover, the operational costs of the intermediary, i.e. STIM's, were insignificant. Consequently, a single aspect of the value to the customer (consumption expressed in minutes watched) came to weigh heaviest. However, as stated earlier, this is merely one aspect of value. It does not say anything about, for example, how much the customer (the TV channel) earns by using the music, or to what extent the music contributes to a larger market share or image building etc.

In reality, there may be a number of other underlying factors that have a strong impact on price setting. One such important situational factor is the product life cycle phase that the good or service has reached. In an early phase, price may be set according to two different principles. Either it is set very high in order to 'skim the market' and attract customers who are highly motivated to buy the product. Later in the product life cycle price is adjusted downwards. Or price is set at a low level from the beginning, in order to penetrate the market. Similarly, there are ideas about price levels in the other phases of the product life cycle (cf. Kotler, 2000).

Another underlying factor that may be important is competition in the form of substitutes. If there are relevant and close substitutes in relation to the product concerned, this may affect price setting, and vice versa obviously; price setting may attract or deter substitutes.

At the beginning of this chapter we stated that the basis for a contractual relationship to arise between buyer and supplier is a certain congruence between the customer's willingness to pay and the supplier's desire to be paid. Obviously, this congruence is not always automatically achieved; quite often it is attained through negotiations, the topic of the next section.

## The impact of negotiation strategies

A consistent supply strategy is based on a buying philosophy that is in line with the overall business strategy. This also implies that the final steps in a business transaction (the negotiations) and the execution of the purchasing operations must be in harmony with the rest of the business process, including the achievement of what has been agreed (deliveries, prices, interactive collaboration etc.). If, for example, a choice has been made to work with one supplier (as a consequence of the business and buying strategy), it is of substantial interest to ensure that the negotiation strategy is in line with earlier choices and assumptions.

This is an overarching reason for having a specific section of this book devoted to negotiation. Some of the other reasons are as follows:

- Well-conducted negotiations can mean a great deal to the results of the business – and these results can be achieved in a relatively short period of time. It is hard to repair by different processes what has been damaged through an unskilfully conducted negotiation.
- It is generally presumed that the representatives of the buying function are skilled negotiators; negotiation is, in other words, one of the buying specialists' core competencies.
- The positive potential of cooperation and relation-oriented buying strategies (see Chapter 10) is often said to be unresolved, since the execution of the negotiation has not been in line with the business and buying strategy.
- In addition to negotiating skills, negotiation strategy is an important condition for influencing others, as well as a significant ingredient in the company's position versus other actors.

As has become apparent from the previous sections on pricing and from previous chapters (such as the discussion on SLAs and specification methods in Chapter 7), there are many aspects to negotiate when buying business services.

## Negotiation defined

Before a contract can be established, i.e. before a legal agreement can be drawn up between the parties involved, the process usually contains one or more sequences of negotiations. These sequences are normally seen as natural and important steps towards establishing a contract.

Negotiations have different purposes and concern different aspects. They work in different ways depending on the context. Scott (1992) uses the term negotiation when referring to a greater 'family of strategies' that a company or, more generally speaking, one actor uses to handle different dependencies. He states that negotiations do not really constitute the actual 'bridge building' between actors, but rather it should be seen as preparation for bridge building. A more concise and much more conventional definition has been given by Lax and Sebenius (1986):

> Negotiation is a process with potential opportunistic interaction, where two or more parties, with certain obvious conflict, try to create better conditions through joint decisions, compared to what they otherwise could have done.

Jonsson (1998) points out that the two authors in this definition do not make any distinction between negotiating and bargaining, a distinction that elsewhere is rather common. Bargaining is part of a process where the partners exchange different possible choices. That part of the negotiation process does of course imply giving and taking, which normally lead to both parties having to make concessions.

Another author, Kremenyuk (1991, p. 64), emphasizes a somewhat different aspect of the term negotiation. He sees it as a metaphor for resource allocation. A consequence of this is that the negotiation process, at least when it comes to bargaining, is about allocating a given collection of resources. The wider meaning of negotiation creates an opening for considering the possibility that the collection of resources can change.

## Negotiation as a zero-sum game or a win–win situation

In the literature on negotiation, for example Bazerman and Neale (1993) and Fisher and Ury (1981), it is common practice to divide negotiations into two main categories: distributive and integrative negotiations.

Distributive negotiation is characterized by usually only including one area to negotiate about, a given amount that can then be distributed between the parties. There is usually a risk in these situations that the result of negotiation will show a 'winner' and a 'loser'. Some of the key elements are as follows:

● Competition.
● Convincing the other party to make concessions.
● Bargaining.
● Claiming value.
● Focusing on evoking concessions.
● Win–lose negotiation.

Integrative negotiation, on the other hand, consists of a process that is created and carried out in such a way that both (or all) parties get a better result than in a distributed process. It is characterized by the parties trying to see the interesting possibilities of combination, synergies and creating win–win situations, results from which both (all) parties gain. This also means that the 'solutions' area can be widened or shrunk depending on the course of the process. It is in fact an important condition that both parties during the negotiations are able to identify possible new developments through an innovative combination of the activity structures and resources of the different parties. The more distinctive the parties' offers and resources are, the more relevant it seems to use integrative negotiation.

A contract based on integrative negotiation, where the foundation is more like a framework for how different aspects should be handled and analysed, becomes an agreement that indicates the boundaries and creates a platform for deciding on how different areas should be negotiated in the future. Some of the key elements are the following:

- Finding possibilities for attaining the goals of both parties.
- Problem solving.
- Cooperation.
- Increasing the overall advantages of existing relationships between the parties.
- Win–win negotiations.

The differences between the two types of negotiation strategies indicate that distributive negotiation best fits a purchasing philosophy and strategy that are aimed at using competition between suppliers (transaction-oriented buying, cf. Chapter 10), while integrative negotiation fits better with a strategy that is more cooperation and relation oriented.

Other alternative negotiation strategies include (Jonsson, 1998):

- *Yielding negotiation.* A yielding strategy is characterized by the fact that one (or all) of the parties is not very persistent in its claims (or its own interests). The negotiation is normally characterized by compliance and a readiness to accommodate the other party and the current situation. There are also attempts to get the other party to yield as well and lower their ambitions.
- *Min–max negotiation.* This is a variant that is influenced by all of the others. It is founded on the assumption that all parties have figured out the most and least profitable outcomes for them. The actual negotiation is then aimed at reaching some sort of compromise and finding solutions that provide both parties with an acceptable outcome. The process is the same whether the negotiation concerns a cooperation- or competition-oriented process.
- *Non-negotiation.* Buying without negotiation is not a real negotiation strategy, but is often used in the phase of 'closing the deal'. The parties have expressed their needs and possible solutions. One of the parties suggests a price and other conditions and the other party accepts without discussion.

Empirical studies show that distributive and integrative negotiations are the dominant strategies (Jonsson, 1998). Nevertheless, it should be emphasized that the variety of strategies between different firms is a reflection of different kinds of buying and marketing strategies, but also of different kinds of purchases, types of products, levels of complexity, scope of business etc. One reason for distributive and integrative strategies being the most common can also be that these (and non-negotiation) are more transparent and thus more easily identified than the yielding and min–max strategies. However, there is nothing to suggest that the various strategies cannot be combined, or that different phases of a negotiation process cannot be dominated by different strategies.

## The process of negotiation

Negotiation can be seen as an 'iceberg' (Carlisle and Parker, 1989), where all attention is directed towards what is said and debated in the dialogue between the parties. Below the surface, however, in preparing and creating the foundation for different calculations, during breaks in the negotiations and so on, important conditions for the contract are created.

A general condition in the negotiation process is the difference in the parties' offerings to each other. If the difference is zero, then there is congruence. In this case, one party's offer is the same as the other party's needs and an agreement can be reached. Until the difference reaches zero there is formally no agreement. It might be that an offer from one party is not answered with a uncomplicated yes or no, but new conditions are brought in. Such a process continues until the negotiation is broken, permanently or temporarily, or closed in such a way that an agreement can be reached. This process of sorting out the differences, moderating and finding possible solutions for coming closer until an agreement can be reached is often seen as the essence of negotiation.

The process can be very complex, difficult to handle and stretched out in time. Recall the presentation of the different methods of specifying services. It is, for example, not always the case that the parties are conscious of what the difference between them looks like. Nor is it always clear what the different offers look like, or if any agreements have been reached during the process. The process can, of course, also be simple, transparent and easy to handle.

There are several ways of describing negotiation processes. One description is *rational calculating*. This resembles a typical rational decision process with a number of steps: preparation, introduction, clarification of positions, bargaining, compromise and closure. Another model emphasizes the negotiation process as something *creative*. As the parties start to deepen their dialogue, possible new opportunities for combining activities and resources are discovered. The creative aspects are, among others, that the negotiating actors, in their dialogue, combine their thinking and their resources, out of which new solutions emerge. It should also be remembered that the interplay itself creates patterns. This has, for example, been convincingly demonstrated by Axelrod (1984) in his discussion of the 'prisoners' dilemma', demonstrating how tit-for-tat patterns emerge. If one party acts cooperatively the other is likely to respond cooperatively and vice versa.

## The result of the negotiation

The result of the negotiation is often described as a question of winning or losing, according to four alternatives: win–win, lose–lose, win–lose, lose–win. Win–win is an interesting case and is possibly the most common in successful integrative negotiations.

It is important to point out, however, that this view is a gross simplification. It does not always have to be a question of winning or losing. It can, for example, be at least as important to reflect on how the conduct of a negotiation influences the company's business in the future. A bad negotiation result, a lost negotiation, can still be an important step towards something better. A process may have been started even though the first step was too short.

It is also the case that a lost negotiation can still be an important element in gaining a relationship. A bad negotiation with a weak result can, in the often irrational processes of economic activities, prove to be of great value later on. It can quite simply be hard to know if a result really is good or bad, a win or a loss. The answer to such a question depends to a great extent on when the result is assessed. What seems like a failure today can from a longer perspective turn out to be the first step in a success story.

Bearing these reflections in mind, we can still ask the 'win–lose question': what is it that can explain the result of the negotiation process? We will limit this discussion to three factors: bargaining power, negotiation strategy, and disposition and tactics of the negotiation.

### Bargaining power

There are always more or less important differences in negotiating power between a customer and a supplier. The customer who buys a large portion of the supplier's production, without being particularly dependent on this supplier, is in a good position for negotiating. The customer who has many business areas and who succeeds in coordinating its buying needs (volume coordination) has a stronger negotiating position than the customer who does not do this.

There are also other power bases, such as different kinds of information advantages. Sako (1992) is talking in those terms when she points out that there is a strong information asymmetry between the parties when they are buying in competition. This is one reason for there being such high expectations that e-commerce will make markets more 'perfect'. In a totally transparent marketplace, all actors should be able to get the same information, thus eliminating information asymmetries (cf. Chapter 6).

Another aspect, which in certain contexts influences the distribution of bargaining power, is how critical the time aspect can be for a product. The customer who needs an important service immediately has a much worse bargaining position than one who can wait. Yet another aspect that can influence bargaining power is if the company is working below capacity or not. The supplier who has a lot of work to do and is using its full capacity can be expected to be less inclined to make concessions than under different circumstances. This is related to the price discussion above: time-based prices are often relevant in services, not least because of the difficulty of storing them.

### Negotiation strategy

Generally speaking, it is hard to say what the choice of any of the five strategies discussed earlier would imply for the results of the negotiation. Nevertheless, it is obvious that it plays an important part, since each strategy focuses on different aspects. The distributive and integrative negotiation strategies in particular should, as they focus on different aspects, lead to different negotiation results.

*Negotiation conduct and tactics*
There are several theoretical and, of course, many practical experiences of suitable methods for conducting a good negotiation. It is to a large extent a question of technique. Let us illustrate this by referring to some of Jonsson's discussions (1998).

A common starting point is to decide how low or high the initial bid should be to reach the best possible price level when the agreement is signed. From a buying point of view, the important part is to get the most beneficial conditions (low price) possible. What tactic should be used? The following are examples of tactical moves:

a) One very common tactic, based on the hypothesis that the lower the customer's initial bid the lower the final price will be, is to start with a low initial bid. Connected to this are often different goals for retreat. These may be quantitatively specified and based on the concept that the contract should end up somewhere between the two parties' initial bids. 'Let us meet half-way' is not an unusual formulation.

b) Another tactic, based on the hypothesis that the longer the preparation the better the result will be, is to thoroughly prepare the entire negotiation and think through all possible variants, as in a game of chess.

c) A third tactic, based on the hypothesis that the longer the negotiating time a negotiator can use the better the result will be, is to allow plenty of time. In this way the negotiator can keep the other party waiting and stressed, and thus more accommodating.

d) A fourth tactic, based on the hypothesis that you like the people you associate with and that those who feel sympathy have more difficulty in being hard on each other, is to work according to the principle 'good guy, bad guy'. The good guy seeks, for example by being interested in and having knowledge about different issues, to achieve and maintain an unconditional and problem-solving discussion. He is complemented in the negotiation by the bad guy who, often at the end of the negotiation, comes in and bargains with a substantially rougher attitude about the issues at stake.

These kinds of tactical manoeuvres have been tested scientifically in different situations. Tactic A, for example, displayed a statistically significant result when buying a used car. Tactics A and C have been shown to be successful when buying an agricultural implement (Min *et al.*, 1995). Which tactic is successful always depends on the circumstances, including the qualifications of the negotiating individuals. But it does not seem unreasonable that these tactics, especially A, will be effective, particularly in distributive negotiations. Jonsson (1998) also points out that an integrative negotiation, distinguished by a cooperation-oriented view, is often conducted totally different under completely different conditions (Carlisle and Parker, 1989).

## Analysing the room for price negotiations in a customer–supplier relationship

It is possible, in principle, to illustrate how different powers are at work in a price negotiation (see Figure 9.4). If the value to the customer of service 1 from supplier A is represented by point VA1, while the costs for A to produce this service can be represented by point CA1, the distance between CA1 and VA1 represents the room for negotiating in which both parties can distribute the 'profits'.

However, this purchasing situation may be complicated when the market in the form of one or more alternative suppliers is taken into consideration. The service may be identical with identical costs for producing it. In that case, the customer has a good opportunity to force the price to a level near the supplier's costs. It is also possible that different suppliers' costs are identical, but the value to the customer of A1 and A2 is different. This also affects the room for negotiation, but it does not have to mean that the customer selects the service with the highest value, because that supplier may want to keep a larger part of the 'surplus'.

In Figure 9.4 the situation is even more complicated. Both suppliers offer different services that have different value to the customer. Additionally, the suppliers have different costs (CA2 versus CA1) in producing the respective services. There may be many different outcomes of such a situation.

Problems to consider are that value and costs are not always easy to calculate; some aspects may be difficult to translate into numbers (economic values) while they still need to be factored in (and sometimes weigh very heavy), and also the time aspect plays a role. What happens to cost structures and value estimates in the short run when conditions change?

Despite these concerns, which may indeed have a strong impact, a combination of value analysis as discussed earlier and along the lines given here may offer, in a specific situation, some guidelines for understanding the conditions for price setting and for the parties involved to come to an agreement regarding price (Anderson and Narus, 1998).

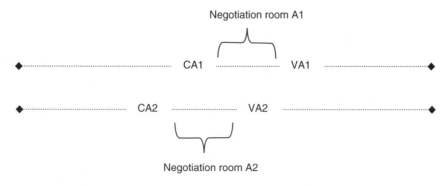

**Figure 9.4** Negotiation room that arises due to the customer's and supplier's respective alternatives

Negotiation is a meaningful activity within the field of purchasing. Fortunately, there is a reasonable amount of knowledge and understanding on how negotiations are performed, what influences the result of the negotiation and what effects can be achieved by a chosen negotiation strategy. An especially important notion is that two general purchasing strategies, transaction oriented and relation oriented (Chapter 10), have their counterparts in distributive and integrative negotiation.

## Payment principles

We have now discussed price, the method of price setting and negotiation strategies as the main elements in contracting business services. We have not yet addressed the principles of payment, or the form of the contract, which are also important. Some common alternatives are a running account, a fixed price or the customer's savings or additional earning capabilities as a starting point. Apparently, there is a clear difference in payment principles for transactions that involve activities that take the form of a project limited in time and will lead to some form of problem solution, and those that take the form of a continuing service, in which case the suppliers have the responsibility for a specific function during a certain period.

In the first case, two payment principles exist: a fixed-price, 'lump-sum' contract, where customer and supplier agree on what should be done and what that may cost; or a 'running account', where customer and supplier agree on a price per unit of time or per activity while the volume (number of days, person-months or similar) is not fixed.

A special variant of the lump-sum contract is the no-cure, no-pay contract, where a supplier will only be paid if the service is successfully executed, i.e. the desired result is achieved (see Boxes 9.12 and 9.14). This payment principle bears a close relationship to the method of specifying output or even outcome (cf. Chapter 7) and the actual level of the lump sum is often determined using some form of value-based pricing.

---

**Box 9.14  No cure, no pay: shipwreck recovery**

Although it has never been a large part of its overall business, Dutch shipping and towing company Wijsmuller has acquired its label 'Dutch Pride' largely on the basis of its shipwreck recovery activities. In the early 1970s, Wijsmuller earned this reputation by being the only firm to offer to recover the bulk carrier *Elwood Meade* off the cliffs of Guernsey on a 'no cure, no pay' basis. Wijsmuller took the contract by signing a Lloyds Open Form and collected, after a successful operation, the equivalent of around €8 million – enough to avoid a pending bankruptcy. In addition, during the Iran–Iraq war in the early 1980s, a new golden era for companies such as Wijsmuller, it was one of the major players in recovering burning oil tankers (*NRC Handelsblad*, 10 October 2001).

Both the lump-sum and running account principles have advantages and disadvantages for the customer and the supplier. A common perception is that it is to the customer's advantage to agree on a specified function for a fixed price. It is seen as an alternative to avoid unpleasant surprises. Similarly, it is argued that a running account is to the supplier's advantage, since every effort spent and activity performed result in compensation. However, these opinions are not beyond dispute and are not always correct. This may be illustrated with the following quotes from a practitioner.

---

**Box 9.15   Which is cheapest, running account or fixed price?**

'I work in a project-intensive company. Over the years, projects with a fixed price have proven to give us the best returns and not the projects that are done on the basis of a running account.

This depends, among other things, on the fact that we always try to create a certain latitude to handle unexpected complications. But the most important reason is that fixed-price projects require more exact specifications: what should be done, what should not be done? However, as these projects are complex, situations will always arise that could not be covered in the specifications. At every such occasion complements are necessary and these are good occasions for us to improve our narrow margins. This is always done in close collaboration with the customer, but the financial consequences of a number of such alterations and additions are often quite significant. If I were a customer, I would always – contrary to common understanding – choose running accounts for this type of projects.'

---

This illustration outlines the trade-off between complexity and the ability to predict the consequences of a project in choosing a payment principle. It also shows that 'simple truths' do not always hold.

An interesting approach could be to contract an intermediary, a purchasing expert, who can represent the buyer. This creates new conditions for the payment principle, as illustrated in the following example.

---

**Box 9.16   Using an intermediary during the negotations can affect the form of payment**

A purchasing manager with extensive experience explains that he currently chooses to 'buy competencies', e.g. to deal with complex IT transactions, rather than, as previously, to carry out the negotiations himself. Experience has shown that there is insufficient ability within the company to specify in great detail the basis for the negotiations. Therefore, at some point a decision was made to buy this type of project on the basis of running accounts. Recently, this has been stopped in favour of buying through an expert. 'We now buy a system integrator that is competent enough to effectively buy, on our assignment, these complex services at a fixed price,' states the purchasing manager.

---

For assignments that are more permanent in nature, payment forms can vary in other ways. The following four principles are examples of how payment arrangements between parties can be structured:

- *No complicated payments.* This implies that the services are offered in a non-differentiated way. The customer has access to all the services that are available. The supplier is compensated by high average margins. This is communicated to customers with the argument that they avoid having to monitor all kinds of complicated details.
- *Package offerings.* Customers, all or within a certain segment, pay a fixed amount per year to have a package of services, e.g. an annual contract for a selection of services from a security company.
- *Pay for consumption.* All customers pay for what they use. Expensive customers that use a large amount of the services offered are not subsidized by cheap customers. The supplier sets prices and is paid for each individual service or service component.
- *Loyalty principle.* In return for certain favours such as a large buying volume, big or otherwise profitable customers avoid certain payments or obtain rebates for various additional services.

A special variety of the loyalty principle, which is especially applicable to long-lasting service exchanges, is the 'bonus/penalty' arrangement, according to which a customer pays a premium if its behaviour creates extra costs for the supplier, and receives a rebate if it behaves in a cost-reducing manner (Box 9.17). These kinds of arrangements nicely illustrate the interactive nature of (most) business services.

---

**Box 9.17   Reward for rapid deployment of temporary employees**

In February 2000, the Dutch Railways (Nederlandse Spoorwegen, NS) announced an innovative contract system for temporary employees. The NS and four employment agencies agreed to an incentive contract that included bonuses for the rapid deployment of temporary workers and a penalty for any delays.

The NS spends about €35 million annually on temporary labour. With the new contract, the NS wanted to enforce a high quality and rapid availability of temporary workers. Neither reducing costs nor the tight labour market were the main reasons for this new system. 'When we need temporary workers, we want them working as soon as possible,' said a spokesperson. Normally temporary staff agencies receive a margin irrespective of the quality of the service they deliver. Under the new contract, the agencies' reward can differ by at most 50 per cent of the normal tariff. The contract with the NS was the first agreement that the agencies reached with a large body such as the Dutch railway company. Because the agencies thought that price-differentiating contracts are relevant to large companies with a fluctuating need for temporary labour, they were convinced that more similar contracts would be established in the future.

The financial incentive was supposed to induce temporary labour agencies to establish a quick service. Because the NS, with the new system, is encouraged to plan the need for temporary workers more effectively, the agencies expected a great advantage. The NS can save a lot of money when it places its request for temporary labour in a timely way. Temporary workers needed for only a short period of time are more expensive than those who are longer seconded to the NS.

Another advantage is that the NS was to use only those four agencies with which the contract was established, although previously only 70 per cent of total temporary labour was requested from these suppliers. The frame contract stimulated the NS to use only these parties as suppliers of temporary labor.

**July 2000: innovative temporary labour contract cancelled**
In July 2000, although all parties expected great advantages from it, the new frame contract with financial consequences for the quick delivery of temporary labour was ended. In practice, the contract was found to have the opposite effect. 'The new system didn't come off the ground as we expected and the plans have been mothballed,' said a NS spokesman. 'Currently we are thinking of adaptations.'

The financial penalty for not delivering temporary labour on time turned out to be counter-productive. 'There is no or just little incentive to second workers to the NS. Because of the penalty regulation in the contract, agencies tend to second the employees to other companies,' said the spokesperson. The railway company itself is not ready for this way of contracting. The agencies hoped to stimulate the NS to better plan its needs for temporary labour. The main problem is that the railway company suffers from too many decentralized units who are themselves responsible for contracting employment agencies. That is why the NS cooperates with more than 50 different agencies. The four contracted agencies and the NS management wanted to force all units to work with those four agencies. The unsuccessful bonus/penalty system is a real disappointment for the agencies involved. They had hoped that the system would become a new trend in temporary labour.

*Source*: *Financieel Dagblad*, various articles, February and July 2000.

The unsuccessful outcome of this payment arrangement demonstrates that, apart from issues around centralized/decentralized buying at the customer, it is important to consider such an arrangement and its effects in the larger context of other customer/supplier relationships that parties involved may have (cf. Chapter 11).

Above all, this section has shown that pricing is not only a matter of agreeing on a certain price level, but has an additional important aspect to do with the payment principles involved.

## Conclusions

Price is always a significant issue in business transactions. There are many important techniques and principles for price setting, some of which have been discussed in this chapter. What is the 'right' price and what is the most appropriate method for determining this price vary from situation to situation. At the same time, it is important to note that many services are heterogeneous and therefore difficult to compare. In those cases value analysis – quantifying the (monetary) worth of a service offered by a specific supplier – is an important tool to apply. This method is technically speaking more difficult to use than the others, but it can nevertheless be carried out according to systematic methods outlined in this chapter and described elsewhere.

Negotiations are likewise an essential part of most businesses. Different strategies and techniques are not equally well fitted to all situations. The integrative method might be better suited to complex, multidimensional transactions, while the distributive approach fits more with a standardized service. There might also be a strong connection between pricing and negotiating strategies. It is likely that integrative strategies often accompany value-based pricing methods.

Another specific aspect of services that affects price setting and principles of payment is the difficulty of storing services. This implies that periodic offers, because they are *available during specific periods*, become more important than in the case of pricing goods.

Despite these concerns with the specific nature of pricing services, our discussion has tried to illustrate that the general underlying principles for setting prices are also relevant to services.

# Part IV

## Reflection

# 10

# Transaction-oriented and Relation-oriented Purchasing

Much of the recent debate in the area of purchasing and supply management has focused on two more or less opposite forms of purchasing behaviour: *transaction oriented* and *relation oriented*. These two forms of behaviour have also been referred to as the 'classical purchasing philosophy' and the 'modern purchasing philosophy'. The difference between purchasing behaviour that is transaction (competition) oriented on the one hand and purchasing behaviour that is relation (collaboration) oriented on the other hand can be illustrated as in Table 10.1.

What is the line of reasoning for each of these philosophies? What are the advantages and disadvantages of adopting one view or the other? In what ways are the pros and cons especially important, related to purchasing business services? These questions are the focus of this chapter.

## Transaction-oriented purchasing philosophy

The transactional view of purchasing behaviour is represented by the key words in the left-hand column of Table 10.1. The buying company strives to have access

**Table 10.1**  Transaction vs relation-oriented purchasing behaviour

| Transactional approach | Relational approach |
| --- | --- |
| Many alternatives | One or few alternatives |
| Every deal is a new business, no one should benefit from past performances | A deal is part of a relationship and the relationship is part of a network context |
| Exploit the potential of competition | Exploit the potential of cooperation |
| Short term; arm's length, avoid coming too close | Long term with tough demands and joint development |
| Renewal and effectiveness by change of partner, choose the most efficient supplier at any time | Renewal and effectiveness by collaboration and 'team effects', combine resources and knowledge |
| Buying 'products' | Buying 'capabilities' |
| → Price orientation, strong in achieving favourable prices in well-specified products | → Cost and value orientation, strong in achieving low total costs of supply and developing new values |

to several different suppliers. Competition between the suppliers leads to them always being willing to do their best. In this way, vitality and quality are fostered at the same time as the prices are kept as low as possible. Another important aspect is to keep the suppliers at a distance, so that strict demands can be maintained over time.

The development of the purchasing function, as touched on earlier (Chapter 1), has led to the creation of an alternative to this transactional view. The alternative, relation-oriented view is characterized by the key words presented in the right-hand column of Table 10.1. Cooperation and long-term relationships are emphasized and the goal is to achieve the lowest costs possible: not only a low price for the actual product purchased, but recognizing many other important costs. We will touch on a few differences between these two models.

In the transactional purchasing model, there is a relatively clear notion of what a rational purchase should look like. First the need, in terms of product or service, must be established. Then a number of potential suppliers will be approached and subsequently compared. Finally the best alternative will be chosen. By using competition between the alternative suppliers, the buyer will get the best conditions, as in the following illustration.

---

**Box 10.1  Stockholm City Council saves 6.5 million a year by using open competition**

For some years Locum, Stockholm city council's estate company, has used open competition for deciding who should get to manage about a fifth of the owned estate.

This has been achieved by Locum's creating a company that has been allowed to compete with private companies for the management of certain hospitals and care centres. An external evaluation has shown that competition has decreased management costs by some 20–30 per cent. At the same time, the evaluation also shows that quality has been maintained at the same level as before. The competition has, however, also meant that Locum has decreased its personnel considerably since the company was formed, from 1100 to 600.

These figures testify to the strength of the transactional purchasing model. It is logical and can give very powerful effects. But in spite of this, it has its weaknesses.

The model can be seen as a logical effect of market thinking where every actor can be seen as free and independent in a market. The market is assumed to contain several actors, purchasers and sellers. From this perspective, efficiency is created *within* every company, with certain restrictions given by the prices on factor (input) and product (output) markets. Efficiency in purchasing is created by the company's acting rationally in every decision, as described above, and using the market mechanisms. It is all about choosing right in every situation – right product, right moment of delivery, right quality, right supplier etc.

The rationality of the model is built on a number of assumptions about the functionality of the marketplace. One of these concerns supply and demand. In the transactional model, these two forces are seen to be well known and matching. In other words, it is assumed that there are suppliers that offer the product requested by the purchasing company – and in the way the purchaser wishes. This is the same as saying that other companies exist with identical needs and wishes to the purchasing firm.

Another assumption is about the conditions that it is important to influence, e.g. how revenues can be increased and costs decreased. In the transactional purchasing model, interest is solely directed outwards, towards the suppliers. Cost pressure on the suppliers is the driving ambition. This is created through lining up the alternatives (i.e. the suppliers) against each other – the customer plays the market.

A third assumption, closely related to the discussion of cost pressure, is the view of which cost factors are relevant. The function of the purchased product or service is standardized, since it is assumed to be offered to and demanded by a number of customers. In addition, the customer's internal costs, which are linked to the purchase, are also assumed to be independent of the chosen product and thereby not to have an influence on the choice of supplier. The price will, under these circumstances, be the only variable that can be influenced at the decision moment (Håkansson, 1989).

The transactional model has certain effects on the company's purchasing behaviour. Some of these are intended and desired, others unintended and undesired. The relation-oriented purchasing model therefore denotes an attempt to reduce the unwanted effects, but also to adapt the behaviour to the new conditions for purchasing discussed previously.

One effect of the transactional view of purchasing can be illustrated by the advice that is often given to purchasers: 'Buy as close to the source and as far back in the supply chain as possible.' Intermediaries are seen as cost drivers and a way of receiving a reduced price is to purchase from the manufacturer directly. This has resulted in a number of administrative and warehousing activities in the purchasing company. The purchaser has taken over the service functions that are normally handled by the intermediary. The number of suppliers with which the customer has direct contact increases and the customer must conduct a considerable amount of coordination work.

Another effect is that the supplier is seen as an opponent to which it is dangerous to come too close. Suppliers should be held at arm's length. It should be possible to switch suppliers at any moment. Independence is seen as a central prerequisite for long-term efficiency.

A third effect is that when discontented, one switches suppliers and chooses a new supplier from the market, without discussing how the present supplier should improve. Yet another effect is that the focus is placed on each actor's own internal costs, not on what could be achieved through teamwork with the purpose of, for example, developing efficient routines for joint administration and quality control.

In conclusion, it can be stated that the transactional view of purchasing has some indisputably strong elements but also several drawbacks. The question is how an alternative view of purchasing could work and in what context the different pros and cons are particularly important.

## Relation-oriented purchasing philosophy

The relation-oriented purchasing model breaks many of the transactional purchasing model's more or less clearly outspoken rules. An important starting point is that the price should not predominantly reflect the given production conditions at the purchaser or seller, but instead the entire functional relationship between customer and supplier. The cost of a product or a function, e.g. the supply of certain materials to a producing unit, is incurred successively, in step with the activities that are needed to order, produce, package and distribute it at various stages: warehousing, transport within the buying company, using the product, taking care of left-over material, invoicing, controlling invoices etc. Some of these costs arise at the producer, others at the distributor and others at the user. When all these costs have been accumulated, the chain of activities has reached a final and total cost.

If the customer purchases in a certain way, wants a certain method of delivery or a particular kind of product (e.g. standard or customized) or a certain delivery time or service, this will have great implications for both the producer and the distributor as well as for the user. The magnitude of the costs can vary, depending on which of the actors is doing which activity. The costs of the total function can also vary because of different possibilities for organizing the required activities. This may also mean that totally different systems can be developed in the interaction between the supplier and the customer. It often becomes clear that, among other things, many of the activities are carried out twice, e.g. when both the supplier and the user test the quality of the products. Such waste could be eliminated by the relation-oriented approach.

From this standpoint, it can easily be questioned whether the price of the product would be the only cost factor to minimize. The result of the supplier's offer should, from this perspective, instead be seen as a result of organizing the total value chain and linking it to exchanges in a number of dimensions, including the costs that follow from using a certain supplier. To make optimal use of the resources that the supplier has available, there are strong elements of long-term thinking in the relation-oriented view. To be able to use all the supplier's capabilities and resources and for it to be able to combine its knowledge and resources in the best way with those held by the buying company, a long-term commitment is usually required.

The relation-oriented view on purchasing can thus be characterized by the following:

- *Long-term perspective*. It is important to choose those suppliers with which the company wants to collaborate over a longer period. Furthermore, the importance of selection and decision making before each purchasing situation is downplayed. Normally, most suppliers are also already involved in other business transactions. There are, in other words, in the short term no available alternatives in the market. It also becomes more important to solve possible problems within the existing relationship, rather than switching to a new supplier.
- *Width*. A number of functional specialists are involved in the supplier relationship, partly because of the more complex content but also to maintain the pressure, or the vitality, in the relationship.
- *Adaptation*. Buyers and sellers develop, so that better cooperation can be achieved, a system within which a number of product, service and behavioural adjustments are made.
- *Technical content*. Buyer–seller relationships often have considerable technical content. The supplier can play a substantial role in product and process development. Between 20 and 25 per cent of the manufacturing industry's technical development takes place through collaboration with suppliers (Håkansson, 1989; Wynstra, 1998).
- *Cooperation*. To achieve the desired effects of the relation-oriented view of purchasing, cooperation is required. Without cooperation it is hard to achieve an optimal combination of the resources of the different parties. Cooperation does not have to mean *tameness*, however; on the contrary. Cooperation and conflict often go hand in hand as creators of dynamic and developing relations (see Laage-Hellman, 1989; and Figure 10.3).

Overall, this approach is about being able to utilize and exploit the heterogeneity in the market, i.e. the differences in the resources (including capabilities) that each actor possesses. The more these resources are created through human competence, the more dependent the result will be on which supplier (with its human competencies) the customer chooses to cooperate with. Likewise, each actor is committed to others in different combinations and thereby has varied access to external resource constellations. This contributes to making each supplier more or less unique as partner. This new way of purchasing has gained more and more ground since the 1980s.

The relation-oriented view of purchasing is founded on the notion that companies within a framework of long-term cooperation are able to save costs and also to create improvements in other aspects. Consider these illustrations.

---

**Box 10.2   Relation-oriented purchasing of financial services**

ABB has an explicit strategy for purchasing financial services. The company wants to decrease the number of suppliers. It wants to have a limited number of banks that can provide service all over the world. In addition, the company is willing to accept a limited number of local suppliers in different countries.

This purchasing philosophy has mostly arisen from debate around the concept of indirect costs. It is expensive to maintain an active and dynamic relationship with a supplier. If the number of suppliers is limited these costs will also be limited. Think of all the supplier representatives who are visiting ABB units all over the country. If it is known that only representatives from a few banks are welcome, this will save a lot of time for many people. The company is ready to pay the price: the risk of missing certain interesting offers. A coordinated general agreement, where the ABB group's purchasing power is used to create the basic conditions for cooperation with selected suppliers, and the savings in working hours are seen to compensate well for the possible risks of losing a great deal.

---

This example is a good illustration of savings on different indirect costs. The potential for value-increasing development that the relation-oriented view of purchasing creates is at least as interesting. Through cooperation the parties can jointly develop their common purpose, as demonstrated in the following examples.

---

**Box 10.3   Joint value creation through relation-oriented purchasing**

**Telia's clean-up of advertising agencies**
Telecom operator Telia has decided to reduce the number of advertising agencies the group hires in order to, among other things, facilitate the creation of a more homogeneous profile. Having fewer suppliers increases the possibility of coordinating activities and communication.

**NCC's purchase of education and other competence development services**
At Swedish construction company NCC, the in-house management development department, NCC University, has a rather selective collaboration profile within the education area. The manager of the NCC University chooses, in collaboration with

internal customers, certain partners and cooperates with these over a considerable period. The purpose is to create, in the best way possible, joint development over time. The advantage for NCC is that the selected partners have a very clear incentive to monitor the company's development and also successively to collect examples. The advantages for the suppliers are that they gain a certain stability in their work and they can invest more time in becoming a better resource for the specific customer.

Other companies have other purchasing profiles. The disadvantage of the method described above is the lack of possibilities to play suppliers against each other and in that way always to get the best offer. The principal of the NCC University emphasizes that, as in most cases, there is no definite right and wrong in this kind of question. Nevertheless, he does emphasize that it is important for these questions to be put and considered in a conscious way so that the company is aware of the complexity of the matter. Furthermore, he also argues that for a service that is as complex and multidimensional as this one, the chosen method is probably the most beneficial. Another advantage is that the customer is more likely to learn what the suppliers' specialisms are and can thus put appropriate demands on each supplier.

Generally, it can be said that the resources of a single company are very small in comparison to the company's environment, even in the case of very large companies. To link the company's own resources and knowledge, in the best way possible, with the resources in the external environment is an important issue.

When considering attitudes to how one should work, it is probable that the change from the left-hand column to the right-hand column in Table 10.1 has been very striking during the last decade or so. This is not the case only in Europe but also in a number of other countries, including the US (see among others Helper, 1991). Many of these changes can be illustrated with statistical data (see among others Gadde and Håkansson, 2001; Brandes *et al.*, 1999). Other indications of change are the expressions of attitudes that many purchasing managers seem to agree on. In spite of altered attitudes and stated changes in behaviour, we may nevertheless not have come as far as some followers of the relation-oriented view have expected. A Swedish study by Jonsson (1998) shows that the dominant view of purchasing is still the transactional one. In addition, in a set of experiments Anderson *et al.* (2000) found that American purchasing managers often still base their purchasing decisions on price rather than on product value (quality).

As suggested earlier, it is definitely not a question of right and wrong when discussing the purchasing function's different methods. At the same time, however, it seems as if the right-hand column with the new line of thinking is more often right today than it was earlier – and is becoming right increasingly often. Generally, it can be said that the new mode of purchasing becomes more right when the indirect costs increase. Indirect costs can appear, for example, in the form of purchasing (transaction) costs, transport, warehousing, waste, rejections and so on. The larger the direct costs, i.e. the costs associated with the actual (well-defined) product or service, the more relevant the transactional view becomes (see Håkansson and Wootz, 1984). Nevertheless, it is also important to point out that the judgement is not only about costs. The two views of purchasing imply different effects in terms of value creation, which we will discuss in more depth later.

## Efficiency in supplier relationships

In Gadde and Håkansson (1993, p. 168) a mathematical expression is formulated to define what kind of costs and revenues should be considered when the economic effects of collaboration with a supplier are to be judged (see Box 10.4).

---

**Box 10.4    The pluses and minuses of a purchasing calculation**

The expression is as follows:

$$V_i = R_i - TC_i$$

Where

$V_i$ = the value of using supplier i
$R_i$ = the revenues in different dimensions, which supplier i creates for the buying company
$TC_i$ = the total cost of using supplier i

The expression only shows that the value of using a supplier equals all positive effects minus the negative effects (the costs). The total cost can be divided into one internal and one external part, that is:

$$TC_i = EC_i + I_{ci}$$

Where

$EC_i$ = the total cost to be paid externally (price + freight, insurance etc.)
$IC_i$ = the costs that arise internally when handling the supplier relationship, i.e. cost of negotiations, contacts, invoice administration etc.
   The total expression will thus appear as:

$$V_i = R_i - EC_i - IC_i$$

Gadde and Håkansson point out that the transaction-oriented mode of purchasing, explicitly or not, assumes that $R_i$ and $IC_i$ are revenues and costs that are equally high (or low) for all possible suppliers. This way of working recommends that the differences in these circumstances are to be minimized before any purchase decision is taken. In the relation-oriented mode of purchasing, all these factors can be influenced and thus are important to consider and work on.

---

Even though it is relatively simple to make this kind of calculation, it must be pointed out that many of these costs and revenues are hard to measure in practice. This is even clearer when considering that, while some costs and revenues can have a considerable impact in the short run, many of them have their full impact only in the long run. An illustration of the different types of costs, which will be used in a later discussion of the two views of purchasing, is given in Figure 10.1.

*Indirect costs* are hard to judge and may consist of the following:

- Basic costs of handling the supplier relationship and the supplier market: contact costs for handling a relationship, general administrative costs of different kinds etc.
- Costs and other effects of the exchange itself: quality problems, e.g. disturbances in quality, warehousing costs, effects of production-adapted purchases, development and product development effects (costs, results) etc.
- Operational costs relating to the purchasing process: number of individuals within the purchasing function, qualifications of these individuals and the cost of having them, time consumption, productivity etc.

An important first issue when deciding what approach should be taken is to try to judge the distribution among direct and indirect costs in relation to the purchase of a certain function. What type of costs is dominant?

Normally, there are reasons to presume that large indirect costs and/or large savings opportunities in indirect costs speak in favour of a relation-oriented purchasing strategy. On the other hand, dominant direct costs and/or savings opportunities, such as direct decreases in price, speak in favour of a transactional purchasing strategy. The latter strategy can efficiently reduce prices for a well-defined product. The former strategy can, as a result of cooperation, better handle the other values (indirect costs).

However, it is not enough to answer that question. Another important, complementary question is: 'Which of these costs is most easily influenced?' Even though the direct costs are dominant, it can be the case that the largest potential for improvement can be in the indirect costs (see Box 10.5).

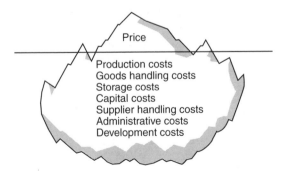

**Figure 10.1**  Total costs: price and indirect costs

*Source*: Gadde and Håkansson, 2001, p. 8.

> ### Box 10.5   What is most easily influenced?
>
> The direct costs in an organization are judged to constitute about 70 per cent of the total costs (effects). Within the company, the judgement is that these costs/effects only can be improved by 5 per cent, since there have already been considerable efforts in these areas. The 30 per cent indirect costs, on the other hand, can possibly be improved by 25 per cent or more, which leads to the conclusion that efforts that decrease these indirect costs should have a higher priority.

Even then, there are still two aspects that should be discussed before a stand can be taken on which view of purchasing is 'the best'. The first is, as mentioned before, that a business exchange around a functional process is not only about different kinds of costs; it is also about creating value. In many cases, additional value can be created through collaboration, for example in the form of new products or work methods, without this having to be connected to different kinds of cost rationalization. These kinds of value also need to be analysed. Generally, it is argued that they can be viewed from two perspectives. The first focuses on the possibilities for creating so-called team effects by realizing that cooperation can create value. The other view holds that a switch of suppliers also can introduce new ideas that would not have happened otherwise (cf. the discussion on outsourcing in Chapter 4). This means that each view on purchasing also becomes ideological. What effects, what kind of dynamics do the managers believe is of higher value?

Finally, it is important to establish that the choice of an approach is also a question of competence. The two approaches to purchasing require different competencies at the buying company. It is not necessarily the case that the purchasing manager and his or her associates can change their working behaviour from one day to another. If the purchasing approach in question is to achieve the desired effect, the purchasing organization should have adequate competencies for the tasks that are to be performed.

The conclusion is that the question of which view is right in a single case is dependent on the following question: 'Which costs are *most easily influenced by us, in our specific situation*, and are we *capable of exploiting* that potential?' This is illustrated in Figure 10.2.

Different measures, which can be in line either with the transaction-oriented and/or the relation-oriented mode of working, will give different effects in different organizations. The reason for this is that the conditions are different in each case, which is something that can be expected to affect the relative shares and the improvement potentials of the direct and the indirect costs, as shown above. But it also depends on the competencies within the various purchasing functions. The result will be that different companies will, as Figure 10.2 shows, demonstrate different *cost–benefit curves* for the effects that the implemented changes can be expected to have.

The illustration of the ability and potential for improvement also means that what is unique today most probably will be standard tomorrow. In the process,

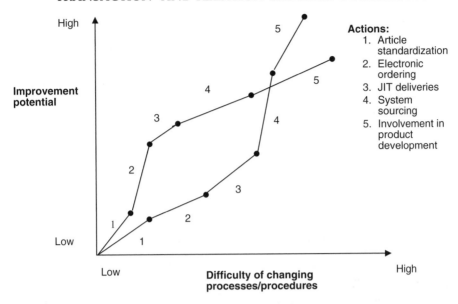

**Figure 10.2** Relationship between improvement potential and difficulty of changing processes/procedures for two suppliers

members of the company will learn – even those working in the purchasing function!

## The efficiency of the relation-oriented view of purchasing: an additional comment

Not all partners are equal. This is obvious if we think about different kinds of service production. Collaboration with consultancy firm X will give a different result to collaboration with consultancy firm Y. Furthermore, we also know that the chance that consultancy firm X will understand our specific situation and that we will know what the supplier can do to help us is greater if we have previous experience with each other. The partners have learned about each other's situation and can adapt and develop their resources accordingly. There are, of course, also instances in which the 'incentives' go in the opposite direction, so that the established supplier becomes too sure of keeping the customer and thus does not do its best.

This is an important issue. It is a common objection that stable relationships become a market imperfection. The supplier is presumed to become more and more complacent and does not commit itself to do its best. In the long run, this becomes harmful. Therefore, it is important that the actors in the market, according to this view, continuously keep the marketplace alive through switching suppliers as soon as something better appears. However, what does the problem really look like? Is it harmful or not to have long-term relationships?

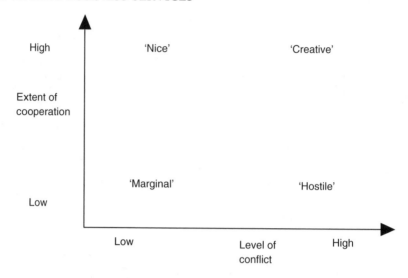

**Figure 10.3** The different characteristics of relationships
*Source*: Gadde and Håkansson, 2001, p. 105.

A first objection is that long-term relationships often are everything but 'nice'. There is a risk of being too nice if the companies do not have any pressure to develop, such as competition, demanding customers or pushy suppliers. Gadde and Håkansson (2001) discuss relationships in terms of cooperation and conflict. They combine these dimensions in the matrix in Figure 10.3.

According to this figure, business relationships can be characterized in two dimensions: cooperation and conflict. Both the level of cooperation and the level of conflict can be either high or low. When the dimensions are combined four situations arise: marginal, nice, hostile and creative. Experience shows that relationships where the demands are very high, there are many issues to cooperate on and also a lot to have possible conflicts about are the strongest or most significant relationships (Gadde and Håkansson, 2001). It is in these relationships that the really big improvements take place.

It is important to point out that the choice between a transaction-oriented and a relation-oriented mode of work will not mean that the other can be totally neglected. The so-called French fries syndrome is a warning for those who work according to a relation-oriented view of purchasing.

---

**Box 10.6   The French fries syndrome**

Since industrial companies are often imbedded in a system of businesses, changes in one part of the system will have impacts on other parts. An illustration of this is the French fries syndrome (Van Weele, 2000). If the harvest is bad one year, the supply of potatoes will decrease. This means that the potato farmer will compensate by raising the price per kilo. The following stages in the supply chain accept this since it reflects an existing market situation. Eventually, after the various stages in the supply chain (the potatoes become French fries, are stored and transported etc.), the final consumer is faced with an increase in the price of French fries.

The next year the harvest is normal. The potato farmer must then accept a lower price per kilo. Again, this reflects the laws of demand and supply on the raw material market and the potato price is probably also reduced in the nearest stages in the supply chain. But when customers get to their local takeaway chip shop, the price level is probably unchanged. The elasticity in the system is generally high when it comes to increasing prices but substantially lower the other way round.

Another important effect, which speaks against the relation-oriented view of purchasing, is lock-in, as illustrated in Box 10.7.

**Box 10.7    In a changing world, who dares to lock themselves in?**

A purchasing manager in an electromechanical company describes his philosophy. 'There is a growing debate on the advantages of well-developed collaborations, and that we can learn so much through cooperating with our suppliers. This may be so. But what happens if our partner does not follow the technical developments? How can a chosen supplier be the best choice for us over a longer time period in an industry that is developing as rapidly as ours and is as diverse as ours? My philosophy is therefore to always keep your back free, to always be able to use the suppliers that are at the leading edge, without being locked in to some kind of alliance.'

## Purchasing philosophy and buying business services

A natural question in a book about buying business services and in which services are characterized according to a number of categories is whether it is possible to say which view on purchasing is the best for purchasing different services.

A first step in discussing this question is to return to the classification of different kinds of services suggested in Chapter 2 and to connect these to the two views on purchasing. We have distinguished two main groups of services: short-term services (A) and long-term or continuously ongoing services (B). We have then related a number of subcategories to these two groups, according to the matrix in Figure 10.4.

It is probably the case that certain of these services, other things being equal, can be perceived to fit more or less with one of the two views. At first sight, one could argue that the transactional view of purchasing would be preferred for services that are simple, non-creative and standardized. For more complex, creative and non-standardized services, it seems reasonable, according to the discussion above, to argue that cooperation can be especially valuable. For creative/developing services there are, as mentioned earlier, obvious arguments

|  | Transaction oriented | Relation oriented |
|---|---|---|
| A. Short contracts, e.g. to complete something during a limited time period. | | |
| B. Long service deliveries<br>● Contract over a long time for many small deliveries<br>● Alternatively long production time for one larger service production | | |
| C. Standardized or non-standardized services | | |
| D. Simple or complex services | | |
| E. Creative services, e.g. to construct a problem solution, or non-creative | | |
| F. Fluctuating or non-fluctuating demands on delivery | | |
| G. Services that are aimed at the members of the company or at the company (or a function) as such | | |

**Figure 10.4**  Different kinds of services combined with the two basic views on purchasing

both for and against the two views (e.g. a change of suppliers can vitalize and give new ideas vs the possibility of creating and exploiting team effects in integrative collaboration).

Even though there can be a certain logic in this kind of reasoning, there is no simple recommendation to be made here. The most fitting purchasing strategy is the result of the overall judgement of a number of factors, of which the characteristics of the service are only one out of many. In summary, we do not give answers to specific situations, but we provide a generic approach for answering such questions in any situation.

## Purchasing philosophy and the use of ICT

In Chapter 6 we discussed the impact of ICT, especially e-commerce, on service operations. We also discussed the impact of ICT on purchasing and supply management and on buying services. If we relate that theme to transaction- versus relation-oriented purchasing, we can be sure that ICT will influence this as well. There are frequent arguments that ICT will make the transaction approach even more 'perfect'. Such an argument is given by Essig and Arnold (2001).

ICT thus enables actors to have almost perfect knowledge and thereby to take rational decisions, as it makes markets and economic conditions transparent. We have noticed a number of techniques and new institutions that are important means of support in this process: virtual marketplaces, auctions and reverse auctions, smart agents, e-tendering, e-informing etc. (Chapter 6).

Does this mean that the transaction-oriented approach will win market share at the expense of the relation-oriented approach? We are not sure. It has become evident from the discussions in Chapter 6 that integrating supply chains, by the use of ICT, should involve the greatest potential for improvement – and that should preferably call for a relation-oriented approach, as it takes time to fine-tune to gain rewards from such systems. Some illustrations have been given to show how entire supply chains and other activity structures could become re-organized and improved thanks to the better availability of accurate information in the entire system. Likewise, we illustrated great possible savings in ongoing information exchange as well as the possibility of generating statistics and knowledge by accumulated experiences (knowledge management). This means that ICT operates in favour of the relationship approach. Thus, both approaches benefit from the new possibilities introduced by the 'e'.

Nevertheless, it is likely that there are situations where previously a transaction-based approach has been preferred that now may be judged differently, and vice versa. The basic analysis and the forces to take into account, however, should still be the same.

In the following section, we will continue the discussion about cooperation-oriented or competition-oriented purchasing, but now looking at some variations.

## Variations on the theme of transaction- vs relation-oriented purchasing strategy

Transaction- and competition-oriented purchasing and relation- and coopera-tion-oriented purchasing have been described as two main alternatives. In practice, there are in fact many more varieties and combinations of the main models in use. There are variations in the number of suppliers. Another variation involves collaborations that are defined for a certain time period, and we will start here.

### The Lopez method: a mixture of cooperation and competition

Another approach that seems to be gaining ground is targeted collaboration for a specific period of time. This model is, as it is normally used, something between real, genuine, open and trustful cooperation, in line with the relation-oriented approach, and tough, opportunistic, closed and suspicious negotiations that are more in line with the transaction-oriented approach to purchasing. This approach is sometimes labelled the Lopez method, after the former purchasing director at

GM and Volkswagen, Ignaçio Lòpez de Arriortua (Van Weele and Rozemeijer, 1996; Van Weele, 2000).

Assessments of Lopez's success vary. During his first years with Volkswagen, a two-digit price reduction in total was achieved on purchased goods and services, at the same time as a great number of improvement possibilities were identified as a result of supplier audits. In earlier processes at General Motors, based on the same philosophy, Lopez had achieved savings of $4 billion in the period 1991 to 1993 (Treece, 1994). The critics say, however, that these savings have been in the short run and that they have created quality problems in the final product, destroyed relationships with suppliers and given rise to distrust and revengefulness among GM's and later VW's suppliers.

---

### Box 10.8  The Lopez method in practice

An important starting point are so-called target prices. The basis for establishing these prices can be the final consumer, say the buyer of a car. How much is the consumer ready to pay for a certain kind of car with a specific performance? The answer is that it depends on the preferences of the consumer, but also on what the alternatives are. This means that for a final product with a defined set of functional characteristics, the manufacturer can expect to obtain a certain price. The following question is how this performance can be achieved for the price that is deemed to be reasonable. In this step the supplier's own business, and how its internal value chain is organized and operates, comes into the picture. Moreover, the organization of the supplier's own supply chains will be investigated.

In practice, this method can mean that a customer invites suppliers to give quotes for the fulfilment of a certain function during a specific time period, e.g. the expected life cycle of a product. The customer puts demands on expected performance both at the start and during the coming period. This can involve annual savings of 5 per cent, which if they are not met will mean that the cooperation with the supplier can be ended or that the supplier must pay a fine. For these savings to be achieved, cooperation between the supplier and customer is expected. The suppliers that not have been able to present a plan of action for major improvements must bear the consequences of their actions.

---

The approach as it is described here can be seen as an extreme form of both the transaction- *and* the relation-oriented view. The transaction-oriented view 'Lopez-style' has without question reached perfection; on the other hand it is more doubtful if the relation-oriented view, in his approach, has reached the same level of perfection. The approach in the Lopez version can be seen as a form of cooperation, but an unequal one marked by an atmosphere that, at its foundation, is not collaboration oriented. Therefore, we choose to see it as a special variety: a competition-oriented way of working, which uses (forced) possibilities for cooperation. This does not prevent the method being very effective in specific circumstances, however, such as the serious financial problems that GM and Volkswagen faced during Lopez's time.

# Variations on the theme of number of suppliers

Regarding the different patterns in the number of suppliers, one can distinguish three main alternatives: a single supplier, two suppliers and several suppliers. Each of these in turn can consist of several variations.

*Choosing several suppliers (multiple sourcing)*
Multiple sourcing can involve everything from having three alternatives to a substantial number of suppliers. There are situations where 10 as well as 100 alternatives are used. The advantages of using several alternatives and 'playing the market' have already been discussed in the section on the transactional view of purchasing.

It is becoming less common for a company to use substantially more than three suppliers for any good or service. Travel and hotel services, rental cars and computers are examples of products where traditionally the preferences of the individual are often allowed to affect purchasing strategy. In these cases, this leads to the risk that the whole company will use such a large number of alternative suppliers that it becomes difficult to monitor (see Box 9.17). In such cases, supplier reduction and restructuring working routines can lead to substantial positive effects.

There are situations, however, where it is obvious that multiple sourcing can be very rational. For example, when it is a matter of generic products that can be purchased on spot markets or regionally, multiple sourcing can be a natural and effective strategy. In other cases, for example when developing new supplier markets, triple sourcing can be a desirable solution. It can also be that, for different reasons, a company that is working with two suppliers today (dual sourcing) has a need to develop a third supplier relationship. The reason can be that one of the two does not work very well or that the additional supplier has a unique competence, a small niche of new solutions to which the others do not have access. Jonsson (1998) found that, except for the triple sourcing alternative, multiple sourcing very seldom occurs as an outspoken strategy, because:

- Purchasing volumes are judged to be too small to be divided between as many as three or more suppliers, i.e. the advantages of scale diminish and the purchaser's negotiation leverage is weakened.
- Transaction costs and the cost of building and handling several suppliers are judged to be too high.

A special problem is that it is sometimes hard to know how many real alternatives there are and which are used and not used by the company, as demonstrated in the following example.

---

**Box 10.9   The company that thought it had twelve suppliers while it had only three**

At a large construction company, 12 well-known subcontractors of construction work were identified. The company's purchasing strategy was aimed at using this competition actively. To be able to do this, the firm worked in a transaction-oriented way.

By pure coincidence, an analysis was conducted, in the form of an examination paper, of the supplier market. The students started out from a network-based approach (see Chapters 3 and 11) and tried to map different types of collaboration agreements, joint ownership etc. between the 12 suppliers. When this mapping was finished, it became clear that the 'tough competition' actually only comprised no more than three independent competitors. All of them were in different ways connected with each other. This led to a review of the current purchasing strategy.

Different alternatives are, in other words, not only a question of different legal entities but can demand a substantially more thorough analysis of other connections between suppliers.

### Choosing two suppliers (dual sourcing)

To choose a purchasing strategy based on more than one alternative is quite common. The arguments for choosing two suppliers are, among others, increased security from disturbances, having the possibility of leveraging the competition between suppliers, the possibility of following up on prices and of using the knowledge and development capabilities of the respective suppliers within the current product areas. It is therefore built on being able to combine and exploit as much as possible the advantages of the transaction-oriented view of purchasing with the advantages of the relation-oriented view. At the same time, the combination should involve as few of the disadvantages of both views as possible.

There are a number of alternatives when choosing two suppliers. Jonsson (1998) classifies possible alternatives into three groups: *double sourcing, seesaw sourcing* and *parallel sourcing*.

### Double sourcing

This simply means that a given purchasing volume for a given product is divided between two suppliers. Market forces will bring about maximum effort from both suppliers so that they can deliver, develop and make money. The competition is also expected to ensure that each supplier invests in developing and making their operations more efficient. Continuously rationalized production should guarantee future deliveries. Prices and total costs will thereby become more and more competitive both in the short and long run. Security is achieved by the purchasing company always being able to switch to the other supplier, for example in the case of strikes, quality disturbances and late deliveries.

Jonsson (1998) does emphasize that an important restriction, which the purchasing company must review when using multiple suppliers, is the analysis of each supplier's cost and revenue curve. If the volumes are improperly distributed, then both suppliers could receive such unfavourable conditions for their respective production operations that none of them is working efficiently, since the volumes are too small. A makeshift solution can in these cases be to allow at least one of the suppliers to work cost effectively. This is usually the supplier that is allowed to supply the largest volume. An important aspect in this kind of situation is that the customer and – above all – the supplier can work with 'open-book accounting', so that the purchasing company can have an insight into the supplier's economic situation.

*Seesaw sourcing*
One way to increase competition when purchasing from two parallel suppliers is to use the so-called seesaw strategy. The total purchasing volume is then used as a clear basis for competition, in which the distribution of the volumes between the suppliers is not balanced, but rather divided according to a 20–80 or 30–70 split. Both of the suppliers are getting information about the total volume and the intended balance and they are also continuously informed about these conditions. By clearly pointing out the fact that additional efforts in service, increased efficiency etc. can increase the next year's share, the seesaw strategy creates a competition where increased effort leads to extra rewards.

*Parallel sourcing*
This purchasing strategy differs from the others in that it involves not the same but similar products, which are distributed between more than one supplier.

---

**Box 10.10   Parallel sourcing**

Bank services can be purchased from several suppliers. Parallel sourcing means that one bank gets to supply certain services, e.g. so called flow services (payments). Another bank gets to handle document administration and a third different special services.
 Temporary labour services may also be sourced in parallel: one supplier gets a contract for delivering temporary engineers and another gets a contract for providing temporary administrative staff.

---

What strategy is applied in a specific case depends on the particular conditions. But contrary to double sourcing, parallel sourcing means that the company concentrates its product on one supplier who thereby can gain advantages of scale. The purchaser does not have to worry about disturbances in quality, which can arise due to differences between the suppliers. The purchaser has at the same time a reasonable safety level, since it is usually possible to switch suppliers if for any reason the first choice does not work out.

*Single sourcing*
The choice of using only one supplier and the basic idea behind this strategy have been discussed in connection with the analysis of the relation-oriented view. The advantages are, as discussed, the possibilities of decreasing indirect costs and creating transaction value. The disadvantages are centred around the buying

company's decreased independence, since it becomes dependent on a single supplier. Other disadvantages are that over time the company can lose specific knowledge about the supplier market. The company becomes less interesting for other suppliers when it has made its choice. The costs increase of eventually switching suppliers, e.g. in a crisis situation. The selected supplier can also become less inclined to do its best all the time when the contract is safely secured.

There are also situations when it is suitable to differentiate between a number of single supplier situations (see Jonsson, 1998): situations created by regulations, in which there is only one supplier available (regulated sole sourcing); or similar situations created by competitors (suppliers) themselves (market-related sole sourcing); and the active choice of a single supplier by the customer (active single sourcing). The basic difference between 'sole' and 'single' is that sole refers to a forced situation, whereas single involves a voluntarily chosen single supplier relationship.

It should be noted, however, that (active) single sourcing may be applied at different levels. For example, a customer firm may decide to have several suppliers for the whole company but to use just a single supplier in the following categories:

- For each division (e.g. a multidivision construction company using just one engineering consultant per division).
- For each production or office location (e.g. a multinational firm using national temporary labour offices for its different operating companies). This may be even more common for buying business services than for goods, since many service industries are not yet as internationalized as most manufacturing sectors.
- For each type of final product (e.g. a tour operator using various airlines for various holiday destinations, but only one per destination).

These special varieties of single sourcing are very similar in purpose and nature to the previously discussed option of parallel sourcing, combining the advantages of both single and multiple sourcing strategies.

## Combining different approaches

It has traditionally been held that companies should choose either the transactional or the relational approach. Today it is equally understood that the approaches need to be combined; some services benefit more from a transactional approach, while others benefit from a relational approach. As a result, it is very common to try to establish some kind of 'purchasing portfolio' in which the purchasing assortment can be divided into separate parts depending on which kind of measures are judged to be most suitable.

The purchasing company can in a more or less conscious way adjust to the situation. A common work method for sorting and separating different categories of purchased products is proposed by Kraljic (1983).

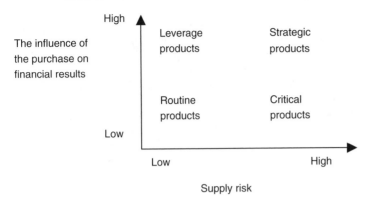

**Figure 10.5** A matrix for sorting purchased products based on the product's influence on the financial result and the supplier risk

*Based on*: Kraljic, 1983, p. 112.

What is purchased can, as one dimension, have a high or low effect on the financial result. The other dimension concerns risk. The product can be related to high or low risk, where high risk means that supply problems can inflict great damage. The four purchasing situations that arise in the matrix in Figure 10.5 can force the work method to be adjusted.

Van Weele (1994, 2000) discusses suitable directions for purchasing given the product's different positions in the matrix. He suggests that leverage products can be purchased after tendering processes where the customer strives towards the lowest price or the best business conditions for a well-defined product. A price reduction greatly influences the financial result and the supply risk is low. For strategic products a deeper, long-term relationship (partnership) is recommended to handle the supply risk and to utilize the development possibilities. Routine products might deserve attention in the way in which the company can or should aim to create efficient purchasing systems. The products do not influence the financial result very much and the supply risk is low, but they might demand extensive handling (to order, deliver, invoice etc.) and thus entail great costs. For critical products it is recommended to ensure supplies in different ways. Since the product's influence on the financial result is low, a certain over-capacity can be accepted. Some illustrations follow.

---

**Box 10.11   From a routine to a strategic business service**

An IT company knew that it had an important role for a large industrial company. The reverse was also true. In spite of this the industrial company still only purchased a limited part of the IT company's range and it purchased standard products. A mutual initiative was taken towards a deeper relationship, based on a closer analysis of the customer's situation and needs. Neither customer nor supplier was initially aware of the customer's real needs and what kind of solutions there were to access or develop.

The initiative entailed that two very knowledgeable individuals from the IT company, together with the purchaser's key people, made an inventory of the company's operations over two weeks. An analysis was done of the customer's operations, the needs for communication and how these were met today, IT currently used, possibilities for other solutions, possible business development through implementing new IT solutions and so on.

The result of the project was that transactions were considerably widened, new combinations of IT solutions were introduced and the relationship was upgraded. More individuals became involved and the contacts became much more continuous. The companies 'hooked up' with each other and developed together.

## Box 10.12   A critical service

LKS Data is a computer company in Sweden that, among other things, supplies system services for a number of specialized trade chains. The service means that the company has a helpdesk function, which the customer contacts when problems arise. This is a critical service. If the computer system is not working the stores cannot sell anything and consequently must close until the system is operational again.

LKS Data's CEO, Leif Lendrup, points out how important this service is when he talks about a newly employed individual in the helpdesk function. This is someone who is functioning especially well, which is partly because he used to be an ambulance driver. He is thus 'used to handling individuals that have a trauma and in are in shock,' argues Lendrup. It is probably the case that this service is not very expensive for the customer, but it is associated with a high-risk situation.

## Box 10.13   A leverage service

Standard temporary labour services are a typical example of leverage services. Increasingly, large corporations, such as Philips Electronics (Box 1.8), realize that they are spending quite a lot of money on these types of services. Hence, they start looking for possibilities of leveraging their purchases in this segment. For example, Philips Electronics decided it would regionally bundle its contracts with temporary labour providers and greatly reduce the number of preferred suppliers in this area.

## Box 10.14   A routine service

Taxi rides can in many businesses function as a routine service. However, they can be purchased in a more or less considered manner. It is common for companies not to have any system for these kinds of services. The employee who is using a taxi can thus freely choose the supplier of this service.

In order for these purchases to be performed in a professional way by a single individual, he or she would have to spend a relatively long time scanning the market.

This is rarely done. On the other hand, it is relatively common for the company to get some control over these purchases through signing a general agreement by which the services are ordered. A company can, for example, have a general agreement with one operator that thus receives a certain volume and can give volume discounts, but it is also relatively easy to add other services such as invoice routines (for example monthly invoicing instead of one invoice per taxi ride etc.) and other service components. This is one way to save both direct as well as indirect costs for this kind of service.

Based on the dimensions in Figure 10.5, different services will thus be handled in different ways. It can also be the case that the design of the entire purchasing organization is heavily influenced by an analysis according to these guidelines. If, for example, 95 per cent of all purchases are considered routine products, it is probably not reasonable to create a purchasing organization that is strongly oriented towards handling strategic products.

These observations imply that the most suitable purchasing approach varies from area to area. Stated differently, it means that the purchasing organization can strive for different kinds of management structures for handling different business transactions. In some cases, the tendency is towards deepened and actor-specific relationships, i.e. the relationships are developed and become more and more individualized. In other cases, the trend is towards transaction-oriented market exchanges. In yet other cases, the development tends towards vertical integration, i.e. hierarchical management structures.

An interesting aspect of this line of reasoning is that the development towards the 'right' management structure will be partly 'organic', since it will turn out to be the most beneficial in the long run. An alternative is that the actors themselves choose to drive development actively towards the structure that seems most adapted to their purposes.

## Conclusions

The traditional, transaction-oriented way of purchasing has been known for a long time. During recent years, an emerging view, the relation-oriented approach, has come to be more and more explicit. Both views have a number of strengths and weaknesses. For some companies and within certain areas of purchasing, the transaction-oriented mode can be preferred, whereas in other cases the opposite is better. Most important considerations are partly which costs and other aspects are most easily influenced and partly what competence the purchasing company has.

There are a number of intermediate forms of the two approaches, in terms of the number of suppliers and the time span of the cooperation. These variations offer nuances in the picture of two main alternatives. They make it possible, to a certain extent, to combine the strengths of one mode with those of the other.

There are some helpful models to guide companies in selecting what services should be bought according to which approach. These and some necessary prerequisites for applying such a differentiated approach have been elaborated in this chapter.

# 11

# Buying Business Services: the Market Perspective versus the Network Perspective

By means of various examples in this book, we have illustrated the wide variety of services that exist. They may involve short-term project-like assignments and long-term assignments, e.g. being responsible for a certain period of time – a month, a year or many years – for a particular function. Services can also vary along a number of other dimensions: standardized–non-standardized, creative –non-creative, seasonally fluctuating–non-fluctuating, oriented towards individuals and/or company oriented etc.

A second notion central to this book concerns the different ways of analysing services in terms of activities, actors and resources. It is a model that we have primarily used to describe the service and the production of specific services. In this chapter we are going to put more emphasis on the same model applied to the analysis of market systems. The A-R-A model is most of all known as a 'network model' (Håkansson and Snehota, 1995; Axelsson and Easton, 1992).

A third important and related notion is that service deliveries are to a large extent realized in an interplay between customer and supplier and other actors. This has important ramifications for our view on specifying and contracting, and for the actual service production and delivery process. In the preceding chapter, we discussed two basic approaches to buying services: the transactional and the relational approach. Each of these is better fitted to certain contexts, but applying the principles also means that the buyer *influences* the market structure in a particular direction. Likewise, the structure as such is an important variable affecting the choice. In this chapter we discuss the outer context of the firm buying business services.

## Outer context: markets vs networks

Some implicit assumptions regarding the outer context of the firm often underlie decision-oriented models of contracting. Håkansson and Snehota (1995) note that the traditional perspective of rational planning of business activities relies on three fundamental assumptions:

- That the organization's environment is more or less 'faceless' and outside the organization's control.
- That the execution of the organization's strategy is enabled by the firm's hierarchical control of these resources. It can, for example, decide to buy certain resources.
- That the environment (market) is constantly changing and that the organization should adapt itself to these developments.

The authors debate all three assumptions. They argue that most organizations operate in an environment with a limited number of identifiable actors. Through interaction (and interplay) between these actors, different relationships emerge and various networks develop. The interaction may result in mutual dependency between the resources of several organizations. This implies, in its turn, that it is difficult to define the boundaries of each organization because, as a result of resource dependency, they 'grow into' each other. By becoming a part of a network with known counterparts, an organization becomes dependent on how well it succeeds in its interactions with others. However, it also becomes dependent on how relationships are developed with other actors in the network.

Based on this argument, it is more correct to talk about a company *being part of* a context rather than *having* an environment. According to that perspective, the company will not adapt itself to its environment, but rather act and react within its own context. This perspective also implies that any development need not be the result of a carefully planned, rational process, but can also be seen as a result of the actions and reactions of the organization and others within its network. Decisions are taken, needs are identified, alternatives evaluated and suppliers selected, but all this happens within the boundaries of a context that resembles a network as described here, rather than traditional ('perfect competition') market structures. Because of that, previous experiences (history) and current dependencies and evaluations of future potential collaboration play a decisive role.

The economic environment, the system within which the purchasing of services takes place, thus creates conditions for purchasing activities, both good and bad. These are conditions that the purchasing company partly must adapt to and partly can try to influence.

In this chapter we discuss two main systems or structures. The first deals with the market system as a fully functional market, based on perfect competition (as it is often described in the literature). The other describes markets as relatively well-organized, connected systems or networks. In both cases suitable work methods and important competencies are discussed.

## Purchasing in a market environment

The market system as a starting point for purchasing activities in a market environment can be illustrated as in Figure 11.1. The figure is based on the following assumptions about the character and function of the market:

- It consists of a relatively large number of actors, buyers and sellers (companies or consumers).
- It is fluid, it being simple to exchange one supplier for another or/and to get new customers, and the offer (product, price etc.) of the moment is the determining factor.
- No single actor can in any significant way influence other actors and/or markets in a wider perspective.
- It is atomistic: relationships between actors are insignificant.

This means that purchasing activities should be aimed at relevant supplier markets, and that they take place in an environment where the suppliers have alternative customers, which they will choose if they offer more. The company chooses certain segments, groups of suppliers, to which it directs its purchasing activities.

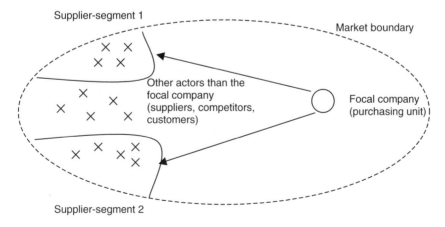

**Figure 11.1** An illustration of a market situation in a typical market environment
*Based on*: Lecture material, Håkan Håkansson, 1997.

The number of producers in a certain situation is important since it represents a reference frame for actions, both in the short and long term. If there are many possible suppliers the company has two choices: to exploit those possibilities in line with the transaction-oriented approach; or, in spite of the possible alternatives, to select only one or two of them (single or dual sourcing). If there only is one producer, then purchasing must act in a completely different way than if there are several alternatives. It is, however, not obvious that the situation with only one supplier has to mean a worse total exchange for the single purchasing company, since it can extract more – for example through skilful negotiations – from the supplier from a development and rationalization perspective than do other purchasing companies. The company can, in other words, work in the relation dimension in line with the relation-oriented approach. It is not certain that this means a lack of competitive pressure on the supplier. The supplier can strive to gain a larger portion of the purchasing company's total purchasing volume (other products) or there can be more or less close substitutes (cf. McMillan, 1990).

The offer's level of standardization is of importance for purchasing from many perspectives. A less standardized offer entails lock-in – at least in the short term. There are costs in breaking a relationship, which means that there are always reasons to analyse whether any existing problems can be solved *within* the relationship before other alternatives are explored.

In a situation with many suppliers, with relatively homogeneous products, the following types of purchasing behaviour and competencies would seem to be appropriate:

● Use existing competition.
● Choose products on a realistic functional level.
● Use standardization arguments for simplifying and making the alternatives continuously comparable.

Important competencies for pursuing such an approach to purchasing and supply management are primarily the following:

For market activities:

● Market knowledge (the possible alternatives).
● Ability to 'play the market'.

For functional aspects of the purchase:

● Assessing the core function to be bought.

The market context in such a situation generally pushes the behaviour towards using existing competition and trying to exploit that opportunity. In essence, a market structure such as this is therefore likely to support the transactional approach to purchasing and supply management (Chapter 10). In order to perform well, the firm should, in line with that, use well-defined specifications of the service. This could involve function (output) or activity (throughput) prescriptive specifications (Chapter 7).

The required purchasing competence thus centres around being able to exploit the market situation and trying to preserve or improve it. Functionally, the purchasing team needs to be competent enough to judge and secure the core function of the product.

To direct and evaluate the performance of purchasing activities in a situation such as this is relatively easy as it forges a transparent business. Price monitoring based on transparent market prices gives a good indication.

We have sometimes argued that this is a 'classical' approach to purchasing. That is true, but it does not mean that it is without innovation. We have already pointed to some possible new practices as a result of ICT applications, but there are other interesting ingredients. In public procurement within the European Union, there are specific laws that the buyers need to adhere to, formed with their point of departure in this approach to purchasing. It is interesting to note that the recently increased attention on these issues has actively contributed to such a renewal of practices. Let us give an example.

---

**Box 11.1    A bidding contest in public procurement exploiting market mechanisms**

Some years ago a public hospital needed to improve its IT support systems for administrative functions. It hired an external consultant to manage the process. The task assigned to the consultant was to develop the requirements and the criteria to apply when choosing between different bidders. The consultant should make possible a professional way of carrying out a bidding race for a complex service such as this, and also manage the bidding process itself. It is also important to note that representatives from the hospital had got permission to use a negotiated deal, i.e. to negotiate with more than one party after the initial bids had been addressed.

The coming deal was announced according to the rules and 15 suppliers applied. All of them were given identical information and if anyone asked a question during the process, that question and the answers to it were immediately distributed to all involved. No one could benefit from better information. In the first phase the buyer chose seven suppliers for continued discussion. They received more detailed information and the possibility of remaining in the process. Due to the responses to that one more was excluded. The remaining six bidders were analysed in five stages:

- Hearing – every supplier got half a day to present its case and respond to questions and doubts. Two companies were excluded after this activity.
- Workshop – four of the remaining suppliers got a full day each for a workshop on functional, business and supplier demands.
- Mini-project – with three of the companies the buyer completed mini-projects when aspects such as organization, supply and price were discussed. This meant complements to all bids.
- Final evaluation – an in-depth analysis with two remaining suppliers. The commitment to quality assurance of systems development was in focus. This was finalized by judgements on the risks involved.
- Negotiations with the winner.

> During the whole process the buyer had been careful to inform all the remaining parties equally and as fast as possible. The buyer was also very explicit about the reasons for the final choice, because it wanted to avoid criticism and also to educate the market.

This is the way to play a market that has some novelty in it – and it also supports market mechanisms.

## Purchasing in a network environment

An illustration of a purchasing company's situation that presents some kind of network structure is given in Figure 11.2. The figure is based on the following assumptions about the market:

● It consists of a few important actors, buyers and sellers (companies and/or consumers).
● It is rigid: it is a difficult process to change suppliers and/or to obtain new customers.
● There are important dependencies between actors and between relationships, which imply that those actions that take place within a specific business relationship influence and are influenced by actions within other relationships. These dependencies can exist both horizontally as well as vertically in a business system.
● Single actors can strongly influence the market.
● It is a more or less well-organized system of actors, activities and dependencies.

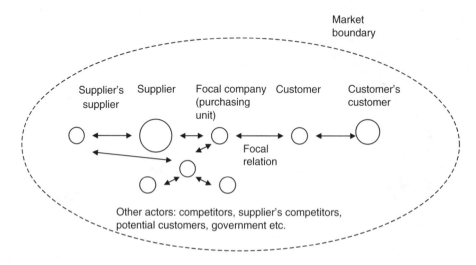

**Figure 11.2**   An illustration of the marketing situation in a typical network environment
*Based on*: Lecture material, Håkan Håkansson, 1997.

A situation like this could trigger efforts to try to create more of a traditional market context, but also to act within the existing frame. It then fosters practices in line with the relation-oriented approach to purchasing and supply management. The company's purchasing activities are aimed at the following particular aspects:

- The *content* of the relationship in the form of the products and problem solutions that are exchanged in the relationship (the activities that take place). This involves the supplier relationship's profitability, i.e. the values in the form of direct and indirect revenues in comparison to the resources used in the relationship, and the supplier relationship's different bonds (social, legal and so on) that keep it together.
- The *functions* of the relationship for the company, e.g. its role in the customer's resource supply system (a profitable supplier and/or an important development supplier, a new or old supplier, a supplier within a certain line of business etc.). This also includes its significance for the company's present and future position in the network, or in various networks related to the relationship in question (actor networks, different resource and knowledge networks etc). Therefore, interest is also directed to how the supplier relationship being focused on is imbedded in a system of other relationships: supplier's suppliers, alternative suppliers, customer's customers and so on. The specific relationship could thus have important functions for the companies involved as actors (capability argument, contribution to better position in certain resource networks); for the dyad, the specific relationship as such; for the wider system, the network in which activities are linked, actors connected and resources tied in specific patterns due to the relationship (Håkansson and Snehota, 1995).

The activities of the company are thus aimed at specific suppliers and other actors instead of at large market segments. The content of the supplier relationship and the function of the specific relationship (the business transactions) is emphasized. But in addition the function in a larger context (the significance of the relationship for the company and the network) will, in a totally different way, be brought into focus more than when acting in the type of market system discussed earlier.

In these network kinds of situations, it is fully reasonable to describe the contents and function of each supplier relationship from a network point of view (as in Figure 11.2).

In situations with a unique relationship and one or a few alternatives, the purchasing function is heavily influenced by the relationship itself. In such a situation it is, from a short-term perspective, more or less impossible to change supplier. All of the work will instead be directed towards building the relationship, learning more about the other party and so on. In such a situation the following way of working (behaviour), competencies and methods seem useful.

The behavior of the purchasing organization should benefit from being oriented towards:

- Seeking other paths than competition to achieve mutuality in negotiations.

- Developing equivalent (supplier–customer) fundamental facts and procedures for assessing (the value of) the business transactions.

Important competencies to perform well are, for market activities:

- Being able to describe, analyse and understand the industrial network's way of functioning.
- Acting in a network-oriented way.

For functional aspects of the purchase:

- High competence in functional aspects of the product/service/offer. How it will fit into the system into which it is to be incorporated (cf. Chapters 7 and 9).

For evaluating the specific supplier:

- Good understanding of production technology.
- Good understanding of production economy.

Appropriate methods that may be helpful in situations such as this include:

- Benchmarking.
- Process value engineering.
- Activity analyses directed towards the business processes.
- Network-oriented activity, actor and resource analyses (according to the A-R-A model with checklists etc. presented in Chapter 3).

From a supplier management and assessment point of view, this situation presents much more complex conditions. The offer is unique and in itself hard to assess, and there is only one supplier. Benchmarking methods, looking at comparable companies' way of handling the corresponding functions, so-called value analyses (see Chapter 9 on pricing) and cost analyses of product or function level etc. are all of interest. The demands on the purchasing function's competence consequently become more complex. Functional, production, technical and market-related aspects need to be assessed.

These two main types of outer business contexts thus impose consequences on purchasing activities, both in terms of behaviour and in terms of required competencies. Since market systems as well as networks involve a great deal of variety, we will now look more closely at network structures. It is also clear that the individual firm can influence the market; it could, for example, act so as to promote more of a traditional market or network structure. The activities in line with a transactional or relation-oriented approach to purchasing clearly have such implications. The extent to which an individual actor is able to drive the market has to do with its power and position in specific contexts.

## Two main categories of networks

In the literature one can find (at least) two main categories of networks:

- The well-organized, *deliberate* network where it is very clear who is inside and who is outside the network. Furthermore, the parties are presumed to have common goals and the network is established with the purpose of improving joint efficiency. These networks can be defined as *constellations of two or more actors, cooperating to (better) achieve common goals.*
- The gradually *emergent* network, where cooperation is established between actors in such a way that they have come to operate within a coordinated system of actors, activities and resources. For these networks, there are no clear boundaries between who is in and who is not. The actors join and enter collaborating relationships by themselves. Even so, the companies within these structures seem to be interrelated through mutual dependencies. These kind of networks can be defined as *constellations of two or more connected exchange processes.*

We would emphasize that those who want to study and analyse a certain network or a certain situation in a network context can do this using either view. The critical issues to be aware of and to manage might, however, differ a great deal. In deliberately organized networks as alliances (the first type), it is a group of actors who come together and agree on common goals and procedures, such as who could qualify to be a member and what kinds of procedures for conflict resolution should apply. In the emergent networks of the second type, many basic aspects are different, such as who is inside and outside the network and how different actors perceive the network. These issues become an empirical question, one of relevance and judgement, of where the analyst chooses to draw the boundaries for the research and what connected exchange processes are considered to be within or outside a network.

There are of course other ways of grouping networks, e.g. individual (personal) versus industrial firm-based networks, and there are also possibilities for fine-tuning the division into the two main categories mentioned (see e.g. Harland *et al.*, 2001). We will not discuss all these varieties here.

We do want to stress that what we have mainly discussed so far are networks from the second category. The whole model of actors, activities and resources is primarily chosen to analyse this second kind of network. Hence as a complement we would like to give an example of a network from the first category.

---

**Box 11.2   Castles in collaboration: an alliance of buying and selling services**

Sixteen castles around the large Swedish lake of Mälaren have for a couple of years cooperated in an association called Mälarslott. An important idea is that the castles cooperate in marketing, but that they should also complement each other and be able to offer tourists an interesting blend of architecture and history. A prerequisite for cooperation is that the parties have good knowledge of each other's attractions and that they thus can sell the others as well as relate their own castle to visitors. The network is well organized and the requirements for entrance are quite strict.

*Source*: Grundén and Westin, 1997.

This is an organized network with an obvious limitation and explicit rules for membership. It thus fits with the definition of deliberate or 'strategic' networks. These kinds of networks have also been subject to research. Among others, Snow *et al.* (1992) have identified a number of roles that need to be fulfilled for the network to function. According to them, some actors (individuals or companies) act as intermediaries who in a creative way connect the resources that other actors have available. They point to three especially important roles, which in their view greatly contribute to a well-functioning network:

- The *architect* that facilitates the creation of the specific network without actually having a complete overview or control over it.
- The driver or *lead operator*, who formally binds the actors together in specific networks.
- The *caretaker*, who focuses on improvements to the common activities that are carried out in the network and who has a wider network horizon.

Many of these roles can be identified in the castle example. There is, for instance, a central figure in the network in the form of a strong, initiative project leader.

These roles are probably in most cases also possible to identify and analyse in the emergent kind of network. In many cases these roles develop spontaneously. The individual firm is likely to be a part of and have to deal with both kinds of networks, and therefore needs to understand some of the logic behind each type. However, there are also a number of issues that are equally applicable to each type of network. We sometimes need, for example, to be able to characterize the structures of relevant networks. For the purchasing party the view of its outer context, not only as a network but as certain kinds of networks, should be an important piece of understanding to guide its behaviour.

## Characterizing network structures

Activity, actor and resource structures can be mapped and described in a more or less systematic way (see Chapter 3). This may provide valuable insights for understanding the company's possibilities for achieving its goals and visions.

Activity, actor and resource structures can also be characterized and classified. A simple division is, as already hinted at in Chapter 3, between *tightly* and *loosely* structured networks. In the tightly structured network, the role division between the actors is clear, the activities are linked and well synchronized with each other and the resource ties are strong. In loosely structured networks, we find the contrary. But that is only one dimension by which to characterize networks. Some of the most common variables that have been used to characterize network structures are the following:

- *Degree of structure*, from very tight to very loose. This may concern actor groupings (in terms of the degree of strength of the actor bonds), activity structures (the strength of activity links) as well as resource structures (the strength of ties between different kinds of resources).

● *Density*, which means that many actors have contact with many others.
● *Concentration*, which means that one or several actors are more densely connected than others.
● *Hierarchy*, which means that one or several actors has a stronger influence and dominates the events in the network.
● *Changeability*, which means that the network is more or less changeable.
● *Degree of internationalization*, which means that the network crosses national boundaries.

Such descriptions not only facilitate decisions on appropriate actions but also help in understanding many questions of 'Why?' and 'How?' in business contexts.

---

**Box 11.3    The network of reverse logistics within electronics – loosely structured in terms of resources and activities**

In Huge-Brodin (1997) we find a description of the structures that have been created to perform reverse logistics within different operations. One of these structures is established for electronic components.

It turns out that the transport involved in the reverse logistics part of the supply chain is not as strongly structured as other parts. In other parts there are very strict driving schedules, requirements for fully loaded trucks etc. In the reverse logistics part of the chain, the goods are loaded and unloaded 'when it suits', i.e. when the capacity is not used by anything else. This is a sign of this part of the resource network not being as well organized as the rest. Return components have not yet been defined as 'resources', at least not as an important resource. Thus the resource network is more loosely structured than it otherwise would have been.

---

In certain situations only one of the variables of actors, activities and resources is relevant to observe. In other situations, a combination of several variables is useful for developing an accurate description of the network's structure. Similarly, it can be said that sometimes just a particular *aspect* of the network structure is interesting, for example the density or changeability, or sometimes this may be a combination of characteristics. These network characteristics are important to understand, as they indicate some of the possibilities for mobilizing actors and resources. Therefore, such an understanding of its surrounding network is also important to the purchasing company.

## Networks of activities, actors and resources

In accordance with the previously discussed A-R-A model (Chapter 3), it can be stated that each of the three main groups of variables – actors, activities and resources – can be seen as a coherent system or network. We can, in other words, talk about structures in the form of actor, resource and activity networks.

Activities as systems mean that the activities, within a certain context, influence, create and are influenced by the existing activity structures. Activity structures can be seen as infrastructures, a kind of 'road system', within which activities in the form of service production take place. Every service production activates a part of this structure.

Resource networks are systems of resources (material and immaterial) formed in connection with the activities through interaction and different kinds of resource mobilization. They constitute structures in the way that they have formed and been reserved for certain fields of application, which in turn will, for better or worse, influence the possibilities of using them for other activities and functions.

Actors as structures mean that there are different kinds of bonds between the actors: technical lock-ins, social ties, contractual regulations etc. Overall this results in structures that can be described as actor networks. These bonds can in some cases create severe barriers to change, while in others they are important enablers of it.

The three main groups of structures are largely overlapping. The activity structures also influence and are influenced by structures of resources and structures of actors, which are being and have been created. Independent of which of these variables we choose to use as a foundation, the others are still important conditions for what can and cannot be done. However, structures of activities, actors and resources can, for example, also make it understandable that what can be carried out on one actor's initiative will not be possible to carry out for another. Consider some illustrations of these structures below. The different dimensions of a network all constitute potentially important conditions for actions.

---

**Box 11.4    The network structure that the customer could see**

An illustration of actor, activity and resource structures (network) can be given for the previously mentioned trip to South Africa by a group of Swedish executive MBA students. Parts of the underlying infrastructure were disclosed when they came to a very isolated boarding house and thought that they were Swedish pioneers, until they looked at the guestbook and found a dominance of Swedish-sounding signatures. The obvious reason for this 'coincidence' was that the service package they had purchased was produced to a great extent within the frames of a longer existing infrastructure. They had been placed in an established structure of activities and resources (as well as actors controlling the resources and performing the activities).

A typical situation is that a need for mobilization arises. It can, using the afore-mentioned trip again as a basis, be a question of solving a new problem. A situation occurred where the customers, the course participants, had a strong wish to visit a particular country. The organizing team, as actor and service producer, had no relevant contacts in South Africa. What should they do? The natural course was to start thinking about the general infrastructure, official Swedish representation such as embassies, the Trade Council etc. In the end, it came to be more about personal networks: who they knew or who might know somebody who could help them. Within a not too long period of time they had, thanks to their own and others' contact networks, been able to solve the problem.

The types of structures discussed are important to understand, influence and create. They limit and enable actions. The example in Box 11.4 might seem special since there is a relatively wide infrastructure where a multitude of activities can be handled. The general line of reasoning is, however, also relevant for operations that take place more continuously and within substantially more limited structures. This means that activity, resource and actor structures are important platforms on which activities (business deals, a trip, a campaign, a transport etc.) can take place.

However, Box 11.4 also indicates that the possibilities of gaining access to structures developed by others are dependent on networking activities. In this case the organizers used known public actors as well as their personal networks to get information as well as recommendations from them. The latter were important prerequisites for making it possible for people to be able and willing to use their capabilities and produce the solutions asked for by the customer. There are thus basic network structures as well as processes of networking that are important to understand and utilize for purchasing organizations.

## The fundamentals of network structures

Håkansson and Snehota (1995) have developed a set of concepts that provide greater conceptual precision for the network model described earlier. They take the division actors/activities/resources further and develop concepts that more clearly distinguish the three main variables. The authors claim that, if we choose to view the cross-section of a relationship between two parties, such a relation can be said to consist of the following:

- *Links* between activities (activity links) that link the purchaser's and seller's activities with each other.
- *Bonds* between actors (actor bonds) that bond actors to each other. These can be technical, administrative, social, legal etc. types of bonds.
- *Ties* between resources (resource ties) that tie the seller's resources with the purchaser's (and other actors') resources.

With the corresponding terminology the single actor (purchaser or seller) can be characterized as:

- An activity system, the actor performs many activities where a part takes place within or in connection to a certain relationship.
- An organizational structure, a system for coordination where a part is directed towards handling the bonds with the single actor.

● A resource bundle, a bundle of technical, human, financial resources, where a part is connected to a certain customer or relationship.

Håkansson and Snehota (1995) also put the single relationship in relation to the surrounding system of other activities, actors and resources. The activity links that exist within a relationship with a customer and supplier are only part of the total activity pattern existing within the network. In a corresponding way, the two actors and their actor bonds form only part of the total system of actors within the network. Furthermore, the actors' resource bundles and resource ties are part of the total resource system in the network. All of this can be summarized in the matrix shown in Table 11.1.

This is a conceptual specification and development of the A-R-A model presented earlier (Chapter 3). It presents a 'language' that enables a precise communication, description and analysis of different business situations. We can relatively easily return to each of our previous illustrations and interpret or translate the descriptions using the terminology in this matrix. We could analyse how the company's activity and organization structures and its bundles of resources connect with parts of the total network of activity patterns, actor groupings and resource constellations. We can also discern what the relationship contents look like in terms of links, bonds and ties. Think, for example, of some of the boxes presented in Chapter 3.

A further element in attempts to systematically understand and evaluate the conditions for maintaining and influencing a network structure is to create a general picture of what influences a single network the most. This can be said to be a result of the forces dominating in a particular network.

## Networks as force fields

Different forces can dominate the specific relationship or the specific network. Sometimes the activity links and changes in these may be dominating the development of the network, and sometimes the strongest force relates to the actor bonds or the resource ties.

An example of a relatively balanced structure (activities, actors and resources are equal in strength) in terms of actors, activities and resources is the following.

**Table 11.1** Matrix of fundamental concepts for analysing business relations

|            | Company                  | Relationship   | Network                |
|------------|--------------------------|----------------|------------------------|
| Activities | Activity structure       | Activity links | Activity pattern       |
| Actors     | Organizational structure | Actor bonds    | Web of actors          |
| Resources  | Resource collection      | Resource ties  | Resource constellation |

*Source*: Håkansson and Snehota, 1995, p. 45.

---

**Box 11.5    Services at Volvo-GM Heavy Truck Corporation**

Volvo-GM Heavy Truck Corporation sells trucks and spare parts within the US through market channels that, among others, include regional warehouses and commercial truck retailers. During the period 1993–95, retailers had reported a stock reduction in critical components even though the total stock was continually increasing. Since the company could not offer predictable and fast deliveries, it lost a lot of contracts.

When the managers of the company eventually understood what the problem was they could start fixing it. Cooperation with Federal Express was initiated, which meant that a totally new and complete central warehouse for all possible components was established in Memphis, Tennessee. Today, when a retailer has an urgent need for a component he or she dials a toll-free number to FedEx, which uses a logistics system constructed to be able to handle a delivery anywhere in the US within 24 hours. The system incorporates some 100 airplanes that converge in Memphis for the sorting of transported goods. A rush order can be loaded by the afternoon of the same day and arrive at the retailer during the night. The spare parts can then be collected at the airport, delivered to the retailer's office or even to the parking lot where the final customer's truck is parked.

Since this system was implemented the company has not lost any more important service deals due to stock shortage. It has been able to close three local warehouses and reduce stocks by 15 per cent. Retailer income has also increased due to faster repairs, for which the customer is willing to pay a substantial premium. The speed represents great value for transportation companies, which this is all about.

*Source*: Narus and Anderson, 1996.

---

In this case there seems to be a relative equilibrium concerning the influence of the three variable groups of actors, activities and resources on how the structure is formed and functions. The illustration demonstrates that the actors are willing to cooperate, that they have the relevant resources and that their activity structures complement each other.

It is obvious that the activity structures in certain situations are very important prerequisites for the possibility of creating fruitful cooperation. Of special importance is the 'rhythm' of these activities or, in other words, their 'timing'. The activities must be synchronized and allowed to 'hook up with each other' easily.

In other situations the force of *resources* dominates.

---

**Box 11.6    The right resources through the right partner – a successful acquisition solved a resource problem**

An IT company, which took part in a tender, was disconnected from the discussion at a critical stage. The customer decided on a fundamentally different system from the one offered by this particular supplier. A quick and active effort with the purpose of mobilizing new, relevant resources was initiated. It turned out to be possible to acquire a couple of specialists from another part of the market. Due to these complementary resources the company once again became a serious player in the tender process.

The example above illustrates the importance of maintaining and nurturing an external resource structure.

In yet other situations, *actors* can constitute the dominant force. Individuals who have similar professional education often have reasons to create contacts over company boundaries to exchange different experiences. Education managers, human resource managers, information managers, logistics managers, lawyers and other experts often establish professional networks in companies of a certain size or within certain industries. An example follows that illuminates how such a network can work.

---

**Box 11.7  Resourcing in actor-dominated networks – or the professional network with a backlash**

A professional network that gathers managers within 20 large Swedish companies and organizations has existed for many years. The managers meet twice a year and exchange experiences. There are several issues of mutual interest and by being part of the network, the individual can also receive support in achieving different kinds of activities. One event may illuminate what can happen if someone breaks the existing pattern.

One of the actors in the network carried out a big tender process. Among the suppliers, there was a long-established individual from the common network who also represented his own company. That company was generally expected to obtain the order; it would have been an obvious choice. But among the candidates were also external suppliers. After elaborate discussions, one of those 'outsiders' was finally selected, causing the 'network favourite' great annoyance. What later happened is more easily understood if the situation is illustrated in a figure.

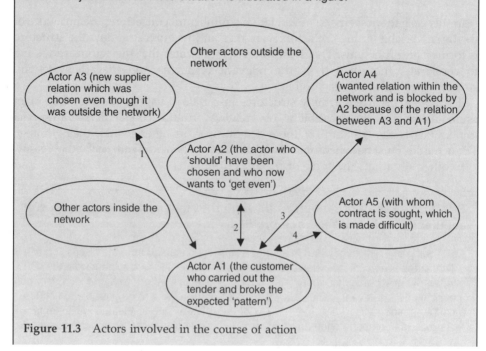

**Figure 11.3**  Actors involved in the course of action

A2 is very disappointed and loses confidence in A1, but A1's relationships with others are also affected by the transaction. This becomes apparent in many situations, for example when A1 wants to establish a new business relationship within the network with A4, with whom no transactions had taken place earlier. A2 lets A4 understand, in different ways, that this is inappropriate and succeeds in blocking the A1–A4 relationship. Contacts in connection to the established relationship with A5 are becoming substantially more difficult as well. The result is that A1 has chosen a supplier, which was seen as the better choice, but which has at the same time effectively chosen to be outside the network. A1 has lost its reputation and its previous possibilities for mobilizing resources for various purposes. Business has become restricted.

Different forces have different weights in different situations. It is also true that, for example, in a system of operations dominated by the activities force, there are normally also strong influences from actors and resources: all three forces are usually present, but to different extents. When several factors pull in the same direction, the joint effect becomes even stronger.

If we relate this discussion to the different categories of services from Chapter 2 we might expect some differences. A complex service executed by a specialist at a professional firm is more likely to be dominated by actors, in such cases often specific individuals and their knowledge, as much of the critical resources are embodied in these professionals. In routine services there might more often be dominance by the activity structures. Such structures make it possible to create changes by networking processes. In loose structures it is normally easier to create changes relative to 'heavy' networks, well-structured and strong activity links as well as actor bonds and resource ties. It is not only important to be aware of the relative ease with which one or more actors by networking actions can create changes as well as resistance to changes, but also to know some of the ways in which such actions could be carried out.

## Networking to influence network structures and processes

The handling of the relationship usually involves at least two actors, customer and supplier: 'It takes two to tango' (Wilkinson and Young, 1991). Sometimes more actors are directly involved but, as has been extensively discussed by now, most often it is a dyadic relationship (customer–supplier), with some consciousness and within the conditions of the context of which the relationship is a part.

A supplier is not always willing to do what the customer suggests. This might be to do with the supplier giving different priorities to these issues, or a lack of resources or will and so on. In these situations, it could be important for the customer to be able to create interest at the supplier in the particular assignment ('reverse marketing' – Leenders and Blenkhorn, 1988; or 'mobilising' – Wynstra, 1998; Wynstra et al., 2002). The customer must thus market its needs.

From a network perspective, there are a number of management problems that are not as apparent in a traditional market perspective. It is, for example, very common that the customer, when managing the specific supplier relationship, actively considers the possible impact on other relationships such as the suppliers' competitors, which can also be established as suppliers of the customer. The specific relationship is conditioned by others, it is dependent on them but it also has a more or less substantial impact on such other, or indirect, relationships. Other actors can be those who supply complementary products, the customer's customer, the supplier's supplier and so on.

Under these circumstances, there are always some situations that need to be addressed or even changed. Smith and Laage-Hellman (1992) have pointed out a number of possible actions (or tactics) in these situations. It may be possible to do the following things to a particular supplier (compare the list of possible actions to change activity structures in Chapter 3):

- *Avoid*. This can partly mean that an actor simply skips a stage, e.g. that the customer directly contacts the supplier's supplier.
- *Flank*. This is two- or multi-step thinking. An alternative can be that the customer establishes a parallel contact with one of the supplier's partners, e.g. with the purpose that the partner should contribute to getting the supplier interested.
- *Combine*. This can concern the case when a customer actively works towards 'pooling' other actors, e.g. supplier B plus supplier C, so that they can jointly offer the desired solution.
- *Change*. To change an actor, e.g. one supplier for another.
- *Develop/strengthen*. An example of this can be to create an additional relationship, e.g. a new supplier relationship without removing any other, or to strengthen and deepen the relationship with an established actor. The latter might, for example, happen through the business transactions being deepened (more links), more actors becoming involved or the personal relationships between the involved actors being deepened (more and/or stronger bonds). Furthermore, more and/or 'better' resources are being reserved for the particular relationship (stronger bonds).
- *Bridge*. This is about using an actor to reach another, similar to flanking. This is a very common element of 'networking' in networks.
- *Block*. This is usually connected to warfare but does also exist in the business environment. Blocking can be expressed in different ways. One can be to acquire a supplier before anyone else does.

What actions are most relevant and fruitful depends on the specific case. Consider the following illustration.

---

**Box 11.8   The IT company that mobilized actors to defend its supplier relationship**

Service Company had for many years had a reliable and stable relationship with IT Company. Strong bonds existed between IT Company's customer support department, including the service technicians, and Service Company's computer department. This customer also had other IT suppliers. At some point, Service Company decided to outsource the computer department. Another IT company, System Company, which was partly competing, partly complementing IT Company as a supplier for Service Company, consequently acquired this part of Service Company's operations and a cooperation contract for several years was signed. As a consequence, Service Company's contacts with IT Company now primarily took place through System Company. The work continued and the business transaction volumes were almost maintained, even though the initial relationship became less deep.

One year later, there was an incident that triggered the 'warning systems' of both Service Company and IT Company. A very large IT company, Competitor, which was one of IT Company's strongest competitors, acquired System Company. IT Company and its contacts, the purchasing managers at the operational level within Service Company who wanted to save the established relationship at any cost, now judged that they were in a situation where they could choose between the following alternatives:

- Wait and see how long the two parties – in spite of the new situation – can go on as before.
- Give up, phase out the relationship and prepare a good exit.
- Attempt offensively to regain and even widen the contacts with each other. The contact network can in this situation be mainly operational, because the most important decision-making contacts were run through System Company.

People within Service Company (and some friends at the old supplier) judged that it would take something extra to regain and deepen the contacts with the original supplier (IT Company). But they in fact decided to 'bet' on the third alternative. The System Company's employees felt more loyalty towards IT Company than to its new owner, Competitor.

---

This is an interesting illustration of a network situation. All of the alternative courses of action above (flanking, bridging etc.) could have been pursued in this situation. The structures of activities, actors and resources need to guide the choice of relevant actions.

Different kinds of incidents and processes continuously occur that influence and change the network. It is obvious that, in the example above, a successive refinement of an established way of working had occurred over a long period of time, which entailed that the actors adapted their resources, physical and personal, to this way of working. It is also obvious that when a change is carried through, it can mean substantial adaptations to activities, resources and the actors involved.

Needless to say, there are a wide variety of ways in which networking activities could be carried out. A basic infrastructure of rich relationships (individual as well as company based) is a great facilitator and could be considered as an 'opportunity network' (Agndal and Axelsson, 2002), as it enables the generation of possible actions. Often when businesspeople are asked about what happened when they managed to generate some important contacts and build coalitions, the typical answer is 'It was just a coincidence', followed by a story that the person, be it a purchasing manager, happened to be at the right place and/or be approached by the right person at the right moment. However, it seems as if luck isn't randomly distributed; some people have more luck than others.

In business markets opportunities for action and coalition building appear at irregular intervals and disappear quickly. When a customer is looking for someone to discuss a new idea or whatever the issue, this could be a strategic 'window of opportunity'. If this is heard of by the right individual, he or she will see it, take the opportunity and act on it. It seems, as a consequence of this, also to be of great importance to be actively present at various meeting places and thereby to capture such opportunities as well as try to influence others. Opportunities for networking do not appear in a desk study but via field or network presence (Axelsson and Johanson, 1992). Likewise, it is important to be able to freeze the possibility of activities. It might be that people in a company know what is the right thing to do, but the timing of it is not right. Håkansson (1987) discusses this using the term 'mummify', trying to stay prepared for a certain activity and being able to wait for the right opportunity. In essence it seems to be a matter of making time work for you, since normally in networks no single actor is able to govern processes.

Markets as networks also mean an aspiration to successively create positions in relation to other actors. An important category of actors is formed by current and potential suppliers. To create an advantageous position in relation to what is judged to be the 'right' kind of supplier should be an important part of the company's purchasing philosophy. Competent suppliers that offer high returns for their money are valuable. But the right supplier can also be a question of a good reference, a bridge to other important actors and markets, and a possibility of gaining experiences – through dialogue – that can be exploited in other situations.

## Creating and designing supply structures

Despite all the limitations discussed so far, the purchasing company has the possibility of deciding if it should actively work towards maintaining the current network situation or if it should try to change it. In a situation with only one supplier and a unique offer, the company may, for example, wish to widen the possibilities through working towards getting more suppliers that offer the same product, for instance by changing the specifications so that it can fit more suppliers. In this case, the company obviously wishes to have more market-oriented transactions with suppliers.

Another course of action can involve a situation where there are many suppliers with similar offers, but the customer wants to change the situation in such a way that the number of choices is narrowed down. The reasons can be that none of the alternative suppliers is good enough and/or that the company, through a well-developed relationship with one of them, wants to develop a unique solution that can give competitive advantages. In this case, the company wishes to have more network-oriented relationships with the chosen suppliers. Obviously, it can also be the case that the company wants to take measures to

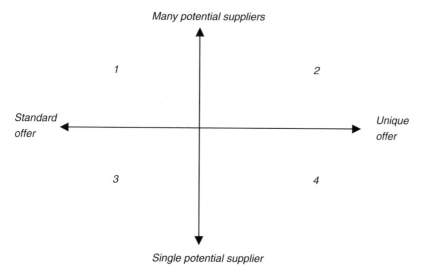

**Figure 11.4**  Alternative purchasing situations

maintain a certain situation, irrespective of whether the original situation offered one or several supplier alternatives.

Consider Figure 11.4, in which we have characterized various alternative situations by means of two variables: the number of potential suppliers and the nature of the product offering in terms of standardization/customization (see Axelsson and Håkansson, 1984). Where the purchasing firm is positioned and in what direction it wishes to go influence and are influenced by its purchasing strategy (see also above).

Situations 1 and 4 differ most from each other. The difference between them is, essentially, a difference in how the different forms of transactions – exchange processes – are carried out. Here, we have called these two forms *market transactions* and *network relations*. What each case strives towards (and enables) can be summed up in Figure 11.5.

|  |  | The function of the business exchange | |
|---|---|---|---|
|  |  | One-dimensional | Multidimensional |
| The substance of the business exchange | Simple/ standard | Market transaction |  |
|  | Complex/ unique |  | Network relation |

**Figure 11.5**  The business exchange's function and substance, and consequently coherent form of transaction

*Source*: Håkansson and Snehota, 1995, p. 331.

Both the market situation and the network situation have their respective problems and possibilities. Exploitation of network relations means a search for the multidimensional and unique aspects of each relationship. This usually implies the development of new solutions. The exploitation of market transactions means a search for the standardized, striving for a solution based on the optimal conditions existing on the market.

## Coordinating and handling business exchanges on a system level

In discussing the four situations in Figure 11.4, only the buyer–seller relationship between two parties (dyads) has been considered. On a system level, where other actors' actions are also considered, the type of structures that were illustrated in Figures 11.1 and 11.2 arise, i.e. market systems as 'markets' or as 'networks' with several actors (three, i.e. triads, or more). The general difference, except for the increasing number of actors, is that the distribution or coordination of activities between actors in the general system is different. In the market situation, exchange/coordination between the different actors' activities is carried out by means of market transactions and in the network by network relations. In any single activity system, there almost always exists a blend of these forms of coordination.

Overall, this means that it can be of great importance for the single actor to try to survey a larger portion of the business system than merely the particular supplier relationship. What happens in the stage before that and even further back? How is the coordination of activities in earlier steps in the supply chain being achieved? Gadde and Håkansson (2001, Chapter 9) discuss various ways to design supply networks. They describe and analyse single and multiple sourcing and combinations of these, as well as more complex systems of networks. One especially interesting mode is the creation of strategic centres (Lorenzoni and Baden-Fuller, 1995), where a strong actor basically designs structures of related actors. The best-known archetype is the Japanese way of organizing suppliers in first-, second-, third-tier levels and so on. But Gadde and Håkansson provide a more diversified picture. One important distinction they make is between high- and low-involvement relationships in network structures (see also Gadde and Snehota, 2000). A firm cannot handle too many high-involvement relationships, but a broader view – a supply network view – is still required for performance enhancement.

## Supply chain management: a special case of building supplier structures

One key aspect of supply chain management is that companies try to coordinate operations across *several* stages along the chain of interrelated buyers and sellers. The second key aspect is that there is a shift in the *form of coordination* of activities away from market forces and towards network relations. It is basically about the organization of activities, which take place between (and within) several actors in an industrial system. SCM treats this system principally from a flow orientation, implying that it does not stop at any individual company's border.

It is also interesting to see that supply chain management focuses on a special subset of networks: the physical product chain and connected information-related activities. The Hewlett-Packard example (Box 3.12) illustrated only one specific part of the company's supply chain. In the illustrations on movie production (Box 3.13) and reverse logistics (Box 11.3) an operational system was described as a chain of production activities.

The network model is more general and more open, and can be used to study both well-organized chains (such as the HP chain) and chains of activities that are connected in other, looser ways. In addition to that, the network model can also be used to see how parallel activities of different kinds are influencing each chain, for example in illuminating the priority problem for the actor who is involved in several chains at the same time. The model allows the analyser to limit the network in relation to what is judged to be relevant in the particular case and to focus on those specific aspects that are seen as the most interesting. Consequently, the network model is compatible with the supply chain management perspective, if it is such a chain of activities that is in focus. It is compatible with the metaphor of value star or value constellation (see Chapter 3) if the company's role in the business system is in focus. The company can, in the model's terms, be described as a meeting place for many activities. Even though – or perhaps since – the model is relatively simple and rough, it is fruitful for analyses of complex operations systems.

## Markets and networks combined

We have already emphasized that, within a specific business system, there are normally several forms of transactions. If we return to the example of movie production, we can easily imagine that the operations system as such – from the script being written to the movie being shown – contains several business exchanges that are dominated by market exchanges as well as network relations. Let us return to this example (see Box 3.13).

---

**Box 11.9   Forms of transactions to coordinate activities within the movie production process**

It is not difficult to imagine that certain parts of the exchange processes in the operations system are dominated by market transactions. Perhaps all movie producers are offered the same conditions when renting a movie studio, purchasing transportation services, costumes etc. If there also are a number of equal alternative suppliers of these services, this would indicate that each production unit is offering its customers standardized offers. In these parts of the operations system, market transactions are dominating. In such a system, an actor's competitive advantages must be created in the internal activities, since all input is purchased at identical conditions and all output is sold under identical conditions as well.

> In other parts of the operations system, we can just as easily think of situations being characterized by network relations. A sponsor, e.g. a soft drink producer, might want to have its product visible in a number of scenes in the movie ('product placement'). If this offer is accepted, then a similar offer by a directly competing soft drink producer cannot be accepted.
>
> Movie actors may have specific demands regarding compensation for their participation in the movie, based on their skills but also on the estimated market value of the movie within the target group. By entering a dialogue with these 'service suppliers', the movie producer's purchases become more differentiated and multi-dimensional. In these parts of the business system, network relations are dominating. In these parts of the system, it is not only the internal activities that create the company's competitive advantage but also how it manages to use the supplier's ability, how it jointly develop resources with suppliers and how it combines the contributions from different 'resource contributors' (synergies).

For the single actor there are two choices. The first option is to accept and in the best possible way try to handle the current situation, partly in the exchange processes that arise with more specific suppliers and partly in the current market system. Depending on the character of the market system two paths can then be distinguished:

● In a system dominated by market transactions, a company ventures everything to become the best in its internal activities (exploiting economies of scale etc.), since all the external (exchange related) conditions are equal for all producers.
● In a system dominated by network relations, a company tries, in a more multidimensional way, to use possible advantages from integrating different activities and processes with suppliers. The company tries to become unique in the way it connects or combines activities, actors and resources.

'Accept the situation' is the motto in both of these cases.

The second alternative is to identify the situation and try to change and develop it in a certain direction. This may involve changes in the specific exchange processes (going from multidimensional/unique to one-dimensional/ standard or the other way around; see Figure 11.5), and also attempts to influence important parts of the existing market system. The latter can, for example, include efforts to create competition at certain stages where it was not present initially, or to start collaboration with the supplier and the supplier's supplier. Following this path, the company tries to work with a wider and deeper overview of the business system and to influence it to create a better position for itself.

Here it should be emphasized once again that the single company – in its purchasing operations – is related to many different operations systems. From this perspective, a purchase of, say, a mechanical component does not only imply a relation with the supplier of such components, but rather with an entire operations system. Similarly, purchases of transport services are not only a question of being related to a supplier of transportation services but rather to another operations system. The total purchasing operation should thus be able to understand, analyse and adapt its behaviour to many different business systems.

A possible effect of analysing purchasing from this perspective, which goes beyond the specific relationship, is that it creates a base for choosing where to purchase: should the company, for example, purchase from a distributor or directly from the manufacturer? Should the company take responsibility for purchase of the components that are part of the system supplier's product? Other, perhaps more obvious questions are: where does the pricing take place, what do the different actors in the system contribute, what stages is it possible to influence?

The single company acts within several such systems and cannot put equal emphasis on all. In certain situations it has to settle for a single supplier contact, in others it is important to survey the whole system. The company must prioritize.

## Conclusions

Performing purchasing activities in a market system, which can be characterized as a network, entails a substantial focus on specific supplier relationships in their network context. For this to be successful, the purchasing function's working methods and competencies need to go hand in hand. Concerning the different ways of working, we have discussed how comparisons can be done to assess if there is a market-oriented situation in which a supplier could be compared with alternatives. Furthermore, we have placed substantial emphasis on the possibilities – in a network-oriented way of working – of creating room for the realization of important ambitions such as establishing new relationships, developing the contents of the current relationships and phasing out relationships. A number of important techniques have been identified.

It is easy for most people to agree that something they call networks often is of great importance for the potential to do business, including suitable purchases. In this chapter we have discussed, in a substantially more penetrating way, some of the basic elements, or languages, for describing and analysing network structures.

Different forces dominate different networks. This is an important insight for those who want to be able to change their own position, but also other parts of the network and the network as a whole. Some principally interesting ways to run changes to networking processes (or resistance to undesired changes) were discussed as well as some of the conditions that might facilitate or obstruct the necessary changes. Furthermore, it was stated that it is a central question for a single company to create activity, resource and activity structures. Those are essential conditions or enablers for the achievement of important ambitions.

# 12

# Summary

In this book we have focused on a corporate function that is gaining ever more attention and recognition, namely purchasing and supply management. Within that scope we have specifically concentrated our attention on a growing and very 'hot' area, namely purchasing of services. If a company's amount of bought-in products corresponds to 50–75 per cent of its sales, the share of services bought should roughly be about 50 per cent of that total. Needless to say, there could be great variations in these figures in individual cases. Buying of services is thus a major issue, and to our knowledge it has been dealt with very little in the literature. Our aim has been to contribute to filling that gap.

In the introduction to this book we stated the general nature of business services and the companies supplying them (Chapters 1 and 2). Between the lines one could also sense the general approach to this study. We have presented a perspective where we do the following:

- Use a model based on three major groups of variables: activities, actors and resources. This is known as the A-R-A model and has been widely employed in studies of business networks, most of all among manufacturing firms. In this book we have applied it to networks of service-producing firms, but also as a tool to penetrate specific services productions. Services consist fundamentally of activities that are performed by actors who need access to resources in order to carry out these activities. Many researchers use that model as an analytical tool. In this book we have used it as a basic framework.

● Utilize much of the existing thinking about purchasing and supply management in general. We have also tried to put our own spin on this, as we are active researchers in this field. In essence one could argue that we have a somewhat more behaviourist approach to activities among business actors than have many other researchers and authors of textbooks in the area. We try not to simply state that 'in a situation like this the company should go for a strategic alliance', our follow-up question would be 'what if the supplier does not want to enter into such a relationship with us?'. This presents what we think is a more realistic view of business life.

● Apply knowledge developed in the service management and services marketing literature, not least due to research by Nordic scholars such as Grönroos, Gummesson and Normann. Of course, we have also utilized much other good thinking. But we find it interesting to notify this characteristic as there have not been too many efforts to merge these two areas of knowledge.

Overall we have tried to draw on the sources mentioned and integrate a great deal of good thinking. We have also tried to position ourselves in between what could roughly be characterized as an 'American' and a 'European' approach to business marketing and purchasing. In our view a typical American textbook is very rationalistic and normative (do it like this: step 1, step 2 etc.), while the European – and possibly we are referring specifically to the so-called IMP tradition – is more descriptive, open to complexities, avoiding normative recommendations and not really (explicitly) emphasizing the economic and financial implications of activities. We have tried to open up greater complexity by not over-simplifying (firms and activities are embedded and dependent on others, no single actor can normally control a market or a network) and at the same explicitly discussing economic effects (e.g. specification methods, pricing, negotiations).

## The contents

As mentioned we have chosen to refer to a definition of services that emphasizes that a service consists of activities (physical or mental) that are sold as a promise or an agreement from the supplier to the buyer, before they are produced. The services are often carried out in some kind of interaction between the parties, which puts the spotlight on the communication, coordination and collaboration between the two (or more) actors involved.

We use the A-R-A model a fair amount in Part II of the book, Analysis (Chapters 3–6):

● To map the activities that form the substance (functions) of specific services and the kind of activity patterns that one or a number of actors together perform in order to carry out a (joint) service production (Chapter 3).

- To discuss allocation of activities between actors, specifically in terms of in- and outsourcing. Which activities are better performed by an outside actor and which are better performed by the user itself? Again, the resources involved and controlled by different actors are important prerequisites to that discussion (Chapter 4).
- To describe and portray the interplay between buyers and sellers due to a classification of services emanating from the ways in which the service is used (as a component etc.) and also what kind of complexity and quality are to be achieved. Here, the focus has turned away from the activities that make the service towards the actions and connections between people involved in the marketing, production and buying of the service (Chapter 5).
- To discuss the impact of ICT on the selling, producing and buying of business services. The new technology will change many things: the ways activities are carried out, the resources needed, the distribution of activities between actors etc. In some areas the influences are likely to be higher, in others there will be less impact (Chapter 6).

We think we have provided a useful tool for obtaining basic descriptions and an overview of different patterns of activities that together constitute specific services. It is also helpful in understanding the underlying reasons for the allocation of activities as well as the distribution of tasks between actors.

In Part III, Application (Chapters 7–10), we still use the basic concepts presented in Part II, but here we use them as a basis for decision making. That applies to the following:

- Specifying a service, including not just the design as activity structures, but also other performance and aspects of the interplay between the parties. We distinguish four methods of specifying and point to the importance of not just the agreement as such but also the service delivery itself (Chapter 7).
- Evaluating, choosing and selecting suppliers. In order to be able to choose, the buying party needs to have an idea of what it needs and what it takes to perform such functions (activities at a certain quality and quantity). For the evaluation of a supplier, we propose a method in which some basic processes (activities) as performed by the supplier need to be mapped. Likewise, we propose a way to identify resources, including knowledge, that the supplier will need to be a capable partner. We also discussed different ways to summarize and utilize the evaluations reached (Chapter 8).
- Pricing and negotiating. Pricing is related to specifications: what the customer gets. There are, however, three principles: cost-plus, market-based and value-in-use pricing. What activities are performed? What is the value of the functions they perform? We discussed those principles and the pros and cons connected with them. Even if there are some general trends in such matters, it is possible to indicate some situations when each of them is the most preferred. Related to this, methods of payment as well as some basic negotiating principles were discussed at some length too (Chapter 9).

The fourth and final part of this book has been meant to be more reflective. We change our focus from specific services and activities to surrounding market conditions. A point of departure is that every business deal is settled within some kind of business context. And the ways in which the deal is settled are likely to have an impact on that market setting.

Two approaches to the purchasing of services were distinguished, the transaction-oriented and the relation-oriented approaches (Chapter 10). These were described and their respective applicability (advantages and disadvantages along a variety of dimensions) was discussed. The transaction-oriented approach fits naturally with a market context, in line with the traditional market view. Applying that approach also means that the buying party will influence the market towards such a structure. Likewise, the relation-oriented approach fits naturally with a business context in line with some kind of network of connected actors and activities. It is also the case that a relation-oriented approach in itself contributes to such structures emerging. In addition to the two basic forms of structures, we took a closer look at different kinds of network structures and how those provide, for good and ill, the context in which business is carried out (Chapter 11).

## Finally

We have used an approach to buying services that we have found fruitful. It is also evident that services incorporate a great variety of products and activity patterns. We have tried to demonstrate this great variation as well as the many dimensions, resources and competences that could be involved in selling, producing and buying services. At the same time it is evident that basic purchasing management principles also apply to services.

There are some things that we have not dealt with, but that are still relevant. This includes, for example, aspects of strategy and capability development. What specific kinds of capabilities are needed for handling the purchase of specific services? Another important area deals with trust: what does the trust-building process look like in services interaction, and for what kind of services is trust a crucial issue? We hope to come back to such issues in our future writing.

# References

Aaker, D.A. and Joachimstahler, E. (2000) *Brand Leadership*, Free Press, New York.

Abrahamsson, M. and Brege, S. (2002) 'E-Commerce', unpublished manuscript.

Adermalm, L., Sjöberg, H. and Wedin, T. (1998) 'Faktorer som påverkar insourcing och outsourcingbeslut', unpublished MBA thesis, Uppsala University, Sweden.

Agndal, H. and Axelsson, B. (2002) 'Internationalisation of the firm: The influence of relationship sediments', in Havila, V., Forsgren, M. and Håkansson, H., *Critical Perspectives on Internationalisation*, Elsevier Science, Amsterdam.

Amin, A. and Malmberg, A. (1995) 'Competing structural and institutional influences on the geography of production in Europe', in Amin, A., *Post-Fordism: A Reader*, Blackwell, London.

Anderson, J.C. and Narus, J.A. (1995) 'Capturing the value of value-added services', *Harvard Business Review*, January–February, pp. 75–83.

Anderson, J.C. and Narus, J.A. (1998) 'Business marketing: Understand what customers value', *Harvard Business Review*, November–December, pp. 53–65.

Anderson, J.C. and Narus, J.A. (1999) *Business Market Management: Understanding, Creating, and Delivering Value*, Prentice Hall, Upper Saddle River, NJ.

Anderson, J.C., Håkansson, H. and Johanson, J. (1994) 'Dyadic business relationships within a business network context', *Journal of Marketing*, Vol. 58, October, pp. 1–15.

Anderson, J.C., Thomson, J.B.L. and Wynstra, F. (2000) 'Combining price and value to make purchase decisions in business markets', *International Journal of Research in Marketing*, Vol. 17, pp. 307–29.

Andersson, D. and Norrman, A. (2002) 'Procurement of logistics services: a minute's work or a multi-year project?', *European Journal of Purchasing and Supply Management*, Vol. 8, No. 1, pp. 3–14.

Andrew, J.P., Blackburn, A. and Sirkin, H.L. (2000) *The Business-to-Business Opportunity: Creating Advantage through E-marketplaces*, Boston Consulting Group, Chicago.

Angehrn, A. (1997) 'Designing mature Internet business strategies: The ICDT model', *European Management Journal*, Vol. 15, No. 4, pp. 361–9.

Axelrod, R.M. (1984) *The Evolution of Cooperation*, Basic Books, New York.

Axelsson, B. (1987) 'Tjänsteporträttering', in Edvardsson, B. and Gummesson, E., *Management i tjänstesamhället*, Liber, Stockholm.

Axelsson, B. (1996a) *Professionell marknadsföring*, Studentlitteratur, Lund.

Axelsson, B. (1996b) *Kompetens för konkurrenskraft*, SNS Förlag, Stockholm.

Axelsson, B. (1998) *Företag köper tjänster*, SNS Förlag, Stockholm.

Axelsson, B. and Berger, S. (1989) 'Informationsteknologi för regional utveckling', in *Data och telekommunikationer: hur påverkas den regionala utvecklingen. En antologi*, Teldok, Länsstyrelsen i Stockholms Iän.

Axelsson, B. and Easton, G. (1992) *Industrial Networks and a New View of Reality*, Routledge, London.

Axelsson, B. and Håkansson, H. (1984) *Inköp för konkurrenskraft*, Liber, Malmö.

Axelsson, B. and Johanson, J. (1992) 'Foreign market entry: The textbook view versus the network view', in Axelsson, B. and Easton, G. (1992) *Industrial Networks and a New View of Reality*, Routledge, London.

Axelsson, B. and Laage-Hellman, J. (1991) *Inköp: en ledningsfråga*, Verkstadsindustriernas Förlag, Stockholm.

Bazerman, M.H. and Neale, M.A. (1993) *Negotiating Rationally*, Free Press, New York.

Berry, L. and Parasuraman, A. (1991) *Marketing Services: Competing through Quality*, Free Press, New York.

Bickerton, P., Bickerton, M. and Simpson-Holley, K. (1999) *Cyberstrategy*, Reed Educational and Professional Publishing, Woburn.

Bitner, M.J. (1992) 'Servicescapes: The impact of physical surroundings on customers and employees', *Journal of Marketing*, Vol. 56, pp. 57–71.

Blomgren, H. (1997) 'Arbetsfördeiningen i produktionskedjan', unpublished PhD thesis, Royal Institute of Technology, Stockholm.

Brandes, H., Lilliecreutz, J. and Jonsson, S. (1999) *Inköpsbarometern*, CMA/Linköping University.

Bryntse, K. (2000) 'Kontraktsstyrning i teori och praktik', unpublished PhD thesis, Department of Business Administration, Lund University, Sweden.

Carlisle, J.A. and Parker, R.C. (1989) *Beyond Negotiation*, Wiley, Chichester.

Chaffey, D. (2002) *E-Business and E-Commerce Management*, Financial Times/Prentice Hall, Harlow.

Chopra, S. and Meindl, P. (2001) *Supply Chain Management: Strategy, Planning and Operation*, Prentice Hall, Upper Saddle River, NJ.

Christopher, M. (1992) *Logistics and Supply Chain Management*, Pitman Publishing, London.

Coase, R. (1937) 'The nature of the firm', *Economica*, Vol. 4, pp. 396–405.

Collins, J.C. and Porras, J.I. (1994) *Built to Last*, HarperCollins, New York.

Cox, R. and Goodman, C.S. (1956) 'Marketing of housebuilding materials', *Journal of Marketing*, July, pp. 36–61.

Croom, S.R. (2000) 'The impact of web-based procurement on the management of operating resources supply', *Journal of Supply Chain Management*, Winter, pp. 4–13.

De Boer, L., Harink, J. and Heijboer, G. (2002) 'A conceptual model for assessing the impact of electronic procurement', *European Journal of Purchasing and Supply Management*, Vol. 8, No. 1, pp. 25–33.

De Geer, H. (1978) *Rationaliseringsrörelsen i Sverige*, SNS, Stockholm.

Dobler, D.W. and Burt, D.N. (1996) *Purchasing and Materials Management: Text and Cases*, McGraw-Hill, New York.

Dubois. A. (1998) *Organizing Industrial Activities across Firm Boundaries*, Routledge, London.

Ellram, L. (1995) 'Total Cost of Ownership: An analysis approach for purchasing', *International Journal of Physical Distribution and Logistics*, Vol. 25, No. 8, pp. 4–23.

Emiliani, M.L. (2000) 'Business-to-business online auctions: Key issues for purchasing process improvement', *Supply Chain Management*, Vol. 5, No. 4, pp. 176–86.

Erramili, M.K. (1989) 'Entry mode choice in service industries', *International Marketing Review*, Vol. 7, No. 5, pp. 50–62.

Essig, M. and Arnold, U. (2001) 'Electronic procurement in supply chain management: An information economics-based analysis of electronic markets, their facilities and their limits', *Journal of Supply Chain Management*, Vol. 37, No. 4, pp. 43–9.

Fasth, G., Gustafsson, J. and Hallefalt, M. (1997) 'Vertikal integration i ett strategiskt perspektiv', unpublished MBA thesis, Uppsala University, Sweden.

Fearon, H.E. and Bales, W.A. (1995) *Purchasing of Nontraditional Goods and Services*, Center for Advanced Purchasing Studies (CAPS), Tempe, AZ.

Fisher, L. (1976) *Industrial Marketing: An Analytical Approach to Planning and Execution* (2nd edn), Business Books, London.

Fisher, R. and Ury, W. (1981) *Getting to Yes and Negotiating Agreement Without Giving in*, Houghton Mifflin, Boston.

Ford, D. (ed.) (1997) *Understanding Business Markets*, Dryden Press, London.

Ford, D., Gadde, L-E., Håkansson, H., Lundgren, A., Snehota, I., Turnbull, P. and Wilson, D. (1998) *Managing Business Relationships*, Wiley, Chichester.

Forrester, J. (1961) *Industrial Dynamics*, MIT Press, Boston.

Gadde, L-E. and Håkansson, H. (1993) *Professional Purchasing*, Routledge, London.

Gadde, L-E. and Håkansson, H. (2001) *Supply Network Strategies*, Wiley, Chichester.

Gadde, L-E. and Snehota, I. (2000) 'Making the most of supplier relationships', *Industrial Marketing Management*, Vol. 29, pp. 305–16.

Grant, R.M. (1996) 'Toward a knowledge-based theory of the firm', *Strategic Management Journal*, Vol. 17 (Winter Special Issue), pp. 109–22.

Grönroos, C. (1979) 'An applied theory for marketing industrial services', *Industrial Marketing Management*, Vol. 8, No. 1, pp. 45–55.

Grönroos, C. (1990) *Service Management and Marketing: Managing Moments of Truth in Service Competition*, Lexington Books, Lexington, MA.

Grönroos, C. (2000) *Service Management and Marketing: A Customer Relationship Management Approach* (2nd edition), Wiley, Chichester.

Grundén, A. and Westin, A. (1997) 'Strategiska nätverk i turistsverige', Master's thesis, Department of Business Studies, Uppsala University, Sweden.

Gummesson, E. (1987) 'Tjänstekvalitet ur kund- och ledningsperspektiv', in Arvidsson, G. and Lind, R., *Ledning av företag och förvaltningar: förutsättningar, former, förnyelse*, SNS Forlag, Stockholm.

Gummeson, E. (1999) *Total Relationship Marketing: Rethinking Marketing Management: From 4 Ps to 30 Rs*, Butterworth Heinemann, Oxford.

Håkansson, H. (1979) 'Marknadsföring av specialstål', Research Report, No. 2, Department of Business Studies, Uppsala University.

Håkansson, H. (ed.) (1982) *International Marketing and Purchasing of Industrial Goods: An Interaction Approach*, Wiley, Chichester.

Håkansson, H. (ed.) (1987) *Industrial Technological Development: An Interaction Approach*, Croom Helm, London.

Håkansson, H. (1989) *Corporate Technological Behaviour*, Croom Helm, London.

Håkansson, H. and Eriksson, A-C. (1993) 'Getting innovations out of supplier networks', *Journal of Business-to-Business Marketing*, Vol. 1, pp. 3–34.

Håkansson, H. and Johanson, J. (1992) 'The network model', in Axelsson, B. and Easton, G. (eds), *Industrial Networks: A New View of Reality*, Routledge, London/New York.

Håkansson, H. and Snehota, I. (1995) *Developing Relationships in Business Networks*, Routledge, London/New York.

Håkansson, H. and Wootz, B. (1975) *Företags Inköpsbeteende*, Studentlitteratur, Lund.

Håkansson, H. and Wootz, B. (1984) 'Lågt pris eller låga kostnader', *Purchasing Magazine*, No. 2, pp. 83–4.

Hallén, L., Johanson, J. and Syed-Mohammed, N. (1991) 'Interfirm adaptation in business relationships', *Journal of Marketing*, Vol. 55, No. 2, pp. 29–37.

Hansen, M.T., Nohria, N. and Tierney, T. (1999) 'What's your strategy for managing knowledge?', *Harvard Business Review*, March–April, pp. 106–16.

Hanson, W. (2000) *Principles of Internet Marketing*, South-Western College Publishing/Thomson Learning, Cincinnati, OH.

Harland, C.M., Lamming, R.C., Zheng, J. and Johnsen, T. (2001) 'A taxonomy of supply networks', *Journal of Supply Chain Management*, Vol. 37, No. 4, pp. 21–7.

Hart, C.W.L., Heskett, J.L. and Sasser, W.E., Jr. (1990) 'The profitable art of service recovery', *Harvard Business Review*, July–August, pp. 148–56.

Hedberg, B., Dahlgren, G., Hansson, J. and Olve, N-G. (1994) *Imaginära organisationer*, Liber, Stockholm.

Heinritz, S.F., Farrell, P.V. and Smith, C.L. (1986) *Purchasing: Principles and Applications*, Prentice Hall, Englewood Cliffs, NJ.

Helmer, T. (1995) 'Outsourcing, ett sätt att öka effektiviteten', unpublished Master's thesis, Department of Business Studies, Uppsala University, Sweden.

Helper, S.R. (1991) 'How much has really changed between US automakers and their suppliers?', *Sloan Management Review*, Summer, pp. 15–28.

Heskett, J.L., Jones, T.O., Loveman, G., Sasser, W.E. and Schlesinger, I.A. (1994) 'Putting the service-profit chain to work', *Harvard Business Review*, March–April, pp. 164–74.

Hiles, A. (1993) *Service Level Agreements*, Chapman and Hall, London.

Holmlund, M. (1997) 'Perceived quality in business relationships', unpublished PhD thesis, Svenska Handelshögskolan, Helsinki.

Huge-Brodin, M. (1997) 'Reverse logistics systems', PhD thesis, Linköping University.

Jismalm, P. and Linder, F. (1995) 'Inköp av industriella tjänster', Master's thesis, Department of Business Studies, Uppsala University, Sweden.

Jonsson, S. (1998) 'Den strategiska försörjningsprocessen med fokus på uppbyggnaden av företagets leverantörsbas', Licentiate thesis, Linköping University.

Kaplan, R.S. and Norton, D.P. (1992) 'The balanced score card: Measures that drive performance', *Harvard Business Review*, January–February, pp. 71–9.

Kaplan, S. and Sawhney, M. (2000) 'E-hubs: The new B2B marketplaces', *Harvard Business Review*, May–June, pp. 97–103.

Kotler, P. (2000) *Marketing Management* (10th international edn), Prentice Hall, Upper Saddle River, NJ.

Kraljic, P. (1983) 'Purchasing must become supply management', *Harvard Business Review*, September–October, pp. 109–17.

Kremenyuk, V.A. (1991) *International Negotiation*, Jossey-Bass, Oxford.

Kvarnemo, A. (1997) 'Felavhjälpning för ökad kundlojalitet', unpublished MBA thesis, Uppsala University.

Laage-Hellman, J. (1989) 'Technological development in industrial networks', PhD thesis, Uppsala University.

Laage-Hellman, J. (1997) *Business Networks in Japan*, Routledge, London.

Lax, D.A. and Sebenius, J.K. (1986) *The Manager as Negotiator*, Free Press, New York.

Lee, H.L. and Billington, C. (1995) 'The evolution of supply chain management models and practice at Hewlett-Packard', *Interfaces*, Vol. 25, No. 5, pp. 42–63.

Leek, S., Turnbull, P.W. and Naudé, P. (2000) 'Is the interaction approach of any relevance in an IT/e-commerce driven world?', *Proceedings 16th IMP Conference* (CD-Rom), IMP, Bath.

Leenders, M.R. and Blenkhorn, D.L. (1988) *Reverse Marketing: The New Buyer–Supplier Relationship*, Free Press, New York.

Levitt, T. (1983) *The Marketing Imagination*, Free Press, New York.

Long, D. and Vickers-Koch, M. (1992) 'Using core capabilities to create competitive advantage', *Organizational Dynamics*, Vol. 24, No. 1, pp 6–20.

Lorange, P. and Roos, J. (1992) *Strategic Alliances*, Blackwell, Oxford.

Lorenzoni, G. and Baden-Fuller, C. (1995) 'Creating a strategic center to manage a web of partners', *California Management Review*, Vol. 37, No. 3, pp. 146–63.

Lovelock, C., Vandermerwe, S. and Lewis, B. (1999) *Services Marketing: A European Perspective*, Financial Times/Prentice Hall, Harlow.

Malone, T., Yates, J. and Benjamin, R. (1987) 'Electronic markets and electronic hierarchies', *Communications ACM*, Vol. 6, pp. 485–97.

Malmgren, H. and Olausson, B. (1997) 'A bird in the hand is worth two in the bush, or: how to use the Telia group's international relationships as a driving force in foreign market entries', MBA thesis, Uppsala University.

McMillan, J. (1990) 'Managing suppliers: Incentive systems in Japanese and US industry', *California Management Review*, Vol. 32, No. 4, pp. 38–55.

Min, H. and Galle, W.P. (1999) 'Electronic commerce usage in business-to-business purchasing', *International Journal of Operations and Production Management*, Vol. 19, No. 9, pp. 909–21.

Min, H., LaTour, M.S. and Jones, M.A. (1995) 'Negotiation outcomes: The impact of the initial offer, team, gender and team size', *International Journal of Purchasing and Materials Management*, Vol. 31, No. 4, pp. 19–24.

Mintzberg, H. (1992) 'The strategy process', in Mintzberg, H. and Quinn, J.B., *The Strategy Process: Concepts and Contexts*, Prentice Hall, Englewood Cliffs, NJ.

Mitchell, V-W. (1995) 'Organisational risk perception and reduction: A literature review', *British Journal of Management*, Vol. 6, pp. 115–33.

Mitchell, V-W. and McGoldrick, P.J. (1995) 'Consumers' risk reduction and strategies: A review and synthesis', *International Review of Retail and Distribtuion Consumer Research*, Vol. 5, No. 4, pp. 504–34.

Narus, J.A. and Anderson, J.C. (1996) 'Rethinking distribution: Adaptive channels', *Harvard Business Review*, July–August, pp. 112–20.

Nayyar, P. (1990) 'Information asymmetry: A source of competitive advantage for diversified service firms', *Strategic Management Journal*, Vol. 11, No. 7, pp. 513–19.

Negroponte, N. (1995) *Being Digital*, Knopf, New York.

Nonaka, I. and Konno, N. (1998) 'The concept of "Ba": Building a foundation for knowledge creation', *California Management Review*, Vol. 40, No. 3, pp. 40–54.

Nonaka, I. and Takeuchi, H. (1995) *The Knowledge Creating Company*, Oxford University Press, New York.

Normann, R. (1992) *Service Management*, Liber, Stockholm.

Normann, R. and Ramirez, R. (1994) *Designing Interactive Strategy: From Value Chain to Value Constellation*, Wiley, Chichester.

OECD (1999a) *OECD in Figures and Related Databases*, OECD, Paris.

OECD (1999b) *Strategic Business Services*, OECD, Paris.

OECD (2000) *The Service Economy*, Business and Industry Policy Forum Series, OECD, Paris.

Ohmae, K. (1995) *The End of the Nation State: The Rise of Regional Economies*, Free Press, London.

Panzar, J.C. and Willig, R.D. (1981) 'Economies of scope', *AEA Papers and Proceedings*, May, pp. 268–72.

Piore, M. and Sabel, C.F. (1984) *The Second Industrial Divide: Possibilities for Prosperity*, Basic Books, New York.

Pitt, L., Berthon, P. and Berthon, J-P. (1999) 'Changing channels: The impact of the Internet on distribution strategy', *Business Horizons*, March–April, pp. 19–28.

Prahalad, C.K. and Hamel, G. (1990) 'The core competence of the corporation', *Harvard Business Review*, May–June, pp. 79–91.

Quinn, J.B. and Hilmer, F.G. (1994) 'Strategic outsourcing', *Sloan Management Review*, Vol. 2, No. 2, pp. 43–55.

Ranson, S. and Stewart, J.D. (1994) *Management for the Public Domain*, Macmillan Press, London.

Rayport, J.F. and Sviokla, J.J. (1995) 'Exploiting the virtual value chain', *Harvard Business Review*, November–December, pp. 75–85.

Reichheld, F.F. (1996) *The Loyalty Effect: The Hidden Force behind Growth, Profit and Lasting Value*, Harvard Business School Press, Boston.

Richardson, G.B. (1972) 'The organization of industry', *The Economic Journal*, Vol. 82, pp. 883–96.

Riesling, R. and Sveiby, K-E. (1986) *Kunskapsföretaget*, Liber, Stockholm.

Robinson, P.J., Faris, C.W. and Wind, Y. (1967) *Industrial Buying and Creative Marketing*, Allyn & Bacon, Boston.

Sako, M. (1992) *Price, Quality and Trust: Inter-Firm Relations in Britain and Japan*, Cambridge University Press, Cambridge.

Sako, M. (1997) 'Does trust improve business performance?', in Lane, C. and Backmann, R. (eds), *Trust Within and Between Organizations*, Oxford University Press, Oxford.

Schary, R.D. and Skjøtt-Larsen, T. (1995) *Managing the Global Supply Chain*, Handelshöjskolens Förlag, Copenhagen.

Scott, W.R. (1992) *Organizations*, Prentice-Hall, Upper Saddle River, NJ.

Shostack, G.L. (1992) 'Understanding services through blueprinting', in Schwartz, T.A., Bowen, D.E. and Brown, S.W., *Advances in Services Marketing and Management*, Vol. 1, JAI Press, Greenwich, CT.

Silander, M. (1997) 'Considerations on total quality in purchasing films and genres to the Swedish TV market windows', unpublished Master's thesis, Department of Business Studies, Uppsala University, Sweden.

Smeltzer, L. and Ruzicka, M. (2000) 'Electronic reverse auctions: Integrating the tool with the strategic-sourcing process', *Practix*, Vol. 3, No. 4, pp. 1–6.

Smith, P. and Laage-Hellman, J. (1992) 'Small group analysis in industrial networks', in Axelsson, B. and Easton, G., *Industrial Networks: A New View of Reality*, Routledge, London.

Snehota, I. (1992) 'A note on a theory of the business enterprise', unpublished PhD thesis, Department for Business Studies, Uppsala University, Sweden.

Snow, C., Miles, R.E. and Coleman, H.J. (1992) 'Managing 21st century network organizations', *Organizational Dynamics*, Winter, pp. 5–19.

Teich, J., Wallenius, H. and Wallenius, J. (1999) 'Multiple-issue auction and market algorithms for the World Wide Web', *Decision Support Systems*, Vol. 26, pp. 49–66.

Thompson, J.D. (1967) *Organizations in Action*, McGraw-Hill, Maidenhead.

Timmers, P. (1998) 'Business models for electronic markets', *Electronic Markets*, Vol. 8, No. 2, pp. 3–8.

Treece, J.B. (1994) 'Hardball is still GM's game', *Business Week*, 8 August, p. 26.

Turban, E., Lee, J., King, D. and Chung, H. (2000) *Electronic Commerce: A Managerial Perspective*, Prentice Hall, Upper Saddle River, NJ.

Utterback, J.M. (1994) *Mastering the Dynamics of Innovation*, Harvard Business School Press, Boston.

Van Weele, A. (1994) *Purchasing Management*, Chapman and Hall, London.

Van Weele, A.J. (2000) *Purchasing and Supply Chain Management* (2nd edn), Thomson Learning, London.

Van Weele, A.J. and Rozemeijer, F. (1996) *Revolution in Purchasing*, Philips Electronics/Eindhoven University of Technology, Eindhoven.

Van Weele, A.J. and Van der Vossen, G.J. (1998) *Purchasing: Dupont Analysis of Some Major Dutch Companies*, Research Report, Holland Consulting Group, Amsterdam.

Venkatraman, N. (1994) 'IT-enabled business transformation: From automation to business scope redefinition', *Sloan Management Review*, Winter, pp. 73–87.

Von Schéele, F. (1996) *Just-In-Case*, Liber-Hermods, Stockholm.

Webster F.E., Jr. and Wind, Y. (1972) *Organizational Buying Behavior*, Prentice-Hall, Upper Saddle River, NJ.

Wernerfelt, B. (1984) 'A resource-based view of the firm', *Strategic Management Journal*, Vol. 5, pp. 171–80.

Wigand, R. (1997) 'Electronic commerce: Definition, theory and context', *The Information Society*, Vol. 13, pp. 1–16.

Wilkinson, I.F. and Young, L.C. (1991) 'Business dancing: The nature and role of interfirm relationships in business strategy', *Asia-Australia Marketing Journal*, Vol. 2, No. 1, pp. 67–79.

Williamson, O.E. (1975) *Markets and Hierarchies: Analysis and Antitrust Implications*, Free Press, New York.

Williamson, O.E. (1985) *The Economic Institutions of Capitalism*, Free Press, New York.

Wittreich, W.J. (1966) 'How to buy/sell professional services', *Harvard Business Review*, March–April, pp. 127–36.

Wymbs, C. (2000) 'How e-commerce is transforming and internationalizing service industries', *Journal of Services Marketing*, Vol. 14, No. 6, pp. 463–78.

Wynstra, F. (1998) 'Purchasing involvement in product development', doctoral thesis, Eindhoven Centre for Innovation Studies, Eindhoven University of Technology, Eindhoven.

Wynstra, F., Weggeman, M. and Van Weele, A J (2002) 'Exploring purchasing integration in product development', *Industrial Marketing Management*, forthcoming.

Zeithaml, V. (1981) 'How consumer evaluation processes differ between goods and services', in Donnelly, J.H. and George, W.R. (eds), *Marketing of Services*, AMA, Chicago.

# Index